FREE & INEXPENSIVE CAREER MATERIALS

A RESOURCE DIRECTORY

FERGUSON PUBLISHING COMPANY

CHICAGO, ILLINOIS

Managing Editor-Career Publications: Andrew Morkes
Editorial Assistant: Nora Walsh
Proofreader: Anne Paterson
Cover Design: Sam Concialdi

Library of Congress Cataloging-in-Publication Data
Free & inexpensive career materials: a resource directory.--3rd ed.
     p. cm.
   Includes bibliographical references.
   ISBN 0-89434-377-7
     1. Vocational guidance--United States--Information services--Directories. I.
   Title: Free & inexpensive career materials.

HF5382.5.U5 F72 2000
016.3317'02'0973--dc21   00-039348

Printed in the United States of America

Published and distributed by:
Ferguson Publishing Company
200 West Jackson Boulevard, 7th Floor
Chicago, Illinois 60606
800-306-9941
http://www.fergpubco.com

X-9

TABLE OF CONTENTS

(Note: Pages are not numbered in order to avoid confusion with the sequence numbers used to identify entries in section IV.)

SECTION I

INTRODUCTION

Ferguson's *Free & Inexpensive Career Materials* offers contact information for more than 660 organizations and associations that provide free or inexpensive ($10 or less) career information. The directory is designed to help individuals planning careers as well as those who guide them. It may also be useful to librarians who wish to expand their resources and to organizations interested in developing career materials.

To update the information published in the previous edition, we contacted every organization. If we were unable to verify the organization's contact information, we deleted its listing from the book. Ten percent of the listings are new to this edition.

This revised edition includes trade associations, professional associations, state occupation-al information committees, academic membership groups, founda-tions, college depart-ments, government agencies, and commercial publishers. These groups are organized alphabetically by name, and each listing includes the following information, when available:

Name of organization
Mailing address
Telephone number
Fax number
E-mail address
Web site address
Name of publication(s)
Price for a single copy, if there is a charge
Number of pages in publication
Description of publication

Organizations in this directory that have a Web site often offer a wealth of infor-mation that can be printed for quick and easy access. In some cases, the full text of publications listed in the entry is available at the Web site. We encourage you to visit the Web sites when possible.

Free and Inexpensive Career Materials

When organizations such as commercial publishers and government agencies distribute dozens of items on careers, only illustrative titles are listed. You may want to contact these organizations to request a catalog listing all their available publications.

We invite readers to notify us of additional free and inexpensive career resources. Just send your suggestions to Editor, Free and Inexpensive, Ferguson Publishing Company, 200 West Jackson Boulevard, Chicago, Illinois 60606. Your assistance will be very much appreciated.

HOW TO USE THIS BOOK

The listings in this directory are organized alphabetically by name and numbered consecutively. If you are looking for a specific organization, just look for its name in alphabetical order in section IV of the directory. If you have a particular career field in mind or just want to browse for ideas, start with the index, which is located in section III. It lists career fields, such as nursing and public relations, and job topics, such as overseas work, and provides a reference to the entry numbers of associated listings. *Because the directory is organized around the listings' entry numbers, the book does not have page numbers.* All numbers you see refer to entry numbers.

Please respect the contribution these organizations make in providing free and inexpensive career material by doing the following:

• Request only a single copy of the material cited unless you are willing to reimburse the organization for the cost of multiple copies.

• Send a self-addressed, stamped business-size envelope to help cover the mailing costs. For items available from Canadian sources, be sure to add the required postage.

• Contact only those organizations whose materials are of specific interest to you. Excessive requests for free and inexpensive material may force some groups to discontinue its availability.

• Include the item number, if given, when requesting information.

• Send a check or money order for the proper amount along with your request for publications that specify a charge. Single copies of publications that do not list a charge are free.

SECTION III

INDEX AND GUIDE TO RESOURCES

Here's a quick guide to the resources cited in this directory. Each number refers to an organization offering free and inexpensive career materials, as listed in section IV.

A

Accounting and auditing, 109, 359, 361, 504, 562
Acoustics, 8
Actuarial science, 254, 584
Acupuncture, 3, 56
Advertising, 10, 46, 166, 290
Aerospace, 332, 384, 418
Agriculture, 12, 32, 71, 81, 152, 222, 285, 327, 331, 391, 419, 420, 429, 620, 642
Agronomy, 153
Air conditioning and refrigeration, 13, 17, 161, 321, 379, 541
Allergy and immunology, 23
American Legion, 115
Anesthesiology, 55, 154
Anthropology, 34, 59, 490, 640
Apparel, 35
Appraising, 189
Apprenticeships, 83, 106, 190, 194, 370, 405, 486, 613, 623, 649
Arboriculture, 422
Archaeology, 192, 574, 576
Architecture, 107, 164, 217, 423, 593, 639
Archival sciences, 585
Army, 197, 633
Art, 36, 37, 106, 424, 447
Art therapy, 36
Astronomy and meteorology, 64, 111, 122
Athletic training, 264, 458
Auctioneering, 459
Automotive services, 232, 384, 460, 461, 588
Aviation, 15, 16, 18, 188, 313, 314, 332, 365, 418, 419

N

Navy, 333, 634
Neurology, 26
Nonprofit employment, 103, 534
Nuclear medicine, 525, 594
Nuclear science, 125, 384, 525
Nursing and midwifery, 27, 49, 55, 76, 223, 257, 343, 403, 443, 484, 507, 527, 616, 634
Nutrition, 89

O

Occupational outlook, 19, 60, 65, 116, 242, 315, 390, 392, 455, 504, 531, 632, 649
Occupational therapy, 126
Operations research, 355, 406
Ophthalmology, 28, 388
Opticianry, 415
Optometry, 127, 224, 343
Oriental medicine, 3, 56
Orthodontics, 57
Osteopathy, 50, 129
Overseas work, 282, 366, 440, 628, 629

P

Packaging, 362
Painting, 370
Paleontology, 243
Paralegal, 42, 441, 485, 491
Pathology, 134, 148, 156, 157, 380
Peace Corps, 536
Peace studies, 324
Pediatrics, 29
Pedorthics, 537
Pest control, 493
Petroleum, 58, 595
Pharmacy, 51, 80, 81, 130, 150, 160, 328, 343, 431, 433
Photogrammetry, 151
Photography, 168, 494, 540
Physical therapy, 30, 132, 403
Physician assisting, 31, 527
Physics, 60, 97, 111, 234, 249, 591
Physiology, 77, 133
Planning, 135, 639

SECTION IV

SOURCES OF FREE AND INEXPENSIVE CAREER MATERIALS

1

9 TO 5, NATIONAL ASSOCIATION OF WORKING WOMEN

1430 West Peachtree Street, Suite 610
Atlanta, GA 30309
404-876-1604
Fax: 404-876-1649
hotline9to5@igc.org
http://www.9to5.org

- *Job Problem Hotline: 800-522-0925.* Provides information about workplace rights and links women with 9 to 5 members in their area.

- *The 9 to 5 Guide to Combating Sexual Harassment.* ($15) Contains step-by-step advice on what to do if you are being sexually harassed; information on how companies can adopt a policy against sexual harassment; suggestions for managers, unions, policy makers, attorneys, and advocates; and useful materials, including interactive exercises and resource lists.

- *Family and Medical Leave: Understanding Your New Rights.* 2 pages. Answers questions regarding the Family and Medical Leave Act.

- *Expanding Family Leave Policies at Your Workplace.* 2 pages. Provides information on the Family Medical Leave Act and how to apply it to your workplace.

- *Sources for Further Information on Family Friendly Policies.* 1 page. Lists organizations offering information on work/family issues.

- *The Sub/Family Challenge: A 9 to 5 Guide.* ($12.95) Not for women only. Includes:

- *9 to 5 Office Supplies.* 2 pages.

- *Computer and Your Health.* 1 page.

2

AACSB

The International Association for Management Education
St. Louis, MO 63141-6762
314-872-8481
Fax: 314-872-8495
http://www.aacsb.edu

• *Value of Accreditation.* Assists accredited institutions articulating and sharing the values of AACSB (Achieving Quality and Continous Improvement through Self-Evaluation and Peer Review). Discusses the accreditation process and the benefits to schools and programs. See Web site for more information on this and other publications and services offered by the AACSB.

3

ACCREDITATION COMMISSION FOR ACUPUNCTURE AND ORIENTAL MEDICINE
1010 Wayne Avenue, Suite 1270
Silver Spring, MD 20910
301-608-9680
Fax: 301-608-9576

• *Accredited and Candidate Programs.* Updated every May and September.

4

ACCREDITING BUREAU OF HEALTH EDUCATION SCHOOLS
803 West Broad Street, Suite 730
Falls Church, VA 22046
703-533-2082
abhes@erols.com
http://www.abhes.org/

• *Accredited Bureau of Health Education Schools/Programs.* Lists ABHES-accredited programs by state and interest .

5

ACCREDITING COMMISSION ON EDUCATION FOR HEALTH SERVICES ADMINISTRATION
730 11th Street, NW, 4th Floor

Washington, DC 20001-4510
202-638-5131
Fax: 202-638-3429
accredcom@aol.com
http://monkey.hmi.missouri.edu/acehsa

The following is available by mail or on ACEHSA's Web site:

• *The Official List of Accredited Programs in Health Services Administration in Canada and the United States.* Includes the program name, date of initial accreditation action, and the degree(s) granted by the accredited program.

6

ACCREDITING COUNCIL FOR INDEPENDENT COLLEGES AND SCHOOLS
750 First Street, NE, Suite 980
Washington, DC 20002-4241
202-336-6780
Fax: 202-842-2593
acics@acics.org

• *Directory of Accredited Institutions.* 80 pages. Lists colleges and schools that offer specific programs, such as accounting and phlebotomy, and provides a state-by-state and international listing of private, postsecondary career colleges and schools. For educational institutions and businesses only (limited supply). Updated annually.

7

ACCREDITING COUNCIL ON EDUCATION IN JOURNALISM AND MASS COMMUNICATIONS
University of Kansas
Stauffer-Flint Hall

Lawrence, KS 66045
785-864-7640
http://www.ukans.edu/~acejmc

Available on ACEJMC's Web site:

• *List of Accredited Programs.* Contains contact information, including Web site links, to over 100 accredited educational programs. Published annually.

8
ACOUSTICAL SOCIETY OF AMERICA
2 Huntington Quadrangle, Suite INO
Melville, NY 11747-4502
516-576-2360
Fax: 516-576-2377
asa@aip.org

• *Acoustics and You.* 12 pages. Discusses career oportunities in the field of acoustics.

• *Directory of Graduate Education in Acoustics.* 24 pages. Lists the schools offering graduate programs in specific acoustical fields, such as architectural, physiological, psychological, and musical acoustics; acoustical instrumentation; noise and noise control; speech communication; ultrasonics; radiation and scattering; structural acoustics and vibration; underwater sound; nonlinear acoustics and aeroacoustics; acoustical signal processing; and bioacoustics. Contact information is also given.

9
ACT PUBLICATIONS
PO Box 1008
Iowa City, IA 52243-1008
800-498-6065 or 319-337-1270

Fax: 319-337-1578
http://www.act.org

• *Preparing for the ACT Assessment.* 62 pages. Includes tips for preparation, a practice assessment test, and a scoring key. Available free at most high schools or directly from ACT.

• *A Guide to College Survival.* ($8) Practical suggestions for overcoming typical freshman problems such as budgeting time and money, establishing a study environment, reading college level texts, taking lecture notes, preparing for and taking college exams, writing research papers, and maintaining a positive attitude. Order online or by phone.

Available at the Web site:

• *Test Preparation.* Online sample questions, testing tips, and frequently asked questions about the ACT Assessment Test.

• *Checklist for College Planning.* Helpful tips to keep in mind from freshman through senior year, scheduled by monthly deadlines.

• *Glossary of College Terms.* Includes definitions ranging from admission terminology to financial aid packages.

• *Choosing a Career.* Breaks down the overwhelming process of planning a career into six manageable steps.

10
ADVERTISING EDUCATION PUBLICATIONS
PO Box 68232
Lubbock, TX 79414
806-798-0616

xnbri@ttacs.ttu.edu
http://www.mcom.ttu.edu/wsig

- *Where Shall I Go to Study Advertising and Public Relations?*

11
ADVOCACY INSTITUTE
1629 K Street, NW, Suite 200
Washington, DC 20006-1629
202-777-7577
Fax: 202-777-7575
publications@advocacy.org
http://www.advocacy.org

- *Why Not Work for a Change: An Introduction to Careers in Social Change.* A booklet of public interest career opportunities.

12
AGRICULTURAL RESEARCH SERVICE
U.S. Department of Agriculture
Information Staff
5601 Sunnyside Avenue, Room 1-2250
Beltsville, MD 20705-5128
301-504-1638
Fax: 301-504-1648
arsinfo@ars-grin-gov
http://www.ars.usda.gov

The following information is accessible through the ARS Web site.

- *Science in Your Shopping Cart.* Describes the research on consumer products developed at the ARS. Applicable to middle school through college students and beyond.

The following online career articles are suitable for younger audiences, grades 4-8:

- *A Really Ugly Fish Makes a Really Tasty Treat.*

- *Lights, Camera, Action!*

- *Fun Careers in a Small Town.*

- *The Plant Hunters.*

13
AIR CONDITIONING CONTRACTORS OF AMERICA
1712 New Hampshire Avenue, NW
Washington, DC 20009
202-483-9370
Fax: 202-234-4721
info@acca.org
http://www.acca.org

- *HVACR: One of the Most Important Industries in the World.* Available by mail or online. Defines HVACR and illustates its importance in society. Includes information on education and training required, future outlook for the field, and lists examples of jobs available within HVACR.

14
AIR FORCE ROTC
Recruiting Branch
551 East Maxwell Boulevard
Maxwell AFB, AL 36112-6106
800-522-0033, ext 2091, or 334-953-2091
Fax: 334-953-6167
http://www.afoats.af.mil

- *Air Force ROTC and Your Future.* 22 pages. Describes the opportunities available through the Air Force ROTC, the qualifications and scholarships, and Air Force career opportunities. Lists colleges and universities offering Air Force ROTC.

15

AIR LINE PILOTS ASSOCIATION INTERNATIONAL

535 Herndon Parkway
PO Box 1169
Herndon, VA 20172-1169
703-481-4440
http://www.alpa.org

The following is available by mail or accessible at the Association's Web site:

• *Looking for a Career Where the Sky's the Limit?* 16 pages. Designed for students interested in a career in aviation. Provides an introduction to aviation; describes the three pilot positions; how to prepare for an airline pilot career; discusses licensing requirements; and provides sources of additional information.

• *What's a Pilot Worth?* Contrasts the costs involved in learning the profession (licenses, training, certification) with the average starting salary of a pilot.

16

AIR TRANSPORT ASSOCIATION OF AMERICA

1301 Pennsylvania Avenue, NW
Suite 1100
Washington, DC 20004-1707
202-626-4000
Fax: 202-626-4181
http://www.air-transport.org

• *The People of the Airlines.* 8 pages. Free booklet describing the necessary skills, education, and types of careers in the field. Contains a list of ATA member airlines.

17

AIR-CONDITIONING AND REFRIGERATION INSTITUTE

4301 North Fairfax Drive, Suite 425
Arlington, VA 22203
703-524-8800
Fax: 703-528-3816
ari@ari.org
http://www.ari.org

• *Career Opportunities in Heating, Air Conditioning and Refrigeration.* 8 pages. Describes job opportunities and required education and training for a career in the HVACR industry.

• *What You Should Know about ARI/GAMA Competency Examinations for Vo-Tech Students/Graduates of HVACR Programs.* 8 pages. Provides details about the competency exam program.

18

AIRCRAFT OWNERS AND PILOTS ASSOCIATION

421 Aviation Way
Frederick, MD 21701-4798
301-695-2000
Fax: 301-695-2375
aopahq@aopa.org
http://www.aopa.org

• *Help Wanted! Careers in Aviation.* 2 pages. Includes career fields and educational requirements. Describes employers in the aviation industry in an easy-to-read chart format.

• *What is General Aviation?* Brochure describing the industry, contrasting general perception with the reality of general aviation.

• *Aviation and You.* Brochure answering your questions about learning to fly, careers in aviation, and much more.

• *Getting Started on Flight Training: Everything You Need to Fly Skyward.* Informational brochure illustrating representative student pilots of all ages and backgrounds.

• *A Teacher's Guide to Aviation.* Brochure including ways to bring aviation into the classroom, the basics of flight and flight training, career information, useful aviation facts, and a guide to additional resources.

19
ALASKA DEPARTMENT OF LABOR AND WORKFORCE DEVELOPMENT
Research and Analysis Section
PO Box 25501
Juneau, AK 99802-5501
907-465-4500
Fax: 907-465-2101
http://www.labor.state.ak.us

The following resources are available online:

• *2000 Alaska Occupational Outlook Table.* Includes statewide and regional occupational estimates and projections, as well as a narrative of the current industry status and outlook.

• *Alaska Wage Rates.* Lists occupational title, region(s) where occupation is found, and links to regional and national wage information.

• *Finding Work in Alaska.* Online guide to job opportunities. Includes helpful information on wages, cost of living, and geography of Alaska.

20
ALASKA SEA GRANT COLLEGE PROGRAM
University of Alaska-Fairbanks
PO Box 755040-MEB
Fairbanks, AK 99775-5040
907-474-6707

• *Careers in Marine Mammal Science.* 12 pages. Booklet addressing questions commonly asked by young people seeking a career in the marine sciences. Covers types of jobs available, salaries, ways to gain experience, and suggested education to prepare for a career in the marine fields.

• *Careers in Oceanography and Marine-Related Fields.* 24 pages. Booklet about technical and professional jobs in the marine sciences requiring a college degree. Aimed at high school and college students interested in environmental discovery through oceanography. Includes information about jobs available, education required, financial tips, job market outlook, and tips on locating a job in marine fields.

21
ALLIANCE OF AMERICAN INSURERS
Publication Sales Department
3055 Highland Parkway, Suite 800
Downers Grove, IL 60515-1289
630-724-2115
Fax: 630-724-2190
pubsales@allianceai.org
http://www.allianceai.org

- *Careers in Insurance.* ($1.15) 22 pages. Provides an overview of career opportunities in the insurance industry, as well as educational requirements and sources for more information.

- *The Insurance Industry: A Key Player in the U.S. Economy.* ($17.95) Focuses on the insurance industry's contribution to the U.S. and state economies as a vital service provider, as employer, as investor, and as taxpayer.

22

ALLIANCE OF CARDIOVASCULAR PROFESSIONALS
910 Charles Street
Fredericksburg, VA 22401
540-370-0102
Fax: 540-370-0015
http://www.acp-online.org

- *Electrocardiograph Technicians: Health Technologist and Health Technicians.* 5 pages. Describes the nature of the work, working conditions, employment, training and advancement, job outlook, earnings, related occupations, and sources of additional information.

- *Cardiology Salary Survey.* 3 pages. National salary survey conducted by the American Academy of Medical Administrators.

- *Accredited Programs.* 4 pages. Lists the 16 programs of cardiovascular technology accredited by the American Medical Association.

23

AMERICAN ACADEMY OF ALLERGY, ASTHMA & IMMUNOLOGY
611 East Wells Street
Milwaukee, WI 53202
414-272-6071
Fax: 414-272-6970
media@aaaai.org
http://www.aaaai.org

- *Academy News.* Highlights from recent and past issues available online. Includes classified ads for positions available in the allergy, asthma, and immunology field, plus other relevant articles regarding the field.

24

AMERICAN ACADEMY OF ENVIRONMENTAL ENGINEERS
130 Holiday Court, Suite 100
Annapolis, MD 21401
410-266-3311
Fax: 410-266-7653
academy@aaee.net
http://www.aaee.net

- *A Crisis in Human Resources in Engineering? Yes, No, Maybe.* 7 pages.

- *Environmental Engineering Selection Guide: A Directory to Board Certified Specialists in Consulting & Education.* 115 pages. Lists institutions with professionally accredited environmental engineering or engineering technology programs.

- *Future Trends in Environmental Engineering.* 5 pages.

25
AMERICAN ACADEMY OF FAMILY PHYSICIANS

11400 Tomahawk Creek Parkway
Leawood, KS 66211-2672
800-944-0000 (orders) or 913-906-6000
fp@aafp.org
http://www.aafp.org

The following publications are all complimentary:

• *U.S. Medical Schools Listing.* (M119) 27 pages. Provides names and telephone numbers of the medical school deans and the coordinators of the family practice predoctoral programs. Also includes a description of the family medicine administration structure of each medical school and the AAFP medical school code.

• *Consider a Career in Family Practice: High School Brochure.* (M146) 6 pages. Describes what family practice is, how to prepare in college for it, and how to choose an undergraduate college.

• *Elementary School Packet.* (M204) Booklet for students wanting to learn more about family physicians. Includes a box of AAFP crayons for activities.

• *Junior/Senior High School Packet.* (M205) Discusses for middle school and high school students careers in medicine, educational preparation, and choosing an undergraduate college. Lists college programs, financial planning, and sources of additional information.

• *Pre-Med Student Packet.* (M206) Provides students with insight on specialty options as well as important information about becoming a family physician. Includes a list of all U.S. LCME-accredited medical schools, admission requirements, and additional materials.

• *Residency Information Packet.* (M105) Designed for students seeking statistical and informative data on family practice residency programs. Additional information includes a listing of all ACGME-accredited family practice residency programs.

• *Specialty of Choice Brochure.* (M110) Designed to provide medical school students information about the specialty of family practice. Discusses practice choices, income expectations, and other interesting facts about the field.

• *Take Another Look at Family Practice.* (M184) Brochure describing family practice and its personal career benefits.

• *Family Practice...A Specialty for Our Time.* (M100) 15-minute video. Follows a group of family physicians and highlights a variety of patient and medical needs that family physicians meet on a daily basis.

• *This Tuesday.* (M209) 30-minute video. Developed to illustrate a day in the life of two family physicians.

• *Can I Afford to be a Family Physician?* (M234) Resource book addressing students' financial concerns about choosing a career in family practice by helping students calculate loan repayment and life-style costs on the average family physician's salary.

• *Heirs of General Practice.* (M170) 119 pages. An in-depth look at what is

involved in family practice by discussing the challenges and professional
obstacles young physicians encounter.

• *Response Article on Questions About
Family Practice.* (M144) Provides answers
to common questions asked by medical
students interested in family practice.

26
AMERICAN ACADEMY OF NEUROLOGY
Customer Service
1080 Montreal Avenue
St. Paul, MN 55116
651-695-1940
Fax: 612-623-2491
http://www.aan.com

• *Choosing the Medical Specialty of
Neurology.* 6 pages. Describes the field of
neurology, the educational and training
requirements, practice options, and
board certification.

• *1999 Directory for Fellowships and
Academic Positions.* 132 pages.
Comprehensive guide of more than 350
post-residency positions, listed by 27
categories of neuroscience research or
subspecialization. Also includes academic position listings. Each entry includes
duration, contact information, salary,
and application/notification dates.

27
AMERICAN ACADEMY OF NURSE PRACTITIONERS
Capitol Station
LBJ Building
PO Box 12846
Austin, TX 78711

512-442-4262
Fax: 512-442-6469
admin@aanp.org
http://www.aanp.org

• *The Nurse Practitioner: A Primary Health
Care Professional.* 8 pages. Provides an
overview of the profession, its specialities, the duties involved, and the working environment.

• *Scope of Practice for Nurse Practioners.* 1
page. Defines the professional role, educational requirements, and responsibilities of nurse practitioners.

• *Standards of Practice.* 4 pages. Lists standards of practice for nurse practitioners.

28
AMERICAN ACADEMY OF OPHTHALMOLOGY
655 Beach Street
PO Box 7424
San Francisco, CA 94120-7424
415-561-8500
Fax: 415-561-8533
http://www.eyenet.org

• *Envision Ophthalmology: A Practical Guide
to Ophthalmology as a Career Choice.* 16
pages. Defines the field and its subspe-
cialities. Provides information on related
topics, such as applying for a residency
and residency program structures.

29
AMERICAN ACADEMY OF PEDIATRICS
141 Northwest Point Boulevard
Elk Grove Village, IL 60007-1098
847-434-4000

Fax: 847-434-8000
pedscareer@aap.org
http://www.aap.org

• *Pediatrics Specialty Fact Sheets.* Online information including a profile of pediatrics, required pediatric residency training, career options and lifestyles, and minority health status indicators.

• *Pediatrics 101: Facts, Figures, and Assorted Intangibles.* Online information covering general pediatrics, subspecialties, practice options, salary data, and larger workforce issues.

• *Selecting a Pediatric Residency: An Employment Guide.* ($.10) Highlights employment opportunities in pediatric residencies.

30
AMERICAN ACADEMY OF PHYSICAL MEDICINE AND REHABILITATION

1 IBM Plaza, Suite 2500
Chicago, IL 60611
312-464-9700
Fax: 312-464-0227
info@aapmr.org
http://www.aapmr.org

• *What is a Physiatrist?* (#PE101) 6 pages. Discusses the types of conditions these specialists treat, their role in treatment, their diagnostic tools, and their work environments.

• *Physical Medicine & Rehabilitation: Diversity in a Profession.* (#PR101)

31
AMERICAN ACADEMY OF PHYSICIAN ASSISTANTS

950 North Washington Street
Alexandria, VA 22314-1552
703-836-2272
aapa@aapa.org
http://www.aapa.org/

• *Financial Aid Resources for PA Students.* 35 pages. Free booklet containing information on finding funds for a physician assistant education. Lists scholarships, traineeships, grants, constituent chapters of the AAPA, and physician assistant programs.

• *Information on the Physician Assistant Profession.* 8 pages. Free information on the profession and a list of the accredited programs located throughout the United States.

32
AMERICAN AGRICULTURAL ECONOMICS ASSOCIATION

415 South Duff, Suite C
Ames, IA 50010
515-233-3202
Fax: 515-233-3101
employment@aaea.org
http://www.aaea.org

• *Careers for the Future...Agricultural Economics and Agricultural Business.* 8 pages. Describes specific career opportunities, the type of work involved, and typical employers in the field of agricultural economics.

33

AMERICAN ALLIANCE FOR THEATRE AND EDUCATION

Arizona State University
Theatre Department
PO Box 872002
Tempe, AZ 85287-2002
480-965-6064
Fax: 480-965-5351
aateinfo@asu.edu
http://www.aate.com

• *Teacher Preparation and Certification Standards.* 8 pages. Offers standards for preparation and certification of theatre specialists, speech/communication/theatre teachers, and speech communication specialists.

34

AMERICAN ANTHROPOLOGICAL ASSOCIATION

4350 North Fairfax Drive, Suite 640
Arlington, VA 22203
703-528-1902
Fax: 703-528-3546
http://www.ameranthassn.org

The following information is available at the Web site:

• *Anthropology: Education for the 21st Century.* Information about the field, major, job opportunities, and typical career paths.

• *Frequently Asked Questions About a Career in Archaeology in the U.S.*

35

AMERICAN APPAREL MANUFACTURERS ASSOCIATION

2500 Wilson Boulevard, Suite 301
Arlington, VA 22201
703-524-1864
Fax: 703-522-6741
grbates@americanapparel.org
http://www.americanapparel.org

• *Careers in the Apparel Manufacturing Industry/College Directory.* 32 pages. Provides brief descriptions and actual case studies of careers in the apparel industry. Also contains a list of colleges offering major programs in apparel manufacturing management and engineering technology, as well as information on curricula and degrees offered.

36

AMERICAN ART THERAPY ASSOCIATION, INC.

1202 Allanson Road
Mundelein, IL 60060
847-949-6064
Fax: 847-566-4580
arttherapy@ntr.net
http://www.arttherapy.org

• *Art Therapy Model Job Description.* ($1)

• *General Information Packet.* ($6 to individuals; no charge to high school guidance counselors and college resource centers) Includes:

• *Art Therapy: The Profession.* ($1 without packet) 4 pages;

• *Art Therapy Educational Program List.* ($2 without packet) 15 pages. Lists AATA-approved graduate degree programs, clinical programs, and institute programs, as well as unapproved undergraduate and graduate programs;

- *Educational Standards for Programs Providing Art Therapy Education.* ($1 without packet) 7 pages; and

- *Resource Sheet.* Lists publication materials available.

37
AMERICAN ARTIST MAGAZINE
Billboard Publications
PO Box 1944
Marion, OH 43305
800-745-8922

- *Directory of Art Schools.* ($5) Contains contact, financial, and enrollment information for art schools, summer schools, class with private teachers, and traveling workshops. Annual supplement appearing every March. Available by mail or at local newstands.

38
AMERICAN ASSOCIATION FOR CLINICAL CHEMISTRY, INC.
2101 L Street, NW, Suite 202
Washington, DC 20037-1526
800-892-1400 or 202-857-0717
Fax: 202-887-5093
http://www.aacc.org

- *Clinical Chemistry: Partnerships in Health Care.* 8 pages. Defines a clinical chemist and describes a typical day as part of a healthcare team.

Available only on the Web site:

- *Graduate and Postdoctoral Training Programs.* Lists only those programs

approved by the Commission on Accrediation in Clinical Chemistry.

39
AMERICAN ASSOCIATION FOR HEALTH EDUCATION
1900 Association Drive
Reston, VA 20191-1599
703-476-3437
Fax: 703-476-6638
http://www.aahperd.org/aahe.html

- *AAHE Directory of Institutions Offering Specialization in Undergraduate and Graduate Professional Preparation Programs in School, Community and Public Health Education.*

40
AMERICAN ASSOCIATION FOR MARRIAGE AND FAMILY THERAPY
1133 15th Street, NW, Suite 300
Washington, DC 20005-2710
202-452-0109
Fax: 202-223-2329
http://www.aamft.org

Available at the Web site:

- *Directory of MFT Training Programs.* Includes listing of marriage and family therapy educational programs in Canada and the United States, as well as information on applying to a marriage and family therapy program.

41
AMERICAN ASSOCIATION FOR MEDICAL TRANSCRIPTION
3460 Oakdale Road, Suite M
Modesto, CA 95355-9690
209-551-0883

Fax: 209-551-9317
aamt@aamt.org
http://www.aamt.org/career.htm

For the following, please send a self-addressed, stamped envelope to the Association or visit the Web site for more information.

• *Frequently Asked Questions About Medical Transcription.* 2 pages.

• *Tip Sheet for Prospective Medical Transciption Students.* 2 pages. Provides questions you should ask before enrolling in a medical transription program.

• *Tip Sheet for Becoming a Self-Employed Medical Transcriptionist.* 2 pages.

42

AMERICAN ASSOCIATION FOR PARALEGAL EDUCATION

2965 Flowers Road, South Suite 105
Atlanta, GA 30341
770-452-9877
Fax: 770-458-3314
info@aafpe.org
http://www.aafpe.org

• *How to Choose a Paralegal Education Program.* ($.50) Recommends factors to consider in choosing a paralegal education program. Available by mail or freely accessible on the Web site.

43

AMERICAN ASSOCIATION FOR RESPIRATORY CARE

11030 Ables Lane
Dallas, TX 75229
972-243-2272
http://www.aarc.org

• *The AARC Career Guide: Climbing the Professional Ladder.* 9 pages. Discusses career planning and employment options.

• *Respiratory Therapy Educational Programs.* 28 pages. Includes a historical summary of the respiratory therapy occupation, occupational and job descriptions, employment characteristics, information about educational programs, and a list of accredited educational programs by state.

• *Decisions.* 6 pages. Details careers in respiratory care. Designed for high school students.

• *Transitions.* 6 pages. Details careers in respiratory care. Designed for adults (college students and beyond).

• *Hello I'm Your Respiratory Care Practitioner.* 4 pages. Provides a basic overview of the respiratory care practitioner.

44

AMERICAN ASSOCIATION FOR STATE AND LOCAL HISTORY

Order Billing Department
1717 Church Street
Nashville, TN 37203-2991
615-320-3203
Fax: 615-327-9013
history@aaslh.org
http://www.aaslh.org

• *Guide to Resource Organizations.* ($8) Booklet containing listings of resource materials and contacts for collections, management, exhibits, educational programming, interpretation, and more. A valuable tool for anyone working with historical sites or museums.

• *Directory of Native American Museums and Cultural Centers.* ($10) Lists over 350 museums, cultural centers, historic houses, and tribal colleges in the U.S. and Canada, with contact information and a listing of key personnel.

45

AMERICAN ASSOCIATION FOR THE ADVANCEMENT OF SCIENCE

Directorate for Science and Policy Programs
1200 New York Avenue, NW
Washington, DC 20005
202-326-6600
Fax: 202-289-4950
science_policy@aaas.org
http://www.aaas.org

• *Guide to Education in Science, Engineering, and Public Policy.* (94-37S) ($10) 144 pages. For each institution lists contact information, background on the program, degrees offered, admission and degree requirements, student and faculty information, positions for graduates, and financial information.

46

AMERICAN ASSOCIATION OF ADVERTISING AGENCIES

Publications Department
405 Lexington Avenue, 18th Floor
New York, NY 10174
212-682-2500
Fax: 212-953-5787
publications@aaaa.org
http://www.aaaa.org

• *Want a Job in Adverstising?* ($3)

47

AMERICAN ASSOCIATION OF BLOOD BANKS

Professional Education Programs Coordinator
8101 Glenbrook Road
Bethesda, MD 20814-2749
301-907-6977
Fax: 301-907-6895
aabb@aabb.org
http://www.aabb.org

Available at the Web site:

• *SBB Programs.* Includes information on SBB education and lists locations of schools and universities that offer SBB programs.

48

AMERICAN ASSOCIATION OF CEREAL CHEMISTS

3340 Pilot Knob Road
St. Paul, MN 55121-2097
612-454-7250
Fax: 612-454-0766
aacc@scisoc.org
http://www.scisoc.org/aacc

Available on the Association's Web site:

• *Careers in Cereal Chemistry.* Defines the field and describes the career opportunities available in cereal chemistry. Includes education requirements and typical training involved to enter the field.

• *U.S. and Canadian Universities That Offer Graduate Education in Cereal Science.* Listing of institutions that offer cereal science degrees or offer education in cereal science as part of a food science degree.

49
AMERICAN ASSOCIATION OF COLLEGES OF NURSING
One Dupont Circle, NW, Suite 530
Washington, DC 20036
202-463-6930
Fax: 202-785-8320
http://www.aacn.nche.edu

The following resources are available at the Association's Web site:

• *Your Nursing Career: A Look at the Facts.* Includes information on statistics showing the high demand for baccalaureate nurses, the changing job market trends, and sources for more information.

• *Listing of AACN-Member Schools.*

50
AMERICAN ASSOCIATION OF COLLEGES OF OSTEOPATHIC MEDICINE
5550 Friendship Boulevard, Suite 310
Chevy Chase, MD 20815
301-968-4100
Fax: 301-968-4101
http://www.aacom.org

• *Osteopathic Medical College Information.* ($2) 35 pages. Identifies 17 member schools and provides a brief description of the campus and the curriculum, admissions criteria, minimum entrance requirements, application material requirements, class size and enrollment, and application deadlines.

• *Osteopathic Medical Education.* 8 pages. Describes osteopathic medicine, education required, and postdoctoral programs and specialities. Provides a list of member colleges of osteopathic medicine.

• *Application Packet.* Information and application materials for applying to the 17 member schools of osteopathic medicine, available also on the Web site.

51
AMERICAN ASSOCIATION OF COLLEGES OF PHARMACY
Publications Department
1426 Prince Street
Alexandria, VA 22314-2841
703-739-2330
Fax: 703-836-8982
lross@aacp.org
http://www.aacp.org/students/students.html

The following information is available free by mail or on the Web site:

• *Shall I Study Pharmacy?* 17 pages. Outlines the field for anyone considering a career in pharmaceuticals. Includes information on typical responsibilities of a pharmacist, education/training required, and job outlook.

• *Academic Pharmacy's Vital Statistics.* Fact sheet listing programs in pharmacy.

• *Pharmacy Education Today.* Brochure of colleges and schools of pharmacy listed by state.

52

AMERICAN ASSOCIATION OF COLLEGES OF PODIATRIC MEDICINE
1350 Piccard Drive, Suite 322
Rockville, MD 20850
800-922-9266 or 301-990-6882
Fax: 301-990-2807
http://www.aacpm.org

All of the following are free of charge:

• *Podiatric Medicine as a Career: What is a DPM?* 12 pages. Defines podiatric medicine; explains what doctors of podiatric medicine do and where they work; lists admission, licensing, and board certification requirements; discusses benefits and income potential; and lists the six colleges that participate in the centralized application service known as AACPMAS.

• *Fact Sheet-Podiatric Medicine.* 2 pages. Describes admission requirements, facts about podiatric medical students and graduates, residency training, licensing and credentialing, and benefits and income potential.

• *Podiatric Medicine's Advising Kit.* Provides help for those who want to present clear and accurate information about podiatric medicine when advising students interested in the health care profession. The kit includes information on podiatric medicine as a career; college information about AACPM's six member colleges; information on APMA; financial aid available; podiatric residencies; and an admissions fact sheet. Also includes application request forms and advisors' order forms.

53

AMERICAN ASSOCIATION OF COMMUNITY COLLEGES
Publications
National Center for Higher Education
One Dupont Circle, NW, Suite 410
Washington, DC 20036-1176
202-728-0200
Fax: 202-223-9390
dcarey@aacc.nche.edu
http://www.aacc.nche.edu

Available in print:

• *Community College Facts...at a Glance.* 2 pages. Provides information on the number of colleges, the background of students, tuition and fees, career programs, and other topics.

• *FACTS.* 4 pages. Contains factual information on AACC.

Check out AACC's Web site, where you can find the latest information on community colleges, government, education, and other helpful resources.

54

AMERICAN ASSOCIATION OF HOMES AND SERVICES FOR THE AGING
901 E Street, NW, Suite 500
Washington, DC 20004-2011
800-508-9442
Fax: 202-783-2255
http://www.aahsa.org

• *Considering a Career in Long-Term Care and Senior Housing.* 4 pages. Describes careers, training required, and salaries for jobs in the field of aging services.

55
AMERICAN ASSOCIATION OF NURSE ANESTHETISTS
Bookstore
222 South Prospect Avenue
Park Ridge, IL 60068-4001
847-692-7050, ext. 3009
Fax: 847-692-6968
http://www.aana.com

• *Focus on Your Future.* (#1024) 6 pages. Includes factors to consider in becoming a nurse, the duties of certified registered nurse anesthetists, how to become a CRNA, educational requirements, program requirements, and advantages of the profession.

• *Questions and Answers about a Career in Nurse Anesthesia.* 1 page. Includes the most frequently asked questions about the profession, the answers to those questions, and suggestions on where to get answers to other questions. Also accessible online.

• *Council on Accreditation of Nurse Anesthesia Educational Programs: List of Recognized Educational Programs.* 10 pages. Lists the programs by state, along with pertinent program information.

• *Certified Registered Nurse Anesthetists and the American Association of Nurse Anesthetists.* 8 pages. Describes the impact of CRNAs on health care, their responsibilities, and their educational requirements.

• *The Best Kept Secrets in Healthcare: Certified Registered Nurse Anesthetists.* ($12) Video: 7 minutes. Informative information for patients and general public.

• *Education of Nurse Anesthetists in the United States.* (#2002)

• *Recruitment Poster.* (14"x 17": #2000; 24"x 30": #2001)

• *Degree Options for CRNAs.* (#1023)

• *Certification Candidate Handbook.* (#1035)

• *Nurse Anesthesia...No Longer the Best Kept Secret in Health Care.* Online information.

56
AMERICAN ASSOCIATION OF ORIENTAL MEDICINE
433 Front Street
Catasauqua, PA 18032-2506
800-500-7999
Fax: 610-264-2768
aaom1@aol.com
http://www.aaom.org

• *Facts.* (donations appreciated) 2 pages. Describes the oriental medicine practice and the training and certification of acupuncturists.

• *Comprehensive Listing of Schools.* 1 page. Lists names, addresses, and telephone numbers of the American Association of Oriental Medicine schools and those offering accredited and candidate programs.

• *State Acupuncture Associations.* 1 page. Lists acupuncture associations by state.

• *Acupuncture: A Successful and Cost Effective Treatment.* 4 pages. Describes acupuncture and compares the costs and results of traditional medicine verses acupuncture.

- *State Licensing.* 2 pages. Lists the licensing requirements for each state.

- *State Listing of Individuals Certified in Acupuncture.* Lists individuals by state.

57

AMERICAN ASSOCIATION OF ORTHODONTISTS

401 North Lindbergh Boulevard
St. Louis, MO 63141-7816
800-222-9969
http://braces.org

The following are available free of charge:

- *Advanced Orthodontic Education Programs Approved by the Commission on Dental Accreditation of the American Dental Association.* 12 pages. Gives contact information, department head, program length, degree granted, number of students accepted, program starting date, and an application deadline for each school.

- *Orthodontics.* Describes the profession, required skills, and career opportunities.

- *Orthodontist.* 2 pages.

58

AMERICAN ASSOCIATION OF PETROLEUM GEOLOGISTS

PO Box 979
Tulsa, OK 74101-0979
918-584-2555
Fax: 918-560-2636
jdawes@aapg.org
http://www.aapg.org

- *Careers in Geosciences.*

59

AMERICAN ASSOCIATION OF PHYSICAL ANTHROPOLOGISTS

Career Development Committee
Department of Anthropology College of Arts and Sciences
University of South Florida, SOC 107
Tampa, FL 33620-8100
813-974-6237
Fax: 813-974-0945
cwienker@admin.usf.edu
http://www.physanth.org/careers

- *A Career in Biological Anthropology.* 6 pages. Defines anthropology and biological anthropology, details a biological anthropologist's duties, and describes the advantages of a career in the field and opportunities for employment.

60

AMERICAN ASSOCIATION OF PHYSICISTS IN MEDICINE

One Physics Ellipse
College Park, MD 20740-3846
301-209-3350
Fax: 301-209-0862
aapm@aapm.org
http://www.aapm.org

- *The Medical Physicist.* 8 pages. Describes the field, the duties, professional position, work environment, training, demand, and occupational outlook of medical physicists.

61

AMERICAN ASSOCIATION OF RETIRED PERSONS

601 E Street, NW
Washington, DC 20049
800-424-3410

member@aarp.org
http://www.aarp.org

Available on AARP's Web site:

- *Paying for College.* Includes information on work/study programs, federal aid, and other tips about budgeting for college expenses.

- *Social Security: The Facts.* Includes facts, issues, and challenges for the federal program and opposing viewpoints about social security.

- *Working Options Home Page.* Includes information about facing and battling age descrimination in the workplace, careers for the future, and tips for searching for and getting the right job later in life.

62
AMERICAN ASSOCIATION OF SCHOOL ADMINISTRATORS
1801 North Moore Street
Arlington, VA 22209-1813
703-875-0748
Fax: 703-841-1543
http://www.aasa.org

- *Voices of Women Aspiring to the Superintendency.* (607) ($14.95) 222 pages. Though a majority of teachers are women, few make it to the powerful and prestigious position of superintendent. This book examines the reasons for this discrepancy through a study of 27 women in high administrative positions aspiring to the executive leadership position.

- *Techniques of Interviewing and Resume Writing for Educators.* (172-001) ($9.95) 31

pages. Education experts in the interviewing process explain how to be an effective communicator, in person and on paper. Tips that will land the job that's right for you.

63
AMERICAN ASSOCIATION OF UNIVERSITY WOMEN EDUCATIONAL FOUNDATION
Customer Service Center
1111 16th Street, NW
Washington, DC 20036
800-326-AAUW
Fax: 202-872-1425
info@aauw.org
http://www.aauw.org

- *Fellowships and Grants.* 15 pages. Describes AAUW Educational Foundation fellowships and grants for women. Encourages women of color to apply for these fellowships and grants.

64
AMERICAN ASTRONOMICAL SOCIETY
Career Brochure
AAS Education Office
University of Chicago
5640 South Ellis Avenue, Room AAC 112
Chicago, IL 60637
http://www.aas.org

- *A New Universe to Explore: Careers in Astronomy.* 19 pages. Describes the astronomy field and employment possibilities and outlines an academic plan for becoming an astronomer.

65

AMERICAN BANKERS ASSOCIATION
1120 Connecticut Avenue, NW
Washington, DC 20036
800-338-0626 or 202-663-5000
Fax: 202-663-5464
eftemp@aba.com
http://www.aba.com

- *Building Your Future? Banking is the Answer.* 8 pages. Describes banking career opportunities, necessary qualifications, training and advancement, and employment outlook.

- *Occupational Outlook Handbook.* 9 pages. Contains information on banking careers. Excerpted from the *Occupational Outlook Handbook,* published by the U.S. Bureau of Labor Statistics.

66

AMERICAN BAR ASSOCIATION
Law Student Division
750 North Lake Shore Drive
Chicago, IL 60611-4497
800-285-2221
Fax: 312-988-5568
abasvcctr@abanet.org
http://www.abanet.org

- *Comprehensive Guide to Bar Admission Requirements.* ($7.50) 58 pages. Details all requirements to be admitted to the bar.

67

AMERICAN BEEKEEPING FEDERATION, INC.
PO Box 1038
Jesup, GA 31598-1038
912-427-4233
Fax: 912-427-8447
info@abfnet.org
http://www.abfnet.org

- *Beekeeper: Career Summary.* Describes beekeeping duties, working conditions, personal qualifications, education and training, earnings, hours, and occupational outlook.

68

AMERICAN BOARD OF FUNERAL SERVICE EDUCATION
38 Florida Avenue
Portland, ME 04103
207-878-6530
Fax: 207-797-7686
gconnic1@maine.rr.com
http://www.abfse.org

- *In Service of Others: The Professional Director.* 6 pages. Lists educational requirements, accredited schools of mortuary science, and responsibilities.

- *Have You Considered...Funeral Service?* 6 pages. Details the duties and responsibilities in the funeral service field, career opportunities, and educational requirements. Lists mortuary science programs.

69

AMERICAN CAMPING ASSOCIATION
5000 State Road 67 North
Martinsville, IN 46151-7902
800-428-2267 or 765-342-8456
Fax: 765-349-6357
bookstore@aca-camps.org
http://www.aca-camps.org

Available at the Web site:

- *Why Work at Camp?* Includes descriptions of typical jobs, benefits, and opportunities available.

- *Careers in the Camp Community.* Includes sources of employment opportunities and contacts for additional information.

- *Colleges and Universities Offering Study in Camp Administration and Related Courses.*

70
AMERICAN CERAMIC SOCIETY
735 Ceramic Place
Westerville, OH 43081-8720
614-890-4700
Fax: 619-899-6109
customersrvc@acers.org
http://www.acers.org

- *Ceramic Engineering: Career Opportunities for You.* 8 pages. Details how to prepare for a career in ceramic engineering. Lists career options and accredited institutions.

- *Ceramic Engineers.* 4 pages. Provides an overview of the ceramic engineering field, including work performed, education and training, personal qualifications, and employment outlook.

71
AMERICAN CHEMICAL SOCIETY
Education Division
1155 16th Street, NW
Washington, DC 20036
800-227-5558 or 202-872-4600
Fax: 202-833-7732
http://www.acs.org/

Career Publications Set available in print and free at the Society's Web site. Includes:

- *Chemistry and Your Career: Questions and Answers.* 16 pages. Answers the questions asked most often by high school students.

- *Futures through Chemistry: Charting a Course.* 64 pages. Designed for undergraduates. Discusses academic preparation, career options, job hunting, how to prepare for and find a graduate school, and financial assistance.

- *I Know You're a Chemist, But What Do You Do?* 11 pages. Includes discussions by chemists in various types of work environments. Provides advice on job hunting.

- *Chemical Careers in Brief.* Discusses responsibilities, working conditions, places of employment, personal characteristics, required education and training, job outlook, and salary range. Briefs available on agriculture chemistry, biotechnology, chemical information, environmental chemistry, food and flavor chemistry, hazardous waste management, materials science, medicinal chemistry, polymer chemistry, and science writing.

72
AMERICAN CHIROPRACTIC ASSOCIATION
1701 Clarendon Boulevard
Arlington, VA 22209
703-276-8800
Fax: 703-243-2593
http://www.amerchiro.org/aca

- *Career Kit.* Complimentary packet about chiropractic careers, including information on future of the profession, opportunities available, and educational information.

Available at the Web site:

- *Educational Requirements.*

- *CCE Accredited Colleges.* Online directory of colleges and universities listed by state.

73
AMERICAN COLLECTORS ASSOCIATION, INC.
PO Box 39106
Minneapolis, MN 55439-0106
612-926-6547
Fax: 612-926-1624
aca@collector.com
http://www.collector.com

Available at the Web site:

- *Careers in Collections.* Describes a career in collection, duties and responsibilities, employment outlook, opportunities, and qualifications.

74
AMERICAN COLLEGE OF HEALTH CARE ADMINISTRATORS
1800 Diagonal Road, Suite 355
Alexandria, VA 22314-3571
703-739-7900
Fax: 703-739-7901
info@achca.org
http://www.achca.org

- *Starting Your Career in Long-Term Health Care Administration.* 8 pages. Describes the field, licensure requirements, and salary.

75
AMERICAN COLLEGE OF HEALTHCARE EXECUTIVES
1 North Franklin Street, Suite 1700
Chicago, IL 60606
312-424-2800
Fax: 312-424-0023
http://www.ache.org

- *Your Career as a Healthcare Executive: A Profile of the Profession Including a List of the Accredited Graduate Programs.* Describes career opportunities for health care executives, academic training, and necessary skills and attributes. Lists related health care organizations and accredited programs in Canada and the United States. The profile is available on http://www.ache.org/carsvcs/ycareer.html.

76
AMERICAN COLLEGE OF NURSE-MIDWIVES
818 Connecticut Avenue, NW, Suite 900
Washington, DC 20006
202-728-9860
Fax: 202-728-9897
info@acnm.org
http://www.midwife.org

Available at the Web site:

- *The CNM Profession.* Describes the career options available in the field.

- *Financing Your Education.* Includes contact information for scholarship opportunities.

- *FAQs for Students.* Addresses questions often asked by students considering a nurse-midwife career.

• *Accredited Programs.* Includes information on certificate and master's programs.

77

AMERICAN COLLEGE OF SPORTS MEDICINE

Public Information Department
PO Box 1440
Indianapolis, IN 46206-1440
317-637-9200
Fax: 317-634-7817
http://www.acsm.org

Single copies of the following brochures are free by sending a business-sized SASE to ACSM:

• *Viewpoint: The Sports Medicine Umbrella.* 2 pages. Describes career opportunities in the field of sports medicine.

• *What is an Exercise Physiologist?* 2 pages. Defines exercise physiology, the duties and responsibilities, work environments, and educational requirements.

• *ACSM Information and Publications Directory.* 27 pages. Contains an overview of the college and a mission statement; information on certification and education; and a publications list.

• *2000 Directory of Undergraduate Programs in Sports Medicine and Exercise Science.* ($15) Contains listings of more than 120 colleges and universities with undergraduate programs. Each listing provides types of degrees each institution offers, areas of specialization, and contact information.

• *Careers in Sport Medicine.*

78

AMERICAN CONGRESS ON SURVEYING AND MAPPING

5410 Grosvenor Lane, Suite 100
Bethesda, MD 20814-2144
301-493-0200
Fax: 301-493-8245
info@acsm.net
http://www.survmap.org

• *Cartography and Geographic Information Systems: A Career Guide.* 20 pages. Lists the jobs available, educational programs with a cartography/GIS emphasis, readings, and federal government agencies related to the field.

79

AMERICAN COUNCIL FOR CONSTRUCTION EDUCATION

1300 Hudson Lane, Suite 3
Monroe, LA 71201
318-323-2816
Fax: 318-323-2413
acce@iamerica.net
http://www.acce-hq.org

• *ACCE Accredited Programs.* 3 pages. State by state listing of colleges and universities with accredited construction education programs.

80

AMERICAN COUNCIL ON PHARMACEUTICAL EDUCATION

311 West Superior Street, Suite 512
Chicago, IL 60610
312-664-3575
Fax: 312-664-4652
shudson@acpe-accredit.org
http://www.acpe-accredit.org

• *Accredited Professional Programs of Colleges and Schools of Pharmacy: Doctor of Pharmacy, Baccalaureate in Pharmacy.* 13 pages. Presents the accreditation status of each professional program, as well as a list of colleges or schools of pharmacy offering professional programs.

81

AMERICAN COUNCIL ON SCIENCE AND HEALTH

1995 Broadway, 2nd Floor
New York, NY 10023-5860
212-362-7044
Fax: 212-362-4919
acsh@acsh.org
http://www.acsh.org

Available at the Web site:

• *Biotechnology and Food.* Describes biotechnology, the challenges for American agriculture with biotechnology solutions, and biotechnology in foods.

• *Biotech Pharmaceuticals and Biotherapy.*

82

AMERICAN COUNSELING ASSOCIATION

5999 Stevenson Avenue, 4th Floor
Alexandria, VA 22304
800-347-6647 or 703-823-9800
Fax: 703-823-0252
cacrep@aol.com
http://www.counseling.org

Available by mail or online:

• *Directory of CACREP Accredited Programs.* Listing of accredited master's and doctoral programs in the United

States and Canada. Includes contact information, updated semi-annually.

Available at the Web site:

• *A Student's Guide.* Includes information on the accreditation process and general information about choosing a career in counseling.

83

AMERICAN CULINARY FEDERATION, INC.

PO Box 3466
St. Augustine, FL 32085-3466
904-824-4468
Fax: 904-825-4758
acf@acfchefs.net
http://www.acfchefs.org

• *ACFEI Apprenticeship Fundamentals/ Program Roster.* 7 pages. SASE. Lists apprenticeship programs available in the United States.

• *ACFEI Accredited Programs.* 1 page. SASE. Lists accredited programs in the United States.

84

AMERICAN DANCE THERAPY ASSOCIATION

2000 Century Plaza, Suite 108
10632 Little Patuxent Parkway
Columbia, MD 21044
410-997-4040
Fax: 410-997-4048
info@adta.org
http://www.adta.org

• *American Dance Therapy Asssociation Clinical Brochure.* ($1.75) Includes ten inserts describing dance movement therapy in a variety of clinical settings with various patient/client populations.

Also available at the Web site:

• *Educational Information.* Includes general information on dance therapy, typical jobs of dance therapists, recommended work experience, and other frequently asked questions. Includes a listing of approved graduate and undergraduate programs in dance/movement therapy.

85

AMERICAN DENTAL ASSISTANTS ASSOCIATION

203 North LaSalle Street, Suite 1320
Chicago, IL 60610-1225
312-541-1550
Fax: 312-541-1496
adaa1@aol.com
http://members.aol.com/adaa1/index.html

• *Careers in the Dental Profession: Dental Assisting.* 10 pages. Provides an overview of training and careers in the dental assisting field. Appropriate for high school students.

• *Fact Sheet: Dental Education and Career Information.* Profiles the career, average salary, and educational requirements.

• *Dental Assisting: Word of Mouth: Careers in the Dental Profession.* 14 pages. General information about the benefits and educational requirements needed for a career in dental assisting.

86

AMERICAN DENTAL EDUCATION ASSOCIATION

Publications
1625 Massachusetts Avenue, NW
Washington, DC 20036-2212
202-667-9433
Fax: 202-667-0642
adea@adea.org
http://www.adea.org

• *Opportunites for Minority Students in the United States Dental Schools.* ($10) 200 pages. Resource of special interest to minority students considering a career in dentistry. Includes information about summer enrichment programs, student aid programs, and more.

Available on ADEA's Web site:

• *Links to Dental Schools.*

87

AMERICAN DENTAL HYGIENISTS' ASSOCIATION

Division of Professional Development
444 North Michigan Avenue, Suite 3400
Chicago, IL 60611
800-243-2342 or 312-440-8900
Fax: 312-440-8929
mail@adha.net
http://www.adha.org

• *Dental Hygiene: A Profession of Opportunities.* 6 pages. Describes a career in dental hygiene and educational requirements.

• *Dental Hygiene Entry Level Education Programs.* 30 pages. Lists educational programs for individuals pursuing a career in dental hygiene.

• *Facts: Dental Hygiene Career Options in a Variety of Settings.* 1 page. Describes the work environments of dental hygienists and typical duties performed in each setting.

• *Facts: Dental Hygiene Education.* 1 page. Discusses admission requirements and prerequisites, degree programs, and curricula.

• *Facts: Dental Hygiene Licensure.* 1 page. Discusses dental hygiene licensure—who grants licenses and how they are obtained.

• *Salary Information for Dental Hygienists.* 1 page. Provides hourly and yearly national average salary ranges for dental hygienists.

88

AMERICAN DESIGN DRAFTING ASSOCIATION
PO Box 11937
Columbia, SC 29211
803-771-0008
Fax: 803-771-4272
national@adda.org
http://www.adda.org

The following information is available online:

• *Schools with Certified Curriculum.* Lists schools currently participating in the ADDA's certification program. The certificate, diploma, or degree level of the program is noted.

• *Drafter Certification Test.* Highlights the importance of certification to a drafter

and an employer. Includes test contents and an online application for certification.

89

AMERICAN DIETETIC ASSOCIATION
216 West Jackson Boulevard
Chicago, IL 60606-6995
800-877-1600, ext. 5400
http://www.eatright.org

• *Your Future with Food and Nutrition.* 6 pages. Defines dietetics, the dietitian, and dietetic technician for 4th to 6th grade students.

• *Check It Out...Careers in Dietetics.* Attempts to increase 6th to 8th grade students' awareness about careers in dietetics. Defines dietetics; describes where registered dietitians (RD) and dietetic technicians, registered (DTR), are employed and their job responsibilities; and lists resources for additional information.

• *Check It Out...Dietetics Educational Programs.* Describes the educational pathways required for students pursuing careers as registered dietitians or dietetic technicians, registered. Provides a list of the Dietetic Programs.

• *Check It Out...a Career as a Registered Dietitian.* 2 pages. Prepared for second career adults or college students who are interested in becoming a registered dietitian. Includes information on job outlook, requirements for registration, employment opportunities, and salary data for registered dietitians.

• *Check It Out...Careers in Dietetics Video.* 7 minutes. Illustrates career opportunities in dietetics by depicting RDs and a DTR in several food and nutrition practice settings. Designed to increase 6th to 8th graders' awareness about careers in dietetics.

90
AMERICAN FARRIER'S ASSOCIATION
4059 Iron Works Parkway, Suite 2
Lexington, KY 40511
606-233-7411
Fax: 606-231-7862
farriers@americanfarriers.org
http://www.americanfarriers.org

• *So You Want to be a Farrier.* Describes duties, working conditions, personal qualifications, training, earnings, and outlook.

• *AFA Certification Study Guide.* Lists the levels of the AFA examination, certification sites on record at the AFA office, and certification rules and study outlines.

• *AFA Certification: Questions and Answers.* Answers the most common questions about the AFA certification program.

91
AMERICAN FEDERATION OF LABOR AND CONGRESS OF INDUSTRIAL ORGANIZATIONS
815 16th Street, NW
Washington, DC 20006
202-637-5000
http://www.aflcio.org

Available at the Web site:

• *AFL-CIO Guide to Union Sponsored Scholarships and Aid.* Online directory organized by state or local union. Includes information about eligibility, application deadlines, and contact information.

92
AMERICAN FISHERIES SOCIETY
5410 Grosvenor Lane, Suite 110
Bethesda, MD 20814-2199
301-897-8616
Fax: 301-897-8096
main@fisheries.org
http://www.fisheries.org

• *Careers in Fisheries.* ($.25) 12 pages. Discusses education, career choices, demand in the field, and employment opportunities.

• *Fisheries Programs and Related Courses at North American Colleges and Universities.* ($.25) 13 pages.

93
AMERICAN FORESTS
PO Box 2000
Washington, DC 20013
202-955-4500
Fax: 202-955-4588
member@amfor.org
http://www.americanforests.org

• *Growing Greener Cities: A Tree Planting Handbook.* ($7.95 plus shipping) 126 pages. A guide for community leaders, teachers or individuals interested in selecting, planting, and caring for trees. Includes easy directions for designing planting plans that are economical and environmental.

• *Growing Greener Cities: Environmental Education Guide.* ($13.95 plus shipping) 60 pages. A companion to the handbook, this teacher guide contains 13 lessons for elementary and secondary school students. Includes activities, a vocabulary list, and game cards.

94

AMERICAN FOUNDATION FOR THE BLIND

11 Pen Plaza, Suite 300
New York, NY 10001
212-502-7661
Fax: 212-502-7774
afbinfo@afb.net
http://www.afb.org

Available at the Web site:

• *Braille Fact Sheet.* Includes information on the alphabet and technological advances made in Braille communication.

• *Educating Students with Visual Impairments for Inclusion in Society.* Report by L. Taylor Leadership Institute.

• *Accessing Education Resources: A Guide for Parents.* Includes information on sources of special education and eligibility requirements.

Available by mail:

• *American Foundation for the Blind Scholarship Program: Application Packet.*

95

AMERICAN FOUNDRYMEN'S SOCIETY, INC.

505 State Street
Des Plaines, IL 60016-8399
800-537-4237 or 847-824-0181
Fax: 847-824-7848
dkanicki@afsinc.org
http://www.afsinc.org

• *Metalcasting: An Art...A Science...A Career!* (#CA-0001) 24 pages. Provides a brief background of the industry; an overview of the specialized careers in the field; scholarship information; a list of universities in the United States offering cast metal studies; and a list of metalcasting organizations.

• *Casting Engineering Guidelines.* (#CA-0002) 27 pages. Provides an introduction to the foundry process. Directed toward the design engineer.

96

AMERICAN GEOLOGICAL INSTITUTE

National Center for Earth Science Education
4220 King Street
Alexandria, VA 22302-1502
703-379-2480
Fax: 703-379-7563
her@agiweb.org
http://www.agiweb.org

Available at the Web site:

• *Careers in the Geosciences.* Describes the field, career opportunities, work environment, and job and salary outlook.

Available by mail:

- *Careers for Geoscientists Brochure.* ($.35) (#550507)

- *Adventures in Geology.* ($5.56) (#300199) 34 pages. Focuses on geology and science teaching and includes activities for upper-elementary and middle-school students to better understand and appreciate the geosciences.

- *Geowriting.* ($6.40) (#300324) 138 pages. Introduction to writing, editing, and printing to help students and scientists cope with the process of publication writing.

- *Sustaining Our Soils and Society Poster.* ($.50) (#300602)

97
AMERICAN GEOPHYSICAL UNION
Education and Research Department
2000 Florida Avenue, NW
Washington, DC 20009-1277
800-966-2481 or 202-462-6900
service@agu.org
http://www.agu.org

Available at the Web site:

- *Survey of Employment Experiences of Recent Doctoral Graduates in Earth and Space Sciences.*

- *AGU Resume Guide.* Information about resume preparation.

98
AMERICAN GERIATRICS SOCIETY
Foundation for Health in Aging
The Empire State Building

350 Fifth Avenue, Suite 801
New York, NY 10118
800-247-4779 or 212-755-6810
staff@healthinaging.org
http://www.healthinaging.org

The following can be viewed online or ordered by mail:

- *What is Geriatrics? An Introduction for Caring for Adults.* 4 pages. Describes the role of the geriatrician, the team approach, choosing a doctor, preventive measures, and tips about taking care of yourself.

99
AMERICAN HEALTH INFORMATION MANAGEMENT ASSOCIATION
233 North Michigan Avenue, Suite 2150
Chicago, IL 60601-5519
312-233-1100
Fax: 312-233-1090
info@ahima.org
http://www.ahima.org

Available at the Web site:

- *Healthcare and Information Technology Career Information.* Includes data on growth, income, educational requirements, and certification.

- *College Directories.* Guide to universities and colleges that offer associate's, bachelor's, and master's programs in health information administration and health information technology.

100
AMERICAN HEALTHCARE RADIOLOGY ADMINISTRATORS
111 Boston Post Road, Suite 105
PO Box 334

Sudbury, MA 01776
978-443-7591
Fax: 978-443-8046
http://www.ahraonline.org

• *Your Career Opportunities in Radiologic Technology.* 17 pages. Describes the duties and responsibilities, certification requirements, educational programs, and career opportunities for a number of careers in the radiologic field.

101

AMERICAN HORTICULTURAL SOCIETY

7931 East Boulevard Drive
Alexandria, VA 22308
703-768-5700
Fax: 703-768-8700
http://www.ahs.org

Available at the Web site:

• *National Education Programs: Youth Garden Resource List.* Online directory includes formal educational programs and curriculum guides and sources for financial assistance and gardening supplies.

102

AMERICAN HOTEL & MOTEL ASSOCIATION

1201 New York Avenue, NW, # 600
Washington, DC 20005-3931
202-289-3100
Fax: 202-289-3199
infoctr@ahma.com
http://www.ahma.com

• *Lodging and Food Service Careers: A World of Opportunities.* 14 pages. Discusses career opportunities in the field and lists sources of additional information.

103

AMERICAN HUMANICS, INC.

4601 Madison Avenue
Kansas City, MO 64112
800-343-6466 or 816-561-6415
Fax: 816-531-3527
http://www.humanics.org

• *Make Your Mark on the World.* 6 pages. Describes AH as a national program devoted to preparing college students for careers in nonprofit youth and human service organizations. Lists requirements of the program and financial assistance and includes an insert on participating campuses and agencies.

104

AMERICAN INDIAN GRADUATE CENTER

4520 Montgomery Boulevard, NE
Suite 1-B
Albuquerque, NM 87109-1291
505-881-4584
Fax: 505-884-0427
aigc@aigc.com
http://www.aigc.com

Available at the Web site:

• *AIGC Graduate Fellowships.* Outlines fellowship eligibility, review and award process, and application procedure and includes application packet order information.

105

AMERICAN INDUSTRIAL HYGIENE ASSOCIATION

2700 Prosperity Avenue, Suite 250
Fairfax, VA 22031
703-849-8888

Fax: 703-207-3561
http://www.aiha.org

- *Careerworks.* (#170-PR-93) Targets students in grades 9 through 12; contains a description of the profession and its objectives; and promotes careers in the hygiene industry.

- *Careerworks for Kids.* (#185-PR94) 12 pages. For 3rd through 8th graders. Delivers a colorful presentation that both entertains and informs young students on hygiene careers.

- *Balancing Work, Health, Technology & Environment: Careers in Industrial Hygiene.* 19 pages. Provides an overview of the profession, a job description, typical employers, educational requirements, and salaries. Lists schools offering industrial programs.

- *Everything You Need to Know about Industrial Hygiene, Version 2.* 17 pages. Discusses the field, salary, educational requirements, work environment, levels of responsibility, and schools with accredited programs.

106
AMERICAN INSTITUTE FOR CONSERVATION OF HISTORIC AND ARTISTIC WORKS
1717 K Street, NW, Suite 301
Washington, DC 20006
202-452-9545
Fax: 202-452-9328
infoaic@aol.com
http://aic.stanford.edu

Available at the Web site:

- *Conservation Training in the United States.* Defines the field and describes the qualifications and responsibilities, work environment, rewards, training and apprenticeship, graduate programs, study abroad, financial aid, and conservation disciplines.

- *Undergraduate Prerequisites for Admission into Graduate Conservation Training Programs.* Includes a listing of programs and the prerequisites in the areas of art, science, language, humanities, and other recommended coursework and experience.

107
AMERICAN INSTITUTE OF ARCHITECTS
1735 New York Avenue, NW
Washington, DC 20006-5292
202-626-7300
http://www.e-architect.com/career/careers/career.asp

Available on the AIA's Web site:

- *Career Decision Stategies.* Career advice including information on the following topics:

- *Career Paths.* Analyzes the growing number of career paths available to architects;

- *The Exploration Process.* Explains how to combine educational foundation with personal values and goals to acquire experience and build expertise;

- *Putting Pen to Paper.* Tips on turning opportunities into jobs by selling yourself and your design philosophy; and

- *Looking Beyond Architecture.* Highlights oppportunities available outside the conventionally defined perimeters of the profession.

108
AMERICAN INSTITUTE OF BIOLOGICAL SCIENCES
AIBS Communications
1444 I Street, NW, Suite 200
Washington, DC 20005
202-628-1500, ext. 261
Fax: 202-628-1509
http://www.aibs.org/careers

Available on the Institute's Web site:

- *What Will You Be Doing in 2020?: Careers in Biology.* Discusses biologists' role in fields such as research, health care, environment, and education. Covers educational and training requirements, outlooks for biology careers, and more.

109
AMERICAN INSTITUTE OF CERTIFIED PUBLIC ACCOUNTANTS
Academic and Career Development Division
1211 Avenue of the Americas
New York, NY 10036-8775
212-596-6200
educat@aicpa.org
http://www.aicpa.org

Available at the Web site:

- *Accounting: A Career Without Limits.* Designed for high school and college students. Contains information on accounting education and CPA careers, technology tools used within the profession, scholarship and internship data, education requirements, and the CPA exam.

110
AMERICAN INSTITUTE OF CHEMICAL ENGINEERS
3 Park Avenue
New York, NY 10016
800-242-4363
xpress@aiche.org
http://www.aiche.org/careers

Profiles of chemical engineers, job descriptions, and salary data are available online.

111
AMERICAN INSTITUTE OF PHYSICS
One Physics Ellipse
College Park, MD 20740-3843
301-209-3100
Fax: 301-209-0843
aipinfo@aip.org
http://www.aip.org

Available at the Web site:

- *Educational Statistics.* Includes information on the latest physics enrollment and degree trends, initial enrollment and average starting salaries for new graduates, recent data on undergraduate physics and astronomy majors, and the latest report on physics in high schools.

112
AMERICAN INSTITUTE OF PROFESSIONAL GEOLOGISTS
8703 Yates Drive, Suite 200
Westminster, CO 80031-3681
303-412-6205
Fax: 303-412-6219

aipg@aipg.com
http://www.aipg.org

• *Education for Professional Practice.* ($9) 16 pages. Provides information to students interested in becoming professional geologists and contains guidelines for curriculum development for university geology departments.

Available at the Web site:

• *Reflections on a Geological Career.*

113
AMERICAN INSTITUTE OF ULTRASOUND IN MEDICINE
14750 Sweitzer Lane, Suite 100
Laurel, MD 20707-5906
301-498-4100
Fax: 301-498-4450
http://www.aium.org

• *Is Sonography for You?* 6 pages. Defines diagnostic and therapeutic ultrasound and discusses education and training, certification, and salary.

114
AMERICAN IRON AND STEEL INSTITUTE
Communications Department
1101 17th Street, NW, Suite 1300
Washington, DC 20036-4700
202-452-7100
Fax: 202-463-6573
http://www.steel.org

• *AISI Statistcal Highlights of the North American Steel Industry.* ($5) Fact-filled folder that opens up to a 20"x 16" chart providing data on production, shipments, employment, finances, and for-

eign trade for the past 10 years. Updated annually.

115
AMERICAN LEGION
National Emblem Sales
PO Box 1050
Indianapolis, IN 46206
888-453-4466
http://www.legion.org

• *Need a Lift?* ($3.95) 152 pages. Discusses college financial aid (loans and scholarships), educational opportunities, and careers. Also includes a financial aid resource application.

116
AMERICAN LIBRARY ASSOCIATION
Office for Library Personnel Resources
50 East Huron Street
Chicago, IL 60611-2795
800-545-2433 or 312-944-6780
http://www.ala.org

Available at the Web site:

• *Directory of Accredited LIS Master's Programs.* Online guide of institutions offering library study programs in the United States and Canada.

• *Guidelines for Choosing a Master's Program in Library and Information Studies.* Includes considerations in making a decision, tips on gathering basic information, and sources of additional information.

The following are available by mail:

• *The Future Is Information: Talented People Wanted.* Folder includes:

- *Careers in Library and Information Science: Academic Librarianship.* 6 pages.

- *Careers in Library and Information Science: Technical Services.* 6 pages.

- *Library and Information Studies Directory of Institutions Offering Accredited Masters Programs.* 33 pages.

- *The Master's Degree for Library and Information Professionals.* 3 pages.

- *ALA Scholarship Application Form.*

- *Youth Services Librarian Information.* 5 pages.

- *Fact Sheet: Libraries Online.* 4 pages.

- *Librarians.* 2 pages. Reprinted from the *Occupational Outlook Handbook.*

- *Librarians: Information Sleuths.* 4 pages. Reprinted from *Career World.*

- *Library and Information Careers: Specialized Areas.* 1 page.

- *Placements and Salaries.* 7 pages. Reprinted from *Library Journal.*

- *You Can Take Your MLS Out of the Library.* 4 pages.

- *Beating Inflation Now: Salary Information.* 7 pages.

- *Job Opportunities Glitter for Librarians Who Surf the Net.* 3 pages.

117
AMERICAN MANAGEMENT ASSOCIATION
1601 Broadway
New York, NY 10019
800-262-9699 or 212-586-8100
Fax: 212-903-8168
http://www.amanet.org

- *Successful Office Skills Series.* ($4 each plus shipping) Available titles for these 64-page booklets include:

- *Coaching and Counseling.* (#07818)

- *Creative Problem Solving.* (#07702)

- *Get Organized!* (#07646)

- *How to Be a Successful Interviewer.* (#07697)

- *How to Deal with Difficult People.* (#07674)

- *How to Delegate Effectively.* (#07700)

- *How to Make an Effective Speech or Presentation.* (#07672)

- *How to Negotiate a Raise or Promotion.* (#07643)

- *How to Read Financial Statements.* (#07644)

- *How to Write an Effective Resume.* (#07669)

118
AMERICAN MATHEMATICAL SOCIETY
PO Box 6248
Providence, RI 02940-6248
800-321-4AMS or 401-455-4000
Fax: 401-331-3842
ams@ams.org
http://www.ams.org/

Available at the Web site:

- *Careers in Mathematics.* Contains helpful information for the college-bound high school student with an interest in mathematics. Discusses the difference between pure and applied mathematics, offers some important considerations when choosing a university, provides information on graduate mathematics programs and undergraduate scholarships and fellowships, and lists sources of additional information.

Available online and by mail:

• *Resources for Undergraduates in Mathematics.* Lists resources available from the AMS and many other organizations. Includes information about fellowships, scholarships, research experience, internships, and math competitions.

• *Seeking Employment in the Mathematical Sciences.* ($5 or free online) Useful resource for new PhD's entering the job market.

119
AMERICAN MEAT SCIENCE ASSOCIATION

1111 North Dunlap Avenue
Savoy, IL 61874
217-356-3182
Fax: 217-398-4119
info@meatscience.org
http://www.meatscience.org

• *Careers in the Meat Industry.* An overview of careers applicable for high school students.

120
AMERICAN MEDICAL STUDENT ASSOCIATION

1902 Association Drive
Reston, VA 20191
703-620-6600
Fax: 703-620-5873
amsa@www.amsa.org
http://www.amsa.org

• *Financial Aid Resources for Minority Medical Students.* ($5) Information on scholarships, fellowships, and loans specifically for minority students. Also lists sources for general financial aid and essay competitions.

• *Study Group on Minority Medical Education: Findings from Literature Search and Anecdotal Data.* ($8) Report highlighting trends in minority medical education, financial issues, ideal programs and research and recommendations from focus groups.

• *Directory of Health Policy Opportunities for Physicians-in-Training.* ($10) Lists organizations in health policy work nationwide that offer internships to physicians-in-training.

• *Training Opportunities in Community-Based Primary Care, Fourth Edition.* ($6) Lists 380 opportunitites for health care professionals-in-training. Also includes an appendix of primary care research opportunities at over 200 community-based cities.

• *Directory of Occupational Medicine Residency Programs.* ($5)

• *Peacework: Opportunities for Medical Students in Peace Promotion.* ($7) Lists internships, rotations, and volunteer opportunities in human rights facilitation, violence prevention, and refugee health.

• *The New Physician: Special Issues, Choosing a Career.* ($3) April 1996 issue: topics include selecting a field, specialism, careers in research, loan repayment options, and an outlook on the field of medicine.

• *Projects in a Box.* A series of short publications available on the Web site. Topics include:

• *The Delivery of Urban vs. Rural Health Care.*

• *The Future of International Health: Exporting Primary Care Medicine.*

• *Leadership Skills and Training.*

• *Physician Supply and Distribution.*

• *The Primary Care Team.*

• *The Senior Boom is Coming: Are Primary Care Physicians Ready?*

• *Student Loan and Debt.*

121
AMERICAN MEDICAL TECHNOLOGISTS
710 Higgins Road
Park Ridge, IL 60068-5765
847-823-5169
Fax: 847-823-0458
amtmail@aol.com
http://www.amt1.com

• *AMT Certification: Standards and Qualifications.* 8 pages. Lists certification requirements for the following positions: medical technologists, medical laboratory technicians, phlebotomy technicians, medical assistants, dental assistants, and office laboratory technicians.

122
AMERICAN METEOROLOGICAL SOCIETY
45 Beacon Street

Boston, MA 02108-3693
617-227-2425
Fax: 617-742-8718
nkassas@ametsoc.org
http://www.ametsoc.org/AMS

• *Challenges of our Changing Atmosphere: Careers in Atmospheric Research and Applied Meteorology.* 12 pages. Describes meteorology and the meteorologist, the duties and responsibilities, tools used, work environments, required education, employment outlook, and typical salaries.

• *Colleges and Universities with Degree Programs in the Atmospheric and Oceanic, Hydrologic, and Related Sciences.* 4 pages. Lists schools in the field.

• *Employment Outlook and Salaries in Meteorology.* 1 page. Includes employment outlook in meteorology and the average annual salaries for meteorologists with varying educational degrees.

123
AMERICAN MONTESSORI SOCIETY
281 Park Avenue South, 6th Floor
New York, NY 10010
212-358-1250
Fax: 212-358-1256
http://www.amshq.org

• *Montessori Education Questions and Answers.* ($.25) 12 pages. Answers questions about the Montessori education philosophy.

• *Affiliated Teacher Education Programs.* ($.25)

• *1999 Salary Survey.* ($7.50) 26 pages.

- *Some Comparisons of Montessori Education with Traditional Education.* ($.25) 1 page.

124
AMERICAN MUSIC THERAPY ASSOCIATION
8455 Colesville Road, Suite 1000
Silver Spring, MD 20910
301-589-3300
Fax: 301-589-5175
info@musictherapy.org
http://www.musictherapy.org

- *Baccalaureate Curriculum in Music Therapy.* 4 pages.

- *Music Therapy as a Career.* 6 pages. Describes the career of music therapy and includes an AMTA school directory.

- *Music Therapy Makes a Difference.* 6 pages. Describes the types of patients who benefit from music therapy, qualifications and skills, employment opportunities, and duties and responsibilities.

- *AMTA Fact Sheet.* 1 page.

125
AMERICAN NUCLEAR SOCIETY
555 North Kensington Avenue
La Grange Park, IL 60525
708-352-6611
Fax: 708-352-0499
nucleus@ans.org
http://www.ans.org

- *Careers for Women in Nuclear Science and Technology.* 28 pages. Discusses career opportunities in education, the government, industry, and national laboratories.

- *Nuclear Technology Creates Careers.* Lists typical duties and responsibilities, career opportunities in the field, income, and employment outlook.

126
AMERICAN OCCUPATIONAL THERAPY ASSOCIATION, INC.
4720 Montgomery Lane
PO Box 31220
Bethesda MD 20824-1220
301-652-2682
Fax: 301-652-7711
http://www.aota.org; click to "student."

The following are available at the Association's Web site:

- *Postprofessional Programs in OT: Master's Degree Programs.*

- *Postprofessional Programs in OT: Doctoral Degree Programs.*

- *Occupational Therapy Careers Outlook.* Article focuses on the recently balancing levels of supply and demand for occupational therapists, and the resulting new fields that OT workers are entering, such as geriatric care.

- *Frequently Asked Questions Regarding Occupational Therapy.* Q & A session covering earnings, degree levels in OT, certificate programs, and the competition finding a job in the industry.

127
AMERICAN OPTOMETRIC ASSOCIATION EDUCATIONAL SERVICES
Educational Services
243 North Lindbergh Boulevard

St. Louis, MO 63141-7881
http://www.opted.org

• *Optometry: A Career with Vision.*
Describes an optometric education,
admission requirements, and financial
aid and offers a statistical profile of students for each accredited school.
Publication available at the Web site.

128
AMERICAN ORTHOPEDIC SOCIETY FOR SPORTS MEDICINE
6300 North River Road, Suite 200
Rosemont, IL 60018
847-292-4900
Fax: 847-292-4905
http://www.sportsmed.org

• *Pathways to Sports Medicine.* 7 pages.
Details the various career opportunities
in the field, the duties, and educational
requirements.

• *Resource Directory for the Disabled
Athletes.* ($2) Lists resources helpful to
the disabled athlete.

129
AMERICAN OSTEOPATHIC ASSOCIATION
Public Relations
142 East Ontario Street
Chicago, IL 60611-2864
800-621-1773 or 312-280-7401
Fax: 312-280-5893
http://www.aoo-net.org
or http://www.am-osteo-assn.org

• *Osteopathic Medical Education.* 6 pages.
Describes admissions, the curriculum,
training, and licensure. Lists accredited
osteopathic medical colleges.

• *Osteopathic Medicine.* 6 pages. Provides
an overview of the field and discusses
education, training, and licensure
requirements.

• *What Is a D.O. (Osteopathic Physician)?* 6
pages. Discusses the difference between
the MD and DO, as well as basic princi-
ples behind osteopathic medicine.

130
AMERICAN PHARMACEUTICAL ASSOCIATION
2215 Constitution Avenue, NW
Washington, DC 20037-2985
202-628-4410
Fax: 202-783-2351
http://www.aphanet.org

Available at the Web site:

• *Pharmacy Student Career Toolkit.*
Resources pharmacy students need for
selecting and landing the perfect first
job. Includes information about writing
your curriculum vitae, what employers
look for, and tips for a successful job
interview.

131
AMERICAN PHILOLOGICAL SOCIETY
291 Logan Hall
University of Pennsylvania
249 South 36th Street
Philadelphia, PA 19104-6304
215-898-4975
Fax: 215-573-7874
http://www.apaclassics.org

• *Careers for Classicists.* ($3)

132
AMERICAN PHYSICAL THERAPY ASSOCIATION

1111 North Fairfax Street
Alexandria, VA 22314-1488
800-999-APTA or 703-684-2782
Fax: 703-684-7343
http://www.apta.org

Available by mail or on the Web:

- *A Future in Physical Therapy.* Outlines the field and provides information on education, training, certification, and employment outlook.

- *Accredited PT Education Programs.* Lists all accredited PT and PTA programs in the United States.

- *Patient Information Brochures.* Various brochures describing specific types of care.

- *Financial Aid Information.*

- *Who Are PTs and PTAs?*

133
AMERICAN PHYSIOLOGICAL SOCIETY

Education Officer
9650 Rockville Pike
Bethesda, MD 20814-3991
301-530-7164
http://www.faseb.org/aps

- *Careers in Physiology.* 8 pages. Discusses the field, education and training, career opportunities, salary levels, and other topics. Available online or by mail.

134
AMERICAN PHYTOPATHOLOGICAL SOCIETY

3340 Pilot Knob Road
St. Paul, MN 55121-2097
651-454-7250
Fax: 651-454-0766
aps@scisoc.org
http://www.scisoc.org

- *Careers in Plant Pathology.* 7 pages. Defines the plant pathologist, typical duties and responsibilities, current technology, and education and training. Lists the departments of plant pathology by state. Also available in Spanish.

135
AMERICAN PLANNING ASSOCIATION

122 South Michigan Avenue, Suite 1600
Chicago, IL 60603-6107
312-431-9100
Fax: 312-431-9985
http://www.planning.org

Career kit includes:

- *Accredited University Planning Programs.* 6 pages.

- *Urban and Regional Planners.* 21 pages. Describes the field, work environment, how to find a planning job, opportunities for women and minority groups, sources of information, and specialties in the field.

- *Urban Planners: Movers and Shakers.* 7 pages. Discusses the profession, salary range, qualifications, the career ladder, and other topics.

136
AMERICAN PODIATRIC MEDICAL ASSOCIATION
Council on Podiatric Medical Education
9312 Old Georgetown Road
Bethesda, MD 20814-1698
301-571-9277
http://www.apma.org

• *Podiatric Medicine: The Physician, The Profession, The Practice.* ($.50) 6 pages. Includes background information on the profession, educational requirements, areas of practice.

• *The Podiatric Medical Assistant.* ($.40) 6 pages. Describes the profession, opportunity and employment outlook, scope of duties, education requirements, and certification.

Available at the Web site:

• *Accredited Colleges of Podiatric Medicine.*

• *Approved Residencies in Podiatric Medicine.*

137
AMERICAN POLITICAL SCIENCE ASSOCIATION
Publications
1527 New Hampshire Avenue, NW
Washington, DC 20036-1206
202-483-2512
Fax: 202-483-2657
apsa@apsanet.org
http://www.apsanet.org

• *Careers and the Study of Political Science: A Guide for Undergraduates.* ($4.50) Discusses how the knowledge and skills political science students acquire can benefit them as they pursue careers in law, government, business, journalism, and teaching.

• *Earning a Ph.D. in Political Science.* ($4) Useful advice for those considering advanced study in political science.

• *Storming Washington: An Intern's Guide to National Government.* ($7) Student guide for finding, planning, and enjoying internships in Washington DC

• *Political Science: An Ideal Liberal Arts Major.* (Single copy is free.)

138
AMERICAN POLYGRAPH ASSOCIATION
PO Box 8037
Chattanooga, TN 37414-0037
800-272-8037 or 423-892-3992
Fax: 423-894-5435
http://www.polygraph.org

• *Polygraph: Issues and Answers.* 12 pages. Presents a few essential facts about polygraph testing. Includes information on polygraph examinations, errors and accuracy of polygraph examinations, and polygraph screening in police agencies.

• *APA Accredited Polygraph Schools.* 1 page. Lists polygraph schools accredited by the APA.

139
AMERICAN PSYCHIATRIC ASSOCIATION
Public Affairs Division
1400 K Street, NW, Suite 501
Washington, DC 20005
202-682-6220
http://www.psych.org

• *What is a Psychiatrist?* 6 pages. Discusses the field, education and training, sub-specialities, work environments, and salaries.

140
AMERICAN PSYCHOLOGICAL ASSOCIATION
Education Directorate
750 First Street, NE
Washington, DC 20002-4242
800-374-2721, ext. 5510 or 202-336-5510
http://www.apa.org

• *Psychology: Careers for the 21st Century.* 20 pages. Single copy available free online or by mail. Provides an overview of psychology, job outlook for the next two decades, educational preparation for work in psychology, and several charts depicting various aspects of the field.

• *Psychology: Careers for the 21st Century.* ($19.95) 14-minute video companion to the free booklet.

Available at the APA's Web site:

• *APA Accredited Graduate Programs in Psychology.*

• *APA Accredited Predoctoral Internships.*

• *An Interesting Career in Psychology: Human Factors and User Interface.* Article outlines the unplanned career path of an experimental psychologist as a human factor specialist.

• *Salaries in Psychology.* Report covering all professional fields in psychology. Includes information on the impact of managed care on net incomes since 1996.

141
AMERICAN PUBLIC WORKS ASSOCIATION
2345 Grand Boulevard, Suite 500
Kansas City, MO 64108
816-472-6100
Fax: 816-472-0405
reporter@apwa.net
http://www.apwa.net

• *Civil Engineering and Other Career Paths into Public Works.* Available online or by writing to the association.

142
AMERICAN SOCIETY FOR BIOCHEMISTRY AND MOLECULAR BIOLOGY
9650 Rockville Pike
Bethesda, MD 20814-3996
301-530-7145
Fax: 301-571-1824
asbmb@asbmb.faseb.org
http://www.faseb.org/asbmb

Available at the Web site:

• *Unlocking Life's Secrets: Career Opportunities in Biochemistry and Molecular Biology.* Addresses career opportunities, duties and responsibilities, education and training, college admission requirements, and financial aid in the biochemistry and molecular biology field.

143
AMERICAN SOCIETY FOR CELL BIOLOGY
9650 Rockville Pike
Bethesda, MD 20814-3992
301-530-7153

Fax: 301-530-7139
ascbinfo@ascb.org
http://www.ascb.org/acsb

- *Exploring the Cell.* 17 pages. Defines cell biology, employment opportunities and outlook, and education and training.

- *Opportunities in Cell Biology.* 13 pages. Contains information pertaining to minority students interested in pursuing a career in cell biology.

- *How to Get a Teaching Job at a Primarily Under Graduate Institution.* 8 pages. Written to assist those seeking "alternative" careers in the field; suggestions for those wishing to obtain employment in cell biology at a primarily undergraduate institution.

- *How to Get a Research Job in Academia and Industry.* 15 pages. Primarily intended for those at the postdoctoral level seeking a position with a large research component. Also helpful for students at an earlier stage in their career who are preparing for their first real job hunt.

144
AMERICAN SOCIETY FOR CLINICAL LABORATORY SCIENCE
7910 Woodmont Avenue, Suite 530
Bethesda, MD 20814
301-657-2768
Fax: 301-657-2909
http://www.ascls.org

- *Clinical Laboratory Science.* Brochure outlining the educational requirements for clinical laboratory science careers. Explains the diverse role of the clinical laboratory professional.

- *Opportunities in Medical Technology Careers (Clinical Laboratory Science).* ($18) 148 pages. Provides current information on training and educational requirements, salary levels, and employment outlook for careers in medical technology.

145
AMERICAN SOCIETY FOR ENGINEERING EDUCATION
1818 N Street, NW, Suite 600
Washington, DC 20036-2479
202-331-3500
Fax: 202-265-8504
pubsinfo@asee.org
http://www.asee.org

Available at the Web site:

- *Engineering: Your Future.* Designed for high school students and others interested in engineering and engineering technology careers. Includes student FAQs, tips on picking the right engineering school, how to finance your education, and more.

146
AMERICAN SOCIETY FOR INDUSTRIAL SECURITY
1625 Prince Street
Alexandria, VA 22314-2818
703-519-6200
Fax: 703-519-6299
http://www.asisonline.org

- *Career Opportunities in Security.* 20 pages. (Available online or in print by request) Describes employment opportunities, careers in the field, certification, education, and training.

147

AMERICAN SOCIETY FOR INFORMATION SCIENCE

8720 Georgia Avenue, Suite 501
Silver Spring, MD 20910-3602
301-495-0900
Fax: 301-495-0810
asis@asis.org
http://www.asis.org

Available at the Web site:

- *Information Science Schools.* Online directory of schools that offer programs in information science and links to their Web sites.

148

AMERICAN SOCIETY FOR INVESTIGATIVE PATHOLOGY, INC.

9650 Rockville Pike
Bethesda, MD 20814-3993
301-530-7130
asip@pathol.faseb.org
http://asip.uthscsa.edu

Available at the Web site:

- *Pathology as a Career in Medicine.* Describes the field, duties and responsibilities, employment opportunities, education, and training.

149

AMERICAN SOCIETY FOR MICROBIOLOGY

Office of Education and Training
1752 N Street, NW
Washington, DC 20036
202-942-9317
Fax: 202-942-9329
http://www.asmusa.org

- *Your Career in Microbiology: Unlocking the Secrets of Life.* 16 pages. Defines the microbiologist and the various career options. Discusses the career avenues for each degree level, possible work environments, salary levels, and high school and college preparation.

- *Colleges and Universities with Programs in the Microbiological Sciences.* 17 pages. Lists schools and contact information.

- *Microbiology—Challenges for the 21st Century.* A poster illustrating microbiologist careers and depicting what a microbiologist does. Suitable for high school students.

- *Seeing the Unseen.* A poster depicting what a microbiologist is. Suitable for middle school students.

- *Heroes of Microbiology.* A poster including short biographies on minorities in microbiology and various experiments to try. Suitable for middle and high school students.

The following are available at the Society's Web site:

- *Careers in Science and Engineering.* Guide to graduate school and beyond.

- *Careers in the Microbiological Sciences.*

150

AMERICAN SOCIETY FOR PHARMACOLOGY AND EXPERIMENTAL THERAPEUTICS

9650 Rockville Pike
Bethesda, MD 20814-3995
301-530-7060
Fax: 301-530-7061

info@aspet.org
http://www.faseb.org.aspet

- *Explore Pharmacology: Graduate Studies in Pharmacology.* 16 pages. Details the number of subdivisions in the field, career opportunities, and required education and training.

- *Graduate Training in Pharmacy Programs in the United States and Canada.* 16 pages. Lists colleges and universities in the United States and Canada and specific fields of study.

151

AMERICAN SOCIETY FOR PHOTOGRAMMETRY AND REMOTE SENSING

5410 Grosvenor Lane, Suite 210
Bethesda MD 20814-2160
301-493-0290
Fax: 301-493-0208
asprs@asprs.org
http://www.asprs.org

Available at the Web site:

- *Career Brochure.* Discusses the field, employment and educational opportunities, and sources of further information.

152

AMERICAN SOCIETY OF AGRICULTURAL ENGINEERS

2950 Niles Road
St. Joseph, MI 49085-9659
616-429-0300
Fax: 616-429-3852
hq@asae.org
http://www.asae.org

- *Careers in Agricultural and Biological Engineering.* Brochure answering commonly asked questions about the fields; includes information on possible employers, skills required, how best to prepare for a job, and suggested courses to take at the university level.

- *Career Options: Agricultural Engineering.* ($.20) 6 pages. Brochure of general information on choosing a career in the field of agricultural engineering.

- *Career Options: Biological Engineering.* ($.20) 6 pages. Brochure of general information about choosing a career in the field of biological engineering. Describes typical duties, opportunities, and educational requirements.

- *Educational Programs in Agricultural Engineering and Related Fields.* A listing of the schools and universities nationwide that offer programs. Additional information available from the facilities listed.

- *Careers for Engineers in Bio-Resource Industries.* ($.20) 6 pages. Describes typical duties, opportunities, and educational requirements.

153

AMERICAN SOCIETY OF AGRONOMY

677 South Segoe Road
Madison, WI 53711
608-273-8080
Fax: 608-273-2021
http://www.asa-cssa-cssa.org

- *Exploring Careers in Agronomy, Crops, Soils, and Environmental Sciences.* 27 pages. Describes the agronomic sciences, duties and responsibilities, education and training, and salary. Lists colleges and universities in the United States.

154
AMERICAN SOCIETY OF ANESTHESIOLOGISTS
520 North Northwest Highway
Park Ridge, IL 60068-2573
847-825-5586
Fax: 847-825-1692
mail@asahq.org
http://www.asahq.org

- *Anesthesiology: Challenge, Diversity, Flexibility, Rewards.* ($.10 per 100 copies) 6 pages. Discusses education and training, residency, employment opportunities, hours, and outlook.

155
AMERICAN SOCIETY OF CIVIL ENGINEERS
Student Services Department
1801 Alexander Bell Drive
Reston, VA 20191
800-548-2723 or 703-295-6300
dconnor@asce.org
http://www.asce.org

- *Our Past, the Present, Your Future...in Civil Engineering.* 8 pages. Describes the civil engineering career. Limited copies available.

- *Civil Engineering: Leading Students into the Future.* ($2) Informational brochure about the career and outlook for the future.

- *Career Guidance Videos.* Free upon request.

- *Civil Engineering Coloring Books.* ($.25)

156
AMERICAN SOCIETY OF CLINICAL PATHOLOGISTS
Board of Registry
PO Box 12277
Chicago, IL 60612-0277
312-738-1336
Fax: 312-738-5808
bor@ascp.org
http://www.ascp.org

- *Careers in Medical Laboratory Technology.* 16 pages. Explores four different career paths in medical laboratory technology.

- *Cytotechnologist: A Career for You!* 1 page. Describes career opportunities, educational requirements, necessary personal characteristics, career preparation, and certification.

- *Histologic Technician: A Career for You!* 1 page. Describes career opportunities, educational requirements, necessary personal characteristics, career preparation, and certification.

- *Medical Laboratory Technician: A Career for You!* 1 page. Describes career opportunities, educational requirements, necessary personal characteristics, career preparation, and certification.

- *Medical Technologist: A Career for You!* 1 page. Describes career opportunities, educational requirements, necessary personal characteristics, career preparation, and certification.

- *BOR Guide to Certification and Careers in the Medical Laboratory.* 12 pages. Provides an overview of all areas of certification.

157

AMERICAN SOCIETY OF CYTOPATHOLOGY
CPRC Secretary
400 West Ninth Street, Suite 201
Wilmington, DE 19801
302-429-8802
Fax: 302-429-8807
lynne@cytopathology.org
http://www.cytopathology.org

• *Consider a Career in Cytotechnology.* Brochure. Describes responsibilities, opportunities, education, certification, and employment.

• *Consider A Career in Cytotechnology.* ($2) A poster depicting career opportunities in cytotechnology.

• *Accredited Programs in Cytotechnology.* Lists accredited cytotechnology training programs in the United States and Puerto Rico. Updated monthly.

158

AMERICAN SOCIETY OF ELECTRONEURODIAGNOSTIC TECHNOLOGISTS
204 West 7th Street
Carroll, IA 51401-2317
712-792-2978
Fax: 712-792-6962
aset@netins.net
http://www.aset.org

Available at the Web site:

• *Career Profile: A Career in Electroneurodiagnostics.* Explains what electroneurodiagnostics do and the studies performed.

• *Schools for Electroneurodiagnostics.* Lists schools in the field that are accredited.

159

AMERICAN SOCIETY OF EXTRA-CORPOREAL TECHNOLOGY
503 Carlisle Drive, Suite 125
Herndon, VA 20170
703-435-8556
Fax: 703-435-0056
http://www.amsect.org

• *AmSECT & Perfusion: The Guide.* Includes the following fact sheets: *Perfusion Education and Training, Career Outlook, Directory of Accredited Educational Programs in Perfusion,* and *Employment Opportunities.* Much of this information also available at the Web site.

160

AMERICAN SOCIETY OF HEALTH-SYSTEM PHARMACISTS
Resident Matching Program
7272 Wisconsin Avenue
Bethesda, MD 20814-1439
301-657-3000
Fax: 301-657-1258
asd@ashp.org
http://www.ashp.org

• *Opportunities: Pharmacy Residencies—Preparing for Your Future.* 26 pages. Provides detailed information on residencies in pharmacy, accredited programs, and specialties.

161
AMERICAN SOCIETY OF HEATING, REFRIGERATING, AND AIR-CONDITIONING ENGINEERS
Education Department
1791 Tullie Circle, NE
Atlanta, GA 30329
404-636-8400
Fax: 401-321-5478
http://www.ashrae.org

Available at the Web site:

• *Visualize a Career in HVAC&R.* Describes the fields of heating, ventilating, air conditioning, and refrigeration, such as construction engineering, technical sales, and more. Addresses environmental issues and answers questions about why to consider a career in engineering.

• *Hot Spots in HVAC&R.* Lists the jobs currently most in demand and lists sources for more information.

• *Frequently Asked Questions About HVAC&R.*

162
AMERICAN SOCIETY OF ICHTHYOLOGISTS AND HERPETOLOGISTS
Maureen Donnelly, Secretary
Department of Biological Sciences
College Of Arts & Science
Florida International University
North Miami, FL 33181
Fax: 305-919-5964
http://www.utexas.edu/depts/asih/pubs/pubs.html

The following information is available at the Society's Web site:

• *Careers in Herpetology.* Profiles careers in the field, employment opportunities, and education and training.

• *Careers in Ichthyology.* Covers education and training, employment opportunities, and schools with graduate programs in ichthyology.

163
AMERICAN SOCIETY OF INTERIOR DESIGNERS
National Headquarters
608 Massachusetts Avenue, NE
Washington, DC 20002-6006
202-546-3480
Fax: 202-546-3240
http://www.asid.org

• *Interior Design Career Guide.* 12 pages. SASE (legal-size envelope). Describes the field, skills and education needed, career options, and future outlook. Includes additional sources of information.

• *Access: Student Newsletter of the American Society of Interior Designers.* Quarterly newsletter aimed at students interested in the field.

• *An Interior Designer Is . . . .* Fact sheet defining the career.

• *Job Opportunities in Interior Design and Design-Related Fields.* Fact sheet illustrating the different types of jobs available withing interior design.

• *ASID Student Chapter Schools By State.* Listing of colleges and universities that offer interior design programs.

• *ASID Student Membership Application.*

• *ASID Scholarship and Awards Program.*

164

AMERICAN SOCIETY OF LANDSCAPE ARCHITECTS
636 Eye Street, NW
Washington, DC 20001-3736
202-898-2444
Fax: 202-898-1185
http://www.asla.org

Available at the Web site:

• *What is Landscape Architecture?* Includes general information about landscape architecture, the early history of the profession, and future outlook for a career in the field.

• *Accredited Programs in Landscape Architecture.* Directory of colleges and universities in the United States and Canada.

165

AMERICAN SOCIETY OF LIMNOLOGY AND OCEANOGRAPHY
5400 Bosque Boulevard, Suite 680
Waco, TX 76710-4446
800-929-2756 or 254-399-9635
Fax: 254-776-3767
business@aslo.org
http://www.aslo.org/

• *Aquatic Science Career Information.* A free article available by mail or online at the Web site. Defines the field of aquatic science and discusses job opportunities, employment outlook, earnings, working conditions, and educational preparation.

166

AMERICAN SOCIETY OF MAGAZINE EDITORS
919 Third Avenue
New York, NY 10022
212-872-3700
Fax: 212-906-0128
asme@magazine.org
http://asme.magazine.org

• *Guide to Careers in Magazine Publishing.* 14 pages. Discusses the industry, finding a job in magazine publishing, careers in the field (e.g., editorial, advertising, circulation, production and distribution, and finance and accounting), and other resources.

167

AMERICAN SOCIETY OF MECHANICAL ENGINEERS INTERNATIONAL
22 Law Drive, Box 2900
Fairfield, NJ 07007-2900
800-843-2763 or 973-882-1167
Fax: 973-882-1717
infocentral@asme.org
http://www.asme.org/careers

• *Mechanical Engineering A-Z.* Brochure for elementary school students that shows everyday items that are created by mechanical engineers.

• *Mechanical Engineering and Mechanical Engineering Technology: Which Path Will You Take?* Available by mail or accessible online. Aimed at high school and college students, brochure describes and contrasts two different career paths available to those interested in mechanical engineering.

• *What is a Mechanical Engineer?* Available by mail or online. Brochure for all ages that explains the field by using everyday devices made possible by mechanical engineers.

168
AMERICAN SOCIETY OF MEDIA PHOTOGRAPHERS, INC.
150 North Second Street
Philadelphia, PA 19106
215-451-2767
Fax: 215-451-0880
http://www.asmp.org

• *Career and School Information.* 1 page. Lists photographic schools and institutions in the United States.

169
AMERICAN SOCIETY OF PLANT TAXONOMISTS
http://www.sysbot.org

Available at the Web site:

• *Careers in Biological Systematics.* Explains the nature of systematics and the important place the field holds in today's society. Includes information on areas of current systematic research, typical salaries, job availability, employers, and the training required to enter the field.

170
AMERICAN SOCIETY OF RADIOLOGIC TECHNOLOGISTS
15000 Central Avenue, SE
Albuquerque, NM 87123-3917
800-444-2778 or 505-298-4500
Fax: 505-298-5063
http://www.asrt.org

• *Discover the Possibilties...The Radiologic Sciences.* 6 pages. Discusses various educational programs, curricula, duties and responsibilities, and specialties for a number of fields in the radiologic sciences.

171
AMERICAN SOCIETY OF SAFETY ENGINEERS
Customer Service
1800 East Oakton Street
Des Plaines, IL 60018-2187
847-699-2929
Fax: 847-296-3769
http://www.asse.org

• *List of Accredited Safety Colleges and Universities Offering Safety and Related Career Programs.* Listing of schools. .

172
AMERICAN SOCIETY OF TRAVEL AGENTS
http://www.astanet.com

Available at the Web site:

• *Choosing a Travel School.* Important considerations for finding a training program.

• *What is a Travel Agent?* Includes frequently asked questions about the job, work environment, benefits and salary, skills necessary, and sources for additional information.

173
AMERICAN SOCIOLOGICAL ASSOCIATION
1307 New York Avenue, NW, Suite 700
Washington, DC 20005

202-383-9005, ext. 319
Fax: 202-638-0882
edwards@asanet.org
http://www.asanet.org

- *Careers in Sociology.* (Available only online) Discusses the specialties; teaching, research, and practice; employment outlook; and career preparation.

- *Directory of Departments of Sociology, 1999.* ($.10 for hard copy; free access online) Provides basic information on over 2,200 departments of sociology and related disciplines, including chair name, department type, mailing address, telephone and fax numbers, e-mail addresses, and existing department home pages.

- *Directory of Programs in Applied Sociology and Sociological Practice.* ($16) 140 pages. List of programs for both the graduate and undergraduate levels.

174
AMERICAN SPEECH-LANGUAGE-HEARING ASSOCIATION
Product Sales
10801 Rockville Pike
Rockville, MD 20852
301-897-5700
Fax: 301-897-7355
http://www.asha.org

- *Careers in Speech-Language Pathology, Audiology, and Speech, Language and Hearing Science Kit.* (# 0111530) ($3.50) The kit includes the following brochures:

- *Careers in Speech-Language Pathology and Audiology.*

- *Exciting Opportunities Ahead for Speech, Language and Hearing Scientists.* 8 pages.

Kit also includes information cards addressing different topics, a list of accredited programs, and an informative question/answer page of FAQ.

175
AMERICAN SPORTSCASTERS ASSOCIATION, INC.
5 Beekman Street, Suite 814
New York, NY 10038
212-227-8080
Fax: 212-571-0556
lschwa8918@aol.com
http://www.americansportscasters.com

Career packet includes:

- *Interview Guidelines.* 1 page.

- *Radio: career profiles for broadcaster, broadcaster producer, engineer, promotions, and sales.* 6 pages.

- *Sportscaster: Career Profile.* 2 pages.

176
AMERICAN STATISTICAL ASSOCIATION
1429 Duke Street
Alexandria, VA 22314-3415
703-684-1221
Fax: 703-684-2037
http://www.amstat.org

Available at the Web site:

- *What Statisticians Do.* Outlines the general duties of a statistician, the educational requirements, employment prospects, and other sources of information.

- *Careers in Statistics.* Describes a career as a statistician.

- *Minorities in Statistics.* Contains information on the field of statistics, job opportunities, programs of study, salaries, and additional topics useful to minority students.

- *Women in Statistics.* Profiles various women that have made valuable contributions in statistics; describes how to become a statistician, job duties, employment outlook and earnings.

177

AMERICAN STUDENT DENTAL ASSOCIATION

211 East Chicago Avenue, Suite 1160
Chicago, IL 60611-2616
312-440-2795
Fax: 312-440-2820
http://www.ada.org

Available at the Web site:

- *Career Brochures and Fact Sheets.* Includes general information on the following fields: dentistry, dental hygiene, dental assisting, dental laboratory technology.

- *ADA Info Pak: Alternative Careers in Dentistry.*

- *Non-Clinical Dental Career Packet.*

- *Dental Schools in the U.S. and Canada.*

- *Advanced Specialty and General Dentistry Education Programs.*

- *Dental Assisting, Dental Hygiene, and Dental Laboratory Technology Education Programs.*

Available only by mail:

- *ASDA Handbook.* Contains useful information on requirements for application and admission to dental schools in the United States.

178

AMERICAN SYMPHONY ORCHESTRA LEAGUE

33 West 60th Street, 5th Floor
New York, NY 10023-7905
212-262-5161
Fax: 212-262-5198
http://www.symphony.org

- *Orchestra Librarian/Music Preparation.* ($7) Packet including two brochures from the Major Orchestra Librarians' Association (MOLA):

- *The Orchestra Librarian: A Career Introduction.* Highlights the duties of orchestra, opera, and ballet librarians and includes the education and training needed for the position.

- *MOLA Music Preparation Guidelines for Orchestral Music.*

179

AMERICAN TEXTILE MANUFACTURERS INSTITUTE

1130 Connecticut Avenue, Suite 1200
Washington, DC 20036
202-862-0500
http://www.atmi.org

- *America's Textiles.* ($2.50) 16 pages. Brochure outlining the social and economical dimensions of today's textile industry in terms of its people, products, and processes.

- *ATMI Textile News and Information Contacts Directory.* ($2) 36 pages. Directory of contacts at textile companies, associations, and colleges. Includes an introduction of the American Textile Manufacturers Institute, as well as industry employment and economic statistics.

- *The High-Tech World of Textiles.* ($1 plus postage and handling) 13 pages. Provides a general overview of careers in the textile industry.

- *ATMI Educator Package.* ($5) Kit including above material and additional information on ATMI.

- *America's Textiles: An Adventure Industry.* ($20 plus postage and handling) Short video showing a coloful sampling of the high-tech products and processes of the U.S. textile industry today. Designed for community/civic groups, high school, and college students.

180
AMERICAN TRANSLATORS ASSOCIATION
225 Reinekers Lane, Suite 590
Alexandria, VA 22314
703-683-6100
Fax: 703-683-6122
ata@atanet.org
http://www.atanet.org

Available at the Web site:

- *A Guide to ATA Accreditation.* Outlines why accreditation is crucial for a career in translation, the nature of the examination, how best to prepare, and how to apply for an examination sitting.

- *Institutions Providing Translation/ Interpretation Courses/Testing.* Directory of institutions with links to their Web sites.

181
AMERICAN TRUCKING ASSOCIATIONS
2200 Mill Road
Alexandria, VA 22314-4677
703-838-1950
http://www.truckline.com/safetynet/ drivers/careers

- *Careers in Truck Driving.* 8 pages. Available by mail or accessible online. Outlines the trucking career, types of truck drivers, choosing a truck driver training school, the necessary qualifications for trucking, and how to get hired and promoted in the trucking field.

182
AMERICAN VETERINARY MEDICAL ASSOCIATION
1931 North Meacham Road, Suite 100
Schaumburg, IL 60173-4360
847-925-8070
Fax: 847-925-1329
avmainfo@avma.org
http://www.avma.org/care4pets

- *Your Career in Veterinary Technology.* SASE. 8 pages. Discusses the required education, curriculum, personal attributes, admission requirements, registration and certification, and salaries.

- *Programs in Veterinary Technology.* SASE. Lists veterinary technology schools. Updated annually.

- *Today's Veterinarian.* SASE. 20 pages. Describes the veterinarian career and lists U.S. schools and colleges of veterinary medicine.

183
AMERICAN WATCHMAKERS-CLOCKMAKERS INSTITUTE
701 Enterprise Drive
Harrison, OH 45030-1696
513-367-9800
Fax: 513-367-1414
http://www.awi-net.org

- *Careers in Horology.* Includes information on career opportunities, salary, and employment outlook.

- *Research and Education Council Roster.* Listing of schools offering training programs for a watchmaking/clockmaking career.

184
AMERICAN WATER WORKS ASSOCIATION
6666 West Quincy Avenue
Denver, CO 80235-3098
303-794-7711
http://www.awwa.org

Available at the Web site:

- *Resume/Cover Letter Tips.*

- *Certification Information.*

- *Job Profiles.* Includes job descriptions, salary statistics, and career outlook for the field.

185
AMERICAN WELDING SOCIETY
550 Northwest LeJeune Road
Miami, FL 33126
800-443-9353, ext. 293 or 305-443-9353
Fax: 305-443-7559
denise@aws.org
http://www.aws.org

- *Welding—So Hot, It's Cool.* 10 minutes. Video designed for students ages 13-15, accompanied by a free full-color poster.

186
AMERICAN YOUTH HORSE COUNCIL
4093 Iron Works Parkway
Lexington, KY 40511
800-TRY-AYHC or 606-226-6011
Fax: 606-299-9849

- *AYHC Source Book.* ($5) 72 pages. Directory of over 200 horse-related organizations and businesses nationwide. Includes educational resources such as books, videotapes, CD-ROMs, and Internet addresses.

- *Career Opportunities in the Horse Industry.* Free brochure outlining the methods for exploring possibilities for a horse-related career. Includes tips for narrowing your search for the right job in the horse industry and lists sources for additional information.

187
AMERICAN ZOO AND AQUARIUM ASSOCIATION
8403 Colesville Road, Suite 710
Silver Spring, MD 20910-3314
301-562-0777

Fax: 301-562-0888
http://www.aza.org

• *A Listing of Universities and Schools Having Courses and Classes Professionally Relevant to Zoo Keeping.* SASE. 15 pages. Lists U.S. and international universities and schools.

Available at the Web site:

• *Zoo and Aquarium Careers.* Describes career opportunities, educational and training requirements, salaries, positions, and other organizations providing more information.

188
AOPA
421 Aviation Way
Frederick, MO 21701
301-695-2000
Fax: 301-695-2375
http://www.aopa.org

• *Choosing a Flight School: A Checklist for Finding Quality Training.* 12 pages. Contains general guidance information. Intended as an aid for anyone interested in learning to fly and for selecting the training organization that will meet specific needs.

• *Six Suggestions for Student Pilots.*

• *Aviation Colleges.* Directory listing colleges, aviation programs, and other collegiate options.

• *A Teacher's Guide to Aviation.* A teacher's guide including information on the following: bringing aviation into the classroom, the basics of flight, flight training, careers in aviation, aviation facts. Also

includes a list of other aviation organizations offering resource materials designed for teachers.

• *Aviation and You: A Student's Guide to Aviation.* Answers the aviation questions of middle and high school students.

• *ABCs of Aviation.* An "Aviation-to-English Dictionary" designed for students in middle school and above. Explains acronyms and jargon that characterize everyday "aviation speak."

• *Airplanes!* A hand-out for elementary and middle school students with diagrams and definitions of airplane structure. Includes general information on airplanes and flight.

• *AOPA's Aviation Fact Card.* Includes statistics on pilots, airplanes, airports, and flight operations.

• *Aviation Education Video List.* A listing of educational videos available on aviation.

• *Careers in Aviation.* Lists 70 different careers and jobs in the aviation industry and includes educational requirements and potential employers.

• *Getting Started on Flight Training.* Article desciding "everything you need to head skyward." For anyone interested in flying.

• *The Mini-Page: Let's Learn About Flying.* Written for elementary school students and their families. Includes an airplane diagram showing its different parts, the four forces of flight, the history of aviation, and more.

• *What is General Aviation?* Brochure designed to increase public understanding of general aviation as "airplanes serving people."

189
APPRAISAL INSTITUTE
875 North Michigan Avenue, Suite 2400
Chicago, IL 60611-1980
312-335-4140
Fax: 312-335-4400
http://www.appraisalinstitute.org

• *Career Opportunities.* 5 pages. Describes duties and responsibilities, qualifications, and employment outlook in the appraisal field.

190
APPRENTICESHIP TRAINING, EMPLOYER AND LABOR SERVICES
U.S. Department of Labor
200 Constitution Avenue, NW
Room N-4649
Washington, DC 20210
202-219-5021
Fax: 202-219-5011
http://www.doleta.gov/bat

The Web site describes the National Apprenticeship System and provides a listing of State Apprenticeship Councils and Bureau of Apprenticeship and Training Offices.

191
ARC: A NATIONAL ORGANIZATION ON MENTAL DISABILITIES
3300-C Pleasant Valley Lane
Arlington, TX 76015
888-368-8009
http://www.thearc.org

• *Make a Difference! Careers in Disability-Related Fields.* (Single copy is free; 100 copies are $11.80) (#30-21-1f) 63 pages. Focuses on the varied career opportunities in the disability-related field. Includes career overviews, salary, educational and certification requirements, and populations served.

192
ARCHAEOLOGICAL INSTITUTE OF AMERICA
656 Beacon Street, 4th Floor
Boston, MA 02215-2006
617-353-9361
Fax: 617-353-6550
http://www.archaeological.org

• *Career Summary.* 2 pages. Covers duties, working conditions, future outlook for the career, and related fields of interest.

• *Anthropologist Fact Sheet.* 4 pages. Covers description of work, earnings, hours, working conditions, and educational training.

• *Archaeological Sites.* 3 pages.

• *Glossary of Archaeological Terms.* 3 pages.

• *Frequently Asked Questions About a Career in Archaeology in the U.S.* 10 pages.

• *Archaeology Programs with Full Description.* 16 pages.

193
ARIZONA DEPARTMENT OF ECONOMIC SECURITY
Research Administration
Labor Market Information Publications
Site Code 733A

PO Box 6123
Phoenix, AZ 85005-6123
800-827-4966 or 602-542-3871
Fax: 602-542-6474

- *Arizona Occupational Employment Forecasts, 1994-2005.* Information for the state and by particular county.

- *Arizona Employer Wage Survey.* (#PAL-542).

- *Arizona's Workforce.* Monthly release.

- *Arizona Economic Trends.* Quarterly review.

- *Employment, Firms, and Wages by Industry.*

- *Job Seekers Kit.*

194
ARIZONA OCCUPATIONAL INFORMATION COORDINATING COMMITTEE
Research Administration
Labor Market Information Publications
Site Code 733A, PO Box 6123
Phoenix, AZ 85005-6123
602-542-3871
Fax: 602-542-6474
vvgruan@de.state.az.us
http://www.de.state.az.us/links/economic

- *Arizona Apprenticeship Data by Training Program.*

- *Arizona Futures.* Includes Career Information Delivery System (CIDS) Information.

195
ARKANSAS EMPLOYMENT SECURITY DEPARTMENT
Occupational Career Information Section
PO Box 2981
Little Rock, AR 72203-2981
501-682-3197

- *Arkansas Labor Market Trends.* 8 pages. Monthly publication concerning non-farm payroll jobs in manufacturing industries and metropolitan areas. Details employment by industry, hours, and earnings.

- *Directory of Licensed Occupations.*

- *Occupational Trends.* Available for the state of Arkansas, the city of Little Rock, and the following regions: Central, Eastern, North Central, Northeast, Southeast, Southwest, West Central, and Western.

- *Staffing Patterns.*

196
ARMSTRONG WORLD INDUSTRIES, INC.
Corporate Relations Department
2500 Columbia Avenue
PO Box 3001
Lancaster, PA 17604-3001
717-396-2436
Fax: 717-396-6056
http://www.armstrong.com

- *A Career as a Lab Technician.* 6 pages. Discusses how to get started in a flooring career, necessary education and knowledge, traits of a good technician, and more.

- *A Career as a Professional Flooring Installer.* 4 pages. Defines a flooring installer, describes the type of work, and suggests ways to learn the flooring trade.

197
ARMY RECRUITING STATION
Contact your local Army recruiter.
http://www.goarmy.com

- *Army Informational Booklet.* Includes general information on opportunities, college loan programs, skills training, benefits, and more.

198
ASPIRA ASSOCIATION, INC.
1444 I Street, NW, Suite 800
Washington, DC 20005
202-835-3600
Fax: 202-835-3613
info@aspira.org
http://www.aspira.org

- *Peparing for College.* ($5) 41 pages. Written for parents. Discusses the importance of college and the parent's role in preparing a child for college.

- *Planning for College.* ($5) 47 pages. Also written for parents. Contains suggestions on when to begin planning for college and the steps to take in the 9th through 12th grades.

- *Paying for College.* ($5) 34 pages. Offers parents suggestions on saving for college, facts about financial aid and how to apply, and the steps to take if the aid received is not enough.

199
ASSOCIATED COLLEGES OF THE MIDWEST
205 West Wacker Drive, Suite 1300
Chicago, IL 60606
312-263-5000
Fax: 312-263-5879
acm@acm.edu
http://www.acm.edu

- *Pre-College Planner.* 13 pages. Offers information on college visits, college evaluation, financial assistance, applications, and other tools students can use to pick the college that best matches their personalities and interests. Available in text or online.

The following are available on ACM's Web site:

- *Make the Most of a Campus Visit.* Guide with tips on things to do and questions to ask when you visit a college campus.

- *Writing a College Application Essay.* Suggestions to help you write the best essay.

- *Together Newsletter.* Back issues of ACM's newsletter available for guidance counselors.

200
ASSOCIATED GENERAL CONTRACTORS OF AMERICA
333 John Carlyle Street, Suite 200
Alexandria, VA 22314
703-548-3118
Fax: 703-548-3119
info@agc.org
http://www.agc.org

Available at the Web site:

• *Occupational Briefs.* Outlines a wide range of jobs available in construction in both the craft and non-craft areas, ranging from accountants, safety directors, draftsmen, electricians, and more. Includes information on the nature of the work, education and training required, and advancement potential.

• *Accredited Construction Degrees.* Online directory of the colleges and universities that offer programs in construction, listed by state.

201
ASSOCIATED LANDSCAPE CONTRACTORS OF AMERICA
150 Elden Street, Suite 270
Herndon, VA 20170
800-395-2522 or 703-736-9666
Fax: 703-736-9668
http://www.alca.org

• *The Landscape Industry: Growing Careers for You!* ($1) 8 pages. Discusses the required education and training, co-op education, the industry outlook, and careers in the industry.

202
ASSOCIATION FOR APPLIED PSYCHOPHYSIOLOGY AND BIOFEEDBACK
10200 West 44th Avenue, Suite 304
Wheat Ridge, CO 80033-2837
303-422-8436
Fax: 303-422-8894
aapb@resourcenter.com
http://www.aapb.org

• *The Psychology Major as Biofeedback Therapist.* 4 pages. Describes biofeedback, necessary training involved, certification requirements, and employment.

203
ASSOCIATION FOR CAREER AND TECHNICAL EDUCATION
1410 King Street
Alexandria, VA 22314
800-826-9972 or 703-683-3111
Fax: 703-683-7424
http://www.avaonline.org

The following are sold in bulk packages only. Call for information on prices and quantities.

• *Get Your Career in Gear!* 6 pages. Explains to students the school-to-career concept.

• *You Can Be What You Want to Be.* 8 pages. Contains career quizzes for middle and high school students on all major career fields.

• *Facts Every Parent Should Know About Vocational Education.* 6 pages. Explains why blending academic and technical courses better prepares high school students for life and career success.

• *Tech Prep for Students: The Success Option.* 8 pages. Shows students that tech prep means focus, applied learning, skills, college, and success.

• *A Parent's Guide to Tech Prep: A Pathway to Success for your Teenager.* 6 pages. Offers seven persuasive reasons why tech prep is an excellent option for students.

- *Learning and Earning Power*. 6 pages. Shows students how the amount and type of education they receive affects their earnings over a lifetime.

- *Life After High School*. Explains how career, technical, and college education work together.

- *Will My Kid Ever Get a Life? A Parent's Guide to Career Exploration*. 4 pages. Simple steps parents can take to help their kids relate their education to realistic career goals.

204

ASSOCIATION FOR CHILDHOOD EDUCATION INTERNATIONAL
17904 Georgia Avenue, Suite 215
Olney, MD 20832
800-423-3563 or 301-570-2111
Fax: 301-570-2212
http://www.udel.edu/bateman/acei

- *Careers in Education*. 6 pages. Describes ways to prepare for careers in education, career possibilities in teaching and related fields, and other sources of information.

205

ASSOCIATION FOR EDUCATION AND REHABILITATION OF THE BLIND AND VISUALLY IMPAIRED
4600 Duke Street, Suite 430
PO Box 22397
Alexandria, VA 22304
703-823-9690
Fax: 703-823-9695
http://www.aerbvi.org

- *Don't Settle for Just a Job—Choose a Career!* (Brochure: $.25 each; Video: $13 plus

shipping) Career information for jobs dealing with teaching and aiding the blind or visually impaired. Includes job outlook, salary information, financial assistance, and educational requirements.

206

ASSOCIATION FOR EDUCATION IN JOURNALISM AND MASS COMMUNICATION
234 Outlet Pointe Boulevard
Columbia, SC 29210-5667
803-798-0271
Fax: 803-772-3509
aejmc@aejmc.org
http://www.aejmc.org

Available at the Web site:

- *Journalism and Mass Communication Directory*. Listing of more than 400 schools and departments of journalism and mass communication. Also features information on organizations, national funds, fellowships, and foundations in journalism.

207

ASSOCIATION FOR GERONTOLOGY IN HIGHER EDUCATION
1030 15th Street, NW, Suite 240
Washington, DC 20005-1503
202-289-9806
Fax: 202-289-9824
aghetemp@aghe.org
http://www.aghe.org

- *Careers in Aging: Consider the Possibilities*. ($.50) 16 pages. An introductory booklet on careers in aging appropriate for high school and college students. Discusses the field of gerontology, jobs and careers available, how to select a program, and how to find jobs in aging.

- *Careers in Aging: Opportunities and Options.* ($2) 28 pages. Defines gerontology, discusses education and training, and provides sources of additional information and suggestions for finding employment in the field.

- *Sources of Information about Fellowships in Gerontology and Geriatrics.* ($4) 9 pages. Descriptions of national fellowship programs at the pre- and postdoctoral level for gerontological education and training. Also includes a list of newsletters and directories that publish fellowship opportunities in aging.

- *Personnel to Serve the Aging in the Field of Occupational Therapy.* ($4) 54 pages. Practitioners in the field of occupational therapy who provide services to older people are described in this study.

- *Gerontological Education & Job Opportunities in Aging.* ($15) 23 pages. Focuses on the links between gerontology education and the work setting of aging studies graduates. Includes practical suggestions for building ties among faculty, students, and employers. Excellent resource for those entering the work field of aging, employers, or for instructors of gerontology.

- *Careers in Aging: Old Friends, New Faces.* ($15) 10-minute video. Focuses on the personal rewards of aging-related careers and the great variety of employment opportunities available.

208
ASSOCIATION FOR INTERNATIONAL PRACTICAL TRAINING
10400 Little Patuxent Parkway, Suite 250
Columbia, MD 21044-3510
410-997-2200
Fax: 410-992-3924
aipt@aipt.org
http://www.aipt.org

- *Solutions for the Global Marketplace.* 8 pages. Outlines the three programs offered to assist companies and individuals with international human resource needs. Describes the different international recruiting and training programs available.

209
ASSOCIATION FOR THE ADVANCEMENT OF COST ENGINEERING
209 Prairie Avenue, Suite 100
Morgantown, WV 26501
304-296-8444
Fax: 304-291-5728
info@aacei.org
http://www.aacei.org

The following is available at the Web site:

- *Education Programs Related to Cost Engineering.* List of U.S. and Canadian colleges and universities that offer coursework in cost engineering.

The following is available by mail.

- *Careers in Cost Engineering and Related Industry Specialities.* 9 pages. Describes the field of cost engineering, the duties, and education and training. Lists industries that typically employ cost engineers.

210
ASSOCIATION FOR THE ADVANCEMENT OF MEDICAL INSTRUMENTATION
3330 Washington Boulevard
Arlington, VA 22201-4598
703-525-4890
Fax: 703-525-1424
http://www.aami.org

- *2000 Applicant Handbook.* Available by mail or accessible on the Web site. For those interested in becoming a certified biomedical equipment technician (CBET), certified radiology equipment specialist (CRES), or a certified laboratory equipment specialist (CLES).

Available online:

- *Biomedical Technology Education Programs.* Listing of universities offering biomedical programs and links to their Web sites.

- *Frequently Asked Questions.* Answers to questions about ICC certification for CBET, CRES, and CLES professions.

211
ASSOCIATION FOR WOMEN IN MATHEMATICS
Career Booklets Order
4114 Computer and Space Sciences Building
University of Maryland
College Park, MD 20742-2461
301-405-7892
awm@math.umd.edu

- *Careers That Count: Opportunities in the Mathematical Sciences.* ($1.50) 18 pages. Describes mathematic careers and pro-files women working in various mathematical fields.

212
ASSOCIATION MONTESSORI INTERNATIONAL-USA
410 Alexander Street
Rochester, NY 14607
716-461-5920
Fax: 716-461-0075
usaami3@aol.com
http://www.montessori-ami.org

- *AMI Invites You...Become a Montessori Teacher.* 6 pages. Contains a brief history of AMI, descriptions of training for prospective teachers and of educational requirements, and a list of AMI training courses in the United States.

213
ASSOCIATION OF AMERICAN GEOGRAPHERS
1710 16th Street, NW
Washington, DC 20009-3198
202-234-1450
Fax: 202-234-2744
gaia@aag.org
http://www.aag.org

- *Geography: Today's Career for Tomorrow.* (first copy free; 50 copies or less: $.25 each; more than 50 copies: $.20 each) 6 pages. Describes the fields in geography and geographers at work.

Other career information is available on the Association's Web site.

214

ASSOCIATION OF AMERICAN MEDICAL COLLEGES

2450 N Street, NW
Washington, DC 20037-1126
202-828-0400
Fax: 202-828-1125
http://www.aamc.org

Available at the Web site:

• *Medicine: a Chance to Make a Difference.*

• *Careers in Medicine: A Guide for High School Students.*

• *31 Questions I Wished I Had Asked.*

• *Medical Schools of the United States and Canada.*

• *Medical Careers.*

• *Careers in Medical Research.*

• *General Information on Admission to U.S. Medical Schools.*

• *Information for High School Students.*

• *Information for Minorities.*

• *Information for Women.*

• *Information on Financial Aid.*

• *U.S. Medical School Tuition and Fees.*

215

ASSOCIATION OF AMERICAN PUBLISHERS, INC.

71 Fifth Avenue
New York, NY 10003-3004
212-255-0200
Fax: 212-255-7007

eharris@publishers.org
http://www.publishers.org

• *Getting into Book Publishing.* 19 pages. Brochure illustrating how to get into the industry, the range of jobs available, and the education or training needed to get a publishing job.

216

ASSOCIATION OF BOARDING SCHOOLS

4454 Connecticut Avenue, Suite A200
Washington, DC 20008
800-541-5908
http://www.schools.com

• *Boarding School Directory.* Published annually to assist families, counselors, and consultants in matching a student with a boarding school. Contains profiles of 283 elementary and secondary boarding schools.

217

ASSOCIATION OF COLLEGIATE SCHOOLS OF ARCHITECTURE

1735 New York Avenue, NW
Washington, DC 20006
800-232-2724 or 202-785-2324
Fax: 202-628-0448
http://www.acsa-arch.org

• *Accredited Programs in Architecture.* 18 pages. Lists accredited architecture programs and indicates program types (by identifying the professional degree received upon the completion of the program).

• *The Education of an Architect.* 24 pages. Contains a brief history of agricultural education, as well as information on high school preparation, architectural programs and degrees, selecting a school, internships, and employment opportunities.

218
ASSOCIATION OF ENERGY SERVICE COMPANIES
10200 Richmond Avenue, Suite 253
Houston, TX 77042
713-781-0758
Fax: 713-781-7542
http://www.aesc.net

• *Consider a Career in Well Servicing.* 6 pages. Describes well servicing crews, their jobs, training programs, and necessary personal traits of a well servicing employee.

219
ASSOCIATION OF FLIGHT ATTENDANTS
1275 K Street, NW, Suite 500
Washington, DC 20005-4090
afatalk@afanet.org
http://www.afanet.org

Available at the Web site:

• *Are You Considering a Job as a Flight Attendant?* Lists U.S. airlines (including contact information) that may be accepting flight attendant applications.

220
ASSOCIATION OF INFORMATION TECHNOLOGY PROFESSIONALS
315 South Northwest Highway, Suite 200
Park Ridge, IL 60068-4278
800-224-9371 or 847-825-8124
Fax: 847-825-1693

aitp_hq@aitp.org
http://www.aitp.org

• *Computer Careers.* 4 pages. Describes education and training available for information technologists; profiles computer careers by listing job titles and descriptions; and describes types of career opportunities available.

221
ASSOCIATION OF MEDICAL ILLUSTRATORS
2965 Flowers Road South, Suite 105
Atlanta, GA 30341
770-454-7933
Fax: 770-458-3314
assnhq@mindspring.com
http://www.medical-illustrators.org

Available at the Web site:

• *Medical Illustration: The Profession and The People.* Information about the profession, becoming a medical illustrator, certification of medical illustrators, and a salary survey.

222
ASSOCIATION OF OFFICIAL SEED ANALYSTS
201 North 8th Street, Suite 400
PO Box 81152
Lincoln, NE 68501-1152
402-476-3852
Fax: 402-476-6547
aosa@assocoffice.net
http://www.zianet.com/aosa

• *Career Opportunities in Seed Analysis.* Discusses responsibilities, education, and training.

223

ASSOCIATION OF OPERATING ROOM NURSES, INC.

2170 South Parker Road, Suite 300
Denver CO 80231-5711
800-755-2676 or 303-755-6300
http://www.aorn.org

Available online:

- *Career Center.* Information on the profession of perioperative nursing, education required, listing of educational programs, career development, job searching, resume tips, and more.

224

ASSOCIATION OF SCHOOLS AND COLLEGES OF OPTOMETRY

6110 Executive Boulevard, Suite 510
Rockville, MD 20852
301-231-5944
Fax: 301-770-1828
admini@opted.org
http://www.opted.org

- *Optometry: A Career with Vision.* 15 pages. Designed for students contemplating a career in optometry. Provides general information about the profession, offers guidelines concerning the recommended course of graduate study, and includes a list of accredited schools and colleges of optometry.

- *Schools and Colleges of Optometry: Admission Requirements, 1999-2000.* 133 pages.

225

ASSOCIATION OF SCHOOLS OF PUBLIC HEALTH

1101 15th Street, NW, Suite 910
Washington, DC 20005
202-296-1099
Fax: 202-296-1252
http://www.asph.org/student.htm

The following are available at the Association's Web site:

- *Accreditation of Schools of Public Health.*

- *List of ASPH Member Schools of Public Health.*

- *Internships and Fellowships for Students of Accredited Schools.*

- *Career Opportunities in Public Health.*

- *10 Most Frequently Asked Questions.*

226

ASSOCIATION OF SURGICAL TECHNOLOGISTS

7108-C South Alton Way
Englewood, CO 80112
303-694-9130
Fax: 303-694-9169
http://www.ast.org

Available at the Web site:

- *Surgical Technology: A Growing Career.* Discusses duties and responsibilities, personal characteristics, working conditions, employment, education, and curriculum. Lists accredited surgical technology programs and career opportunities.

227
ASSOCIATION OF SYSTEMATICS COLLECTIONS
1725 K Street, NW, Suite 601
Washington, DC 20006-1401
202-835-9050
Fax: 202-835-7334
asc@ascoll.org
http://www.ascoll.org

• *Careers in Biological Systematics.* 12 pages.

228
ASSOCIATION OF THEOLOGICAL SCHOOLS
10 Summit Park Drive
Pittsburgh, PA 15275-1103
412-788-6505
Fax: 412-788-6510
ats@ats.edu
http://www.ats.edu

• *Directory and Membership List.* ($8 plus shipping) 148 pages. Provides brief descriptions of the major institutional and organizational resources for graduate theological education in North America.

229
ASSOCIATION OF UNIVERSITY PROGRAMS IN HEALTH ADMINISTRATION
730 11th Street, NW, 4th Floor
Washington, DC 20001-4510
202-638-3429
Fax: 202-638-3429
aupha@aupha.org
http://www.aupha.com

Available at the Web site:

• *FAQs About Health Administration.* Includes information about types of careers available, education required, typical study programs, what employers are looking for, and sources of additional information.

• *Academic Programs.* Contains links to colleges and universities that offer both graduate and undergraduate programs in health administration.

230
ASSOCIATION OF WOMEN SURGEONS
414 Plaza Drive, Suite 209
Westmont, IL 60559
630-655-0392
Fax: 630-655-0391
info@womensurgeons.org
http://www.womensurgeons.org

• *Pocket Mentor: A Manual for Surgical Interns and Residents.* A guide for women in the surgical specialties. Available in print form or accessible online.

231
ASSOCIATION ON HIGHER EDUCATION AND DISABILITY
University of Massachusetts, Boston
Boston, MA 02125
617-287-3880
Fax: 617-287-3881
http://www.ahead.org

• *College Students with Learning Disabilities.* ($.35) 8 pages. Offers suggestions for college students with learning disabilities and for faculty dealing with students with learning disabilities.

• *Ready, Set, Go: Helping Students with Learning Disabilities Prepare for College.* ($.35) 6 pages. Lists activities that high school students with learning disabilities can do as they prepare for college.

232
AUTOMOTIVE SERVICE ASSOCIATION
PO Box 929
Bedford, TX 76095-0929
800-ASA-SHOP or 817-283-6205
Fax: 817-685-0225
asainfo@asashop.org
http://www.asashop.org

• *Automotive Technician: A Challenging and Changing Career.* 10 pages. Contains job description and discusses areas of speciality, employers of technicians, employment outlook, career advancement, training, earnings, and opportunities for women and minorities.

• *Career Opportunities...in the Automotive Collision Repair and Refinishing Industry.* 10 pages. Includes job description and discusses earn while you learn programs, advancement opportunities, opportunities for women, areas of speciality, and outlook and earnings.

233
BIOMEDICAL ENGINEERING SOCIETY
8401 Corporate Drive, Suite 110
Landover, MD 20785-2224
301-459-1999
Fax: 301-459-2444
http://www.mecca.org/BME/BMES/society/

Available at the Web site:

• *Planning a Career in Biomedical Engineering.* Outlines typical duties, the specialty areas, employment opportunities, career preparation, and lists sources for additional information.

234
BIOPHYSICAL SOCIETY OFFICE
9650 Rockville Pike
Bethesda, MD 20814-3998
301-530-7114
Fax: 301-530-7133
society@biophysics.faseb.org
http://www.biophysics.org/biophys

• *Careers in Biophysics.* 20 pages. Provides an introduction to careers in biophysics for high school and college students, as well as the nature of the work, employment opportunities, and education.

235
BIOTECHNOLOGY INDUSTRY ORGANIZATION
1625 K Street, NW, Suite 1100
Washington, DC 20006-1604
202-857-0244
Fax: 202-857-0237
http://www.bio.org

Available at the Web site:

• *Editors' and Reporters' Guide to Biotechnology.* Online information about the industry, legislative issues, biotechnology's role in various industries, and careers.

236
BOTANICAL SOCIETY OF AMERICA
Business Office
Department of Botany
Ohio State University
1735 Neil Avenue
Columbus, OH 43210
614-292-3519
http://www.botany.org

• *Careers in Botany: A Guide to Working With Plants.* Available by mail or online. Discusses specialties in the field, employment opportunities, salary, job availability, educational requirements and preparation, and additional sources of information.

237
BOY SCOUTS OF AMERICA
Professional Selection Service
1325 West Walnut Hill Lane
PO Box 152079
Irving, TX 75015-2079
972-580-2188
Fax: 972-580-2549
cdelhier@netbsa.org
http://www.bsa.scouting.org

• *Have You Thought about Being an Executive with the Boy Scouts of America?...A Career of Character.* 4 pages. Explains professional BSA work, philosophy, and compensation.

• *Why Not Consider Something Different?...A Career in the Boy Scouts of America.* 6 pages. Explains the work, qualifications, and advantages of the BSA for those considering a career change.

• *Why Not Make the Boy Scouts of America Your Life's Work?...A Career of Character.* 6 pages. Describes a career in the Boy Scouts. Suitable for those still in high school.

238
BRICK INDUSTRY ASSOCIATION
11490 Commerce Park Drive
Reston, VA 20191-1525
703-620-0010
Fax: 703-620-3928
brickinfo@bia.org
http://www.brickinfo.org

• *Playing in the Big Leagues as a Brick Mason.* Outlines the benefits and advantages of a mason and how to get started in the field.

• *Brick Laying.* A poster showing brick laying tools and providing brief statements about the brick laying craftsman. Suitable for school counselors and career centers.

239
BUREAU FOR AT-RISK YOUTH
135 Dupont Street
PO Box 760
Plainview, NY 11803-0760
800-99-YOUTH
Fax: 516-349-5521
info@at-risk.com
http://www.at-risk.com

• *Becoming a Civilian Family: Successfully Getting Through the Transition.* ($3) 14 pages. Discusses the obstacles facing a military family returning to civilian life and how to avoid them.

- *How to Be a Successful Young Military Family.* ($3) 14 pages. Discusses the military lifestyle and how to prepare for and deal with its unique set of challenges.

- *Set of six leaflets for teens.* ($4) Titles include: *Choosing a Career Path, Finding a Part-Time or Summer Job, How to Keep Your Job Once You're Hired, Interviewing Techniques that Get the Job, Matching Your Talents to Employers' Needs, Where and How to Find Job Opportunities.*

240
BUREAU OF INDIAN AFFAIRS
Office of Indian Education Programs
U.S. Department of the Interior
18th and C Streets, NW
Washington, DC 20240
202-208-4234

Call or write the Bureau for a list of current publications.

241
BUREAU OF LABOR STATISTICS
Office of Compensation and Working Conditions
U.S. Department of Labor
Postal Square Building, Room 4175
2 Massachusetts Avenue, NE
Washington, DC 20212
202-691-6199
Fax: 202-606-6647
ocltinfo.bls.gov
http://stats.bls.gov/ocshome.htm

- *Occupational Compensation Surveys.* Cites salary wages and hourly wages for a number of occupations in various U.S. cities.

242
BUREAU OF LABOR STATISTICS
U.S. Department of Labor
Washington, DC 20212
202-691-5700
oohinfo@bls.gov
http://stats.bls.gov/emphome.htm

The following are available in print form for a nominal fee or can be accessed on the Web site free:

- *The College Labor Market: Outlook, Current Situation, and Earnings.*

- *Matching Yourself with the World of Work.*

- *Resumes, Applications, and Cover Letters.*

- *Core Subjects and Your Career.*

- *High Earnings Workers Who Don't Have a Bachelor's Degree.*

- *Occupational Outlook Handbook.*

- *The Career Guide to Industries.*

- *Occupational Outlook Quarterly.*

243
BUREAU OF LAND MANAGEMENT
Colorado State Office
2850 Youngfield Street
Lakewood, CO 80215
303-239-3600
http://www.co.blm.gov/pdf/brochures.htm

Available at BLM's Web site:

- *Set in Stone. A Teacher's Resource to Paleontology.*

244
CALIFORNIA EMPLOYMENT DEVELOPMENT DEPARTMENT
Labor Market Information Division
Information Services Group
Publications and Information Unit
7000 Franklin Street, Suite 1100
Sacramento, CA 95823
916-262-2162
Fax: 916-262-2443
http://www.calmis.ca.gov

• *California Occupational Guide Series.* Set available for career counselors; individual titles available upon request. These 2-page fact sheets describe typical duties; working conditions; employment outlook; wages, hours, and fringe benefits; entrance requirements and training; advancement; finding the job; and related occupational guides for a number of occupations, including bell person, copywriter, numerical-control machine operator, and tool designer.

• *California Career Notes Set: Careers with a Future.* ($12.50) Provides "at-a-glance" information about occupations for entry level job seekers. All jobs have a large number of openings and provide career growth potential. The set contains 50 occupations.

• *Labor Market Conditions in California.* ($6) Includes the current population survey data, and wages and salaries by industry, both seasonally adjusted and unadjusted.

• *Small Business in California: A Resource Guide for Starting and Improving Your Small Business.* ($10) A resource tool for small business owners and those who

dream of sometime owning their own business.

• *Emerging Occupations in California: A Sampler.* (1995) ($9).

• *Emerging Occupations in California: Environmental Hazardous Waste Occupations.* (1994) ($9).

• *Emerging Occupations in California: Robotics and Related Automated Systems.* (1994) ($9).

245
CALIFORNIA LIBRARY ASSOCIATION
717 K Street, Suite 300
Sacramento, CA 95814-3477
916-447-8541
Fax: 916-447-8394
info@cla-net.org
http://www.cla-net.org

• *From Books to Bytes: Careers for Librarians and Information Professionals.* Covers careers in public libraries and children's librarianship, as well as opportunities for minorities.

246
CALIFORNIA SEA GRANT COLLEGE
University of California
9500 Gilman Drive, Department 0232
La Jolla, CA 92093-0232
858-534-4444
Fax: 858-453-2948
http://www-cgsc.uscd.edu

• *Directory of Academic Marine Programs in California.* 82 pages. Lists and describes for students, teachers, and counselors, the marine programs at 48 two- and four-year schools of higher learning in California.

247
CALIFORNIA STUDENT AID COMMISSION
Publications
PO Box 419026
Rancho Cordova, CA 95741-9026
916-526-7590
Fax: 916-526-8002
http://www.csac.ca.gov

Available at the Web site:

• *Fund Your Future: The Financial Aid Workbook for Students.* Guide containing application information for California state grants, federal aid, and other financial aid programs.

• *ABCs of Financial Aid.* Answers common questions about financial aid eligibility and application requirements.

• *Internet Tools for Students and Schools.* Contains links to the best financial aid calculators on the Web.

248
CAMPUS COMPACT
Brown University
PO Box 1975
Providence, RI 02912
401-863-1119
Fax: 401-863-3779
campus@compact.org
http://www.compact.org

• *Campus Compact: Higher Education in Service to the Nation.* Publishes a list of fellowships for those involved in volunteer service projects.

249
CANADIAN ASSOCIATION OF PHYSICISTS
150 Louis Pasteur, Suite 112
McDonald Building
Ottawa, Ontario K1N 6N5, Canada
613-562-5614
Fax: 613-562-5615
cap@physics.uottawa.ca
http://www.cap.ca

• *Careers in Physics.* 9 pages. Describes the main fields of physics and lists Canadian universities offering physics programs.

250
CANADIAN VETERINARY MEDICAL ASSOCIATION
Communications Officer
339 Booth Street
Ottawa, Ontario K1R7K1, Canada
613-236-1162
Fax: 613-236-9681
admin@cvma-acmv.org
http://www.cvma-acmv.org

• *Veterinary Medicine in Canada: Your Career Choice.* ($.75) 4 pages. Describes the various fields and types of practice, educational requirements, necessary personal attributes, and salary range. Lists the four veterinary colleges in Canada. In English or French.

• *Veterinarians Caring for Animals.* ($1.25) For children to age 11. Includes a basic introduction to veterinarians and animal care. In English or French.

• *Jr. Veterinarian Club Kit.* ($.50) Contains activity book suitable for elementary and middle school students, with basic facts about veterinarians. Includes ruler and pin. In English or French.

251
CAREER COLLEGE ASSOCIATION
750 First Street, NE, Suite 900
Washington, DC 20002
202-336-6700

• *Accredited Vocational and Technical Schools.*

252
CAREER PUBLISHING, INC.
Order Department
PO Box 5486
Orange, CA 92863-5486
800-854-4014
order@careerpubinc.com
http://www.careerpubinc.com

• *20/20 Career Planning: How to Get a Job & Keep It!* ($3.50) 32 pages. Gives guidelines for analyzing job potential and provides specific instructions to help the job seeker get the right job. Lists 20 steps toward getting a job and 20 tips on keeping a job.

• *15 Tips on Handling Job Interviews.* ($2.95) 24 pages. Provides information on how to succeed at a job interview. Includes advice on how to handle every part of the interview from preparation to follow-up.

• *15 Tips on Writing Resumes.* ($2.95) 24 pages. Offers an easy-to-follow method to help plan, write, and prepare a resume that will get noticed. Includes sample resumes.

253
CAREER TRANSITION FOR DANCERS
200 West 57th Street, Suite 808
New York, NY 10019-3211
212-581-7043
Fax: 212-581-0474
ctfd@aol.com
http://www.careertransition.org

• *CareerLine.* A national career consultation line (800-581-2833) for dancers seeking information about a career transition. Schedules career counseling sessions with a member of the counseling staff.

• *Career Transition for Dancers: For Life After Dance.* Brochure describing free programs and services available for eligible professional dancers.

• *Moving On.* Semi-annual newsletter.

• *Dancers on the Move.* Semi-annual newsbrief.

• *After the Final Curtain.* Magazine article describing transition stories of former dancers.

254
CASUALTY ACTUARIAL SOCIETY
1100 North Glebe Road, Suite 600
Arlington, VA 22201
703-276-3100
Fax: 703-276-3108
office@casact.org
http://www.casact.org
or http://www.beanactuary.org

• *Actuaries Make a Difference.* 22 pages. Profiles actuaries in various actuarial careers. Discusses an actuary's duties, work environment, employment outlook, and qualifications, as well as how to prepare for a career, achieve professional status, the exams, and related organizations.

• *Actuarial Training Programs.* 30 pages. Provides information on some of the actuarial training programs in Canada and the United States available for actuaries. Suitable for those entering the actuarial profession.

• *Canadian and United States Schools Offering Actuarial Science Courses Including Actuarial Mathematics.* 4 pages. Identifies schools in Canada and the United States offering actuarial courses.

255

CENTER FOR FUTURES EDUCATION, INC.

PO Box 309
Grove City, PA 16127
724-458-5860
Fax: 724-458-5962
info@thectr.com
http://www.thectr.com

• *How to Become a Futures Broker.* ($3) 24 pages. Booklet discussing alternatives for entering the futures industry with step-by-step directions. Includes information on the industry, ethics training, and the National Commodity Futures Exam.

• *A Guide to Futures and Options Market Technology.* ($3.95) Over 300 futures and futures options terms defined for anyone interested in becoming familiar with the industry jargon. Available in English, Spanish, Portuguese, German, and Japanese.

• *Futures Trivia: Do You Know?* ($2) Contains little known facts about how the futures world really operates by dispelling myths about futures trading.

• *The Fundamentals and Techniques of Trading Futures.* ($3) Booklet addressing the basic aspects of futures trading, including how to open an account, the mechanics of a trade, the proper way to place an order, and how to review your confirmations.

• *Understanding Commodity Futures.* ($3) Introduction to the futures markets, including information on exchange functions, how future contracts work, the difference betweeen speculators and hedgers, and much more. Also available in German.

• *Making Sense of Futures Options.* ($3.50) Introduction to futures trading, including definition of terms, components of premiums, calculating break-even, placing and tracing orders, types of strategies, reading the newspaper, calculating gains and losses, and hedgers and spectators. Also available in German.

256

CENTER FOR WOMEN POLICY STUDIES

1211 Connecticut Avenue, NW, Suite 312
Washington, DC 20036
202-872-1770
Fax: 202-296-8962

• *The SAT Gender Gap: Action Kit.* ($25)

• *The SAT Gender Gap: Identifying the Causes.* ($13)

- *Women of Color in Math, Science, and Engineering.* ($10)

- *Getting Smart About Welfare: Post-Secondary Education.* ($8)

257
CHANNING L. BETE COMPANY, INC.
200 State Road
South Deerfield, MA 01373
800-628-7733 or 413-665-7611
Fax: 800-499-6464
custsvcs@channing-bete.com
http://www.channing-bete.com

The following booklets are each 16 pages (add $6.25 for shipping).

- *Career Planning.* (42267) ($1.05)

- *Job Interview Skills.* (42242) ($1.05)

- *About RNs.* (37101) ($1.05)

- *Setting Goals to Reach Your Potential.* (73221) ($1.05)

- *Writing Your Resume.* (42259) ($1.05)

- *Adult Learners.* (40808) ($1.05)

- *Be a Volunteer.* (18382) ($1.05)

- *Women and the Work Force.* (55218) ($1.60)

- *Financing the Cost of College Education.* (55137) ($1.60)

- *Landing a Job.* (55129) ($1.60)

- *How to Balance Work and Family.* (48835) ($1.05)

- *How to Choose a College.* (55087) ($1.60)

- *How to Develop Your Leadership Skills.* (18465) ($1.05)

- *How to Have Successful Meetings.* (18507) ($1.05)

- *Improving Your Interpersonal Skills.* (18556) ($1.05)

- *Decision-Making Skills.* (15867) ($1.05)

- *Improving Communication Skills.* (74465) ($1.05)

- *Developing Workplace Skills.* (44438) ($1.05)

- *A Guide for Single Mothers Entering the Work Force.* (71548) ($1.05)

258
CHICAGO MERCANTILE EXCHANGE
Education Department
30 South Wacker Drive
Chicago, IL 60606-7499
312-930-6937
edu@cme.com
http://www.cme.com

Available online or by mail:

- *Do You Have a Career in Futures?* Resource of information about the individual positions that comprise the exchange staff, employment opportunities with members and clearing firms, and sources of more information.

259
CHILD CARE ACTION CAMPAIGN
330 Seventh Avenue, 14th Floor
New York, NY 10003
212-239-0138

Fax: 212-268-6515
info@childcareaction.org
http://www.childcareaction.org

CCAC Information Guides (up to 3 guides free). SASE business-size. Titles include:

- *Careers in Child Care.* (#23)

- *Child Care Liability Insurance.* (#25)

- *Current State Day Care Licensing Offices.* (#28)

- *Employer Supported Child Care: Current Options and Trends.* (#10)

- *How to Start a Child Care Center.* (#24)

- *How to Start a Family Day Care Home.* (#26)

- *Speaking with Your Employer about Child Care Assistance.* (#9)

- *Wages and Benefits in Child Care.* (#27)

- *Family Child Care as a Job Opportunity for Welfare Recipients.*

- *7 Work and Life Trends Likely to Impact Child Care.*

260
CHRONICLE GUIDANCE PUBLICATIONS, INC.

66 Aurora Street
PO Box 1190
Moravia, NY 13118-1190
800-899-0454
Fax: 315-497-3359
customerservice@chronicleguidance.com
http://www.chronicleguidance.com

- *Career Preparation.* ($5.95) 58 pages. Emphasizes the important role education and training play in your later career plans. Includes a career interest checklist, money-managing tips, train-

ing and education options after high school, and sources of additional career information.

- *Knowing Yourself.* ($5.95) 57 pages. Learn to define your success by identifying your educational and personal skills. Includes tips on building upon your skills and creating a successful lifestyle.

- *Making Decisions.* ($5.95) 57 pages. Learn to take control of your life by making educated decisions through a three-step method.

- *Your Career.* ($5.95) 58 pages. Good resource for students to think about their career paths and potential ideal jobs. Includes interviewing tips and a guide for researching employers.

261
CLEARINGHOUSE ON DISABILITY INFORMATION

Office of Special Education and Rehabilitive Services
U.S. Department of Education
330 C Street, SW
Switzer Building, Room 3132
Washington, DC 20202-2425
202-205-8241
Fax: 202-410-2608
http://www.ed.gov/offices/osers

- *Federally Supported Clearinghouses on Disability.* Lists clearinghouses offering information on disability.

- *Pocket Guide to Federal Help for Individuals with Disabilities.* 27 pages. Summarizes benefits and services available to individuals with disabilities.

- *OSERS Magazine.* A collection of various articles on disability. No longer published, although individual copies of back issues are still available.

262
COLLEGE BOARD
45 Columbus Avenue
New York, NY 10023-6992
212-713-8000
http://www.collegeboard.org

Available at the Web site:

- *Planning for College.* Issues both students and parents should consider.

- *Career Search.* Information on various fields to help those just beginning to explore.

- *The Path from Home School to College.* Guide to help home school students make the transition easier.

- *College Applications: Step by Step.* Practical guide for applying to college.

- *Finding a College that Fits.* Four-step process to selecting the college that best suits the student.

- *What Admission Officers Look for in Students.* Information to help students put their best foot forward in the admissions office.

- *Considering Community Colleges.* Learn the benefits of attending a local college.

- *Your College Essay.* Tips on writing an essay that grabs attention.

Available to order online:

- *Campus Visits and College Interviews.* ($9.95) 130 pages. Tips on how and when to plan visits, whether to go alone, and what to look for during a visit. Includes interviewing tips.

- *Choosing a College: The Student's Step-by-Step Decision-Making Workbook.* ($9.95) 165 pages. Through exercises, quizzes, and worksheets students can identify their priorities and apply them to choosing a college.

- *Coping with Stress in College.* ($9.95) 172 pages. Offers guidance on how to manage the pressures of college life.

- *The College Board Guide to Going to College While Working.* ($9.95) 142 pages. Helps adult students to access their plans, locate appropriate colleges, organize admission and financial aid, and juggle the demands of school with those of work and home.

263
COMMERCE CLEARING HOUSE, INC.
4025 West Peterson Avenue
Chicago, IL 60646
800-248-3248
Fax: 800-224-8299
http://www.cch.com

- *Social Security Benefits—Including Medicare.* (5335) ($5) 48 pages.

264
COMMISSION ON ACCREDITATION OF ALLIED HEALTH EDUCATION PROGRAMS
35 East Wacker Drive, Suite 1970
Chicago, IL 60606-2208
312-553-9355

Fax: 312-553-9616
caahep@caahep.org
http://www.caahep.org

Available at the Web site:

• *Accredited Programs.* Directory to accredited academic programs nationwide for the following professions: anesthesiologist assistant, athletic trainer, emergency medical technician/paramedic, kinesiotherapist, medical assistant, physical assistant, and more.

265
COMMISSION ON MASSAGE THERAPY ASSOCIATION
820 Davis Street, Suite 100
Evanston, IL 60201-4444
847-869-5039

• *Accreditation.* Provides updated information on the Commission, upcoming workshops, helpful tips, and more.

• *What is Accreditation?* Brochure explaining the benefits and process of accreditation and includes information about COMTA and its services.

• *A Student Guide to Accreditation.* Brochure listing COMTA accredited institutions by state. Includes background information about accreditation and COMTA.

266
COMMISSION ON WOMEN IN THE PROFESSION
Publications Orders
American Bar Association
PO Box 10892
Chicago, IL 60611

800-285-2221
Fax: 312-988-5528
abacwp@abanet.org
http://www.abanet.org/women

• *Options and Obstacles: A Survey of the Studies of the Careers of Women Lawyers.* ($10) 60 pages. Identifies issues that continue to create barriers in women's careers and points out where gathering more information would assist the profession in understanding and eliminating those barriers.

• *Pathways to Leadership: An ABA Roadmap.* ($9.95) 28 pages. Provides information on the various paths to leadership positions within the American Bar Association.

• *The Basic Facts from Women in Law: A Look at the Numbers.* ($6) 6 pages. A quick summary of the most asked questions regarding statistics on women in the legal profession.

• *Goal IX Report Card.* Free. Issued by the Commission. Provides statistics on women's involvement in the ABA and measures women's progress in attaining leadership positions in ABA sections and divisions and in ABA governance.

267
COMMITTEE ON ACCREDITATION FOR RESPIRATORY CARE
1248 Harwood Road
Bedford, TX 76021-4244
800-874-5615 or 817-283-2835
Fax: 817-252-0773
http://www.coarc.com

Available by mail or at the Web site:

• *CoARC Accredited Programs.* Lists programs in respiratory therapy education by state.

268
COMMUNITY SERVICE SOCIETY
Office of Information
105 East 22nd Street
New York, NY 10010
212-614-5322
Fax: 212-614-5390

• *Youth Enterprises: A How-to Manual for Starting a Youth Businesss in Your Community.* ($5) 41 pages. Helpful to the staff in youth programs and organizations serving youth. Provides a general approach for community-based enterprise development.

• *Critical Choices: Education and Employment among New York City Youth.* ($10) 115 pages. A study on New Yorkers between the ages of 16 and 24. Provides a detailed analysis of their connection to education and employment and evaluates school enrollment, labor force participation, educational attainment, work history, fertility, and poverty status by race, ethnicity, age, and sex.

269
COMPUTING RESEARCH ASSOCIATION
1100 Seventeenth Street, NW, Suite 507
Washington, DC 20036
202-234-2111
Fax: 202-667-1666
info@cra.org
http://www.cra.org

• *The Supply of Information Technology Workers in the United States.* Online study to improve the understanding of the supply of and demand for informational technology workers in the U.S. and the surrounding contextual issues.

270
CORNELL UNIVERSITY
Publications Resource Center
7-8 Business and Technology Park
Ithaca, NY 14850
607-255-2080
Fax: 607-255-9946
http://www.cce.cornell.edu/
publications/catalog.html

• *Your Teen's Career: A Guide for Parents.* ($2) 6 pages.

271
COSMETOLOGY ADVANCEMENT FOUNDATION
4262 Northlake Boulevard, PMB 102
Palm Beach Gardens, FL 33410-6224
561-630-7766
Fax: 561-630-0344
http://www.cosmetology.org

• *Where Do I Go from Here?* 12 pages.

272
COUNCIL FOR ACCREDITATION OF COUNSELING AND RELATED EDUCATIONAL PROGRAMS
5999 Stevenson Avenue
Alexandria, VA 22304
703-823-9800, ext. 301
http://www.counseling.org/CACREP

The following is available at the Web site:

• *Directory of Accredited Programs.* Lists accredited master's and doctoral degree programs in counseling (community, career, gerontological, marriage and family counseling/therapy, mental health, and school), and student affairs practice in higher education.

273

COUNCIL FOR EXCEPTIONAL CHILDREN

1920 Association Drive
Reston, VA 20191-1589
888-CEC-SPED or 703-620-3660
Fax: 703-264-9494
service@cec.sped.org
http://www.cec.sped.org

Available at the Web site:

• *Student CEC.* Contains special education career information, including recommended questions to ask in a job interview, resume tips, building professional experience, and more.

274

COUNCIL FOR PROFESSIONAL RECOGNITION

2460 16th Street, NW
Washington, DC 20009-3575
800-424-4310
Fax: 202-265-9161
http://www.cdacouncil.org

• *Improving Child Care.* Describes the history, functional areas, and competency goals of the CDA Credentialing Program.

• *CDA Information Brochure.* Contains information about the assessment processes for center-based, family child care and home visitor personnel.

Provides information on the CDA Professional Preparation Program and state regulations related to CDAs.

• *Council News & Views Newsletter.* Published three times a year. Provides program updates, profiles of CDAs, and news affecting the early care and education professional.

• *National Directory of Early Childhood Teacher Preparation Institutions, Fourth Edition.* ($8) Directory containing nationwide listings of two-and four-year colleges and vocational-technical postsecondary schools that offer early childhood education courses.

275

COUNCIL FOR THE ADVANCEMENT OF SCIENCE WRITING

PO Box 404
Greenlawn, NY 11740
631-757-5664
http://www.casw.org

Available by mail or at the Web site:

• *Careers in Science Writing.* Defines science writers, their job duties, how stories are developed, average salary, and tips on getting started in a career in scientific writing.

276

COUNCIL OF AMERICAN SURVEY RESEARCH ORGANIZATIONS

3 Upper Devon, Belle Terre
Port Jefferson, NY 11777
631-928-6954
Fax: 631-928-6041
casro@casro.org
http://www.casro.org

- *Surveys and You.* ($.25) 7 pages. Available by mail or online. Answers questions about survey research: what it is, who does it, how it involves people, and how it helps people.

277
COUNCIL OF GRADUATE SCHOOLS
One Dupont Circle, NW, Suite 430
Washington, DC 20036-1173
202-223-3791
Fax: 202-331-7157
http://www.cgsnet.org

- *Graduate School and You: A Guide for Prospective Graduate Students.* ($10 plus shipping) 36 pages. Designed for people of all ages considering graduate study. Discusses the purpose of graduate education and contains information on career options, choosing a school, timetables for applying, and guidelines for financing graduate education.

- *Graduate Studies in the United States: A Guide for Prospective International Graduate Students.* ($5) 19 pages. Written expressly for students from other countries interested in American graduate education. Provides information on appropriate backgrounds for graduate education, how to apply, points about living in the United States, and other topics related to raduate study.

278
COUNCIL OF LOGISTICS MANAGEMENT
2805 Butterfield Road, Suite 200
Oak Brook, IL 60523
630-574-0985
Fax: 630-574-0537

clmadmin@clm1.org
http://www.clm1.org

Available by mail:

- *Careers in Logistics.* 20 pages. Describes the field, required education and training, career profiles, and where the jobs are.

- *Executive Placement Guide.* 7 pages.

- *Career Patterns in Logistics.* 20 pages.

Available at the Web site:

- *Transportation & Distribution College/ University Directory.* 13 pages.

279
COUNCIL ON CHIROPRACTIC EDUCATION
8049 North 85th Way
Scottsdale, AZ 85258-4321
480-443-8877
Fax: 480-483-7333
cce@adata.com
http://www.cce-usa.org

General Information Packet includes:

- *Chiropractic Programs & Institutions Holding Accredited Status.* 2 pages.

- *General Information Letter.* 3 pages. Includes information on preprofessional requirements, transfer students, transfer of credit from foreign health profession institutions, and licensure.

- *CCE—The Council on Chiropractic Education.* 6 pages. Includes information on CCE and a list of CCE accredited institutions.

• *Preparing to be a Doctor of Chiropractic: Answers to Questions About Chiropractic Education.* Includes sources of additional information and an online list of the programs and institutions accredited by the Council on Chiropractic Education.

These publications are also available at the Council's Web site.

280

COUNCIL ON EDUCATION FOR PUBLIC HEALTH

800 Eye Street, NW
Washington, DC 20001
202-789-1050
Fax: 202-789-1895
http://www.ceph.org

• *United States Schools of Public Health and Graduate Public Health Progams Accredited by the Council on Education for Public Health (CEPH).* 2 pages. Lists schools of public health and graduate public health programs accredited by the CEPH.

281

COUNCIL ON HOTEL, RESTAURANT AND INSTITUTIONAL EDUCATION

1200 17th Street, NW
Washington, DC 20036-3097
202-331-5990
Fax: 202-785-2511
info@chrie.org
http://www.chrie.org

• *United States and International Directory of Schools.*

282

COUNCIL ON INTERNATIONAL EDUCATIONAL EXCHANGE

Council Travel Service
205 42 Street, 15th Floor
New York, NY 10017
888-COUNCIL
http://www.ciee.org

Available by mail or online:

• *Student Travels Magazine.* Includes information on studying, working, and traveling abroad for students.

• *Work Abroad.* Describes working abroad opportunities for college students. Includes information on applying for programs, the jobs available, and frequently asked questions.

283

COUNCIL ON REHABILITATION EDUCATION

1835 Rohlwing Road, Suite E
Rolling Meadows, IL 60008
847-394-1785
Fax: 847-394-2108
http://www.core-rehab.org

Available by mail or online:

• *CORE Recognized Master's Degree Programs in Rehabilitation Counselor Education.*

284

CUNA & AFFILIATES

Credit Union and Consumer Publications
5710 Mineral Point Road
PO Box 431
Madison, WI 53701-0431

800-356-8010
Fax: 608-231-1869
ccsd@meteor.org

• *Your Guide to Careers in Credit Unions.* Describes credit unions and careers in credit unions.

285
CURRICULUM PUBLICATIONS CLEARINGHOUSE
Horrabin Hall 46
Western Illinois University
1 University Circle
Macomb, IL 61455-1390
800-322-3905 or 309-298-1917
Fax: 309-298-2869
cpc@wiu.edu
http://www.wiu.edu/useres/micpc/cpc

• *A Guide to Free Career Guidance Materials.* (#186) ($3.25) Consists of a listing of free career-related materials produced and made available by national associations, corporations, and governmental agencies.

• *Exploring Career Paths: A Guide for Students and Their Families.* (#499) ($1) Assists students to make smart decisions for career exploration by helping them learn more about themselves and their potential career paths that fit their talents and interests.

• *1999 Guide to Career Choices.* (#536) ($6) Set of 26 career brochures providing information on the following occupational interest areas: agriculture and natural resources; arts and communications; business and administrative; health care; human and family services; and industrial and engineering.

286
DADANT & SONS, INC.
51 South Second Street
Hamilton, IL 62341-1399
217-847-3324
Fax: 217-847-3660
dadant@dadant.com
http://www.dadant.com

• *Beginning with Bees.* ($3 plus shipping) A set of five pamphlets on beekeeping.

• *First Lessons in Beekeeping.* ($4 plus shipping) A beginner's manual to beekeeping.

• *Me? Beekeeping?* (Free.) Details how to get started in beekeeping.

287
DANCE MAGAZINE
111 Myrtle Street, Suite 203
Oakland, CA 94607
510-839-6060
Fax: 510-839-6066
dancemag@dancemagazine.com
http://www.dancemagazine.com

• *Summer Study Issue.* ($3.95 for current issue available every January or back issues for $5 each) Lists summer dance programs at colleges, universities, and dance schools in the United States and abroad. Available at your local newstand.

288
DEVRY, INC.
One Tower Lane
Oakbrook Terrace, IL 60181
800-73-DEVRY or 630-571-7700

Fax: 630-571-0317
obtweb@dpg.devry.edu
http://www.devry.edu

Available at the Web site:

• *Academic Catalog.* Describes a variety of different fields as a career choice, including information on the job, the future outlook for the career, and lists potential entry-level positions found in the field. Careers include: accounting, business administration, computer engineering technology, computer information systems, electronics engineering technology, electronics technician, information technology, technical management, and telecommunications management.

289
DIETARY MANAGERS ASSOCIATION
406 Surrey Woods Drive
St. Charles, IL 60174
800-323-1908
Fax: 630-587-6308
http://www.dmaonline.org

Available online:

• *How to Become a Certified Dietary Manager (CDM).* Outlines the dietary manager credentialing exam and eligibility requirements.

• *DMA Approved Schools.* Online directory of approved schools, listed by state.

• *Certification: What Does it Mean?* Explains the benefits of certification to you, your facility, and addresses the importance of continuing education.

290
DIRECT MARKETING EDUCATIONAL FOUNDATION
1120 Avenue of the Americas
New York, NY 10036-6700
212-768-7277, ext. 1329
Fax: 212-302-6714
dmef@the-dma.org
http://www.the-dma.org

For copies of the following, send an e-mail to dmef@the-dma.org, including the name of the requested publication and your name and mailing address.

• *The 2000 Directory of Direct Marketing Summer Internships.* Includes job profiles of 132 organizations in 23 states and the District of Columbia. Unpaid and paid opportunities range from database marketing, sales, and account work to E-commerce.

• *Your Career in Direct Marketing & Direct Response Advertising.* Brochure presenting an overview of the field and contains information about resources, salaries, and brief information on how to market yourself.

• *Careers in Magazine Circulation and Marketing.* Introduction on magazine circulation marketing, including information on necessary credentials, entry-level and higher career paths, and sources for further education and information. Lists recruiters accepting resumes from entry-level candidates and profiles industry representatives.

• *Career Opportunities in Retailing Direct Marketing, Database Marketing, and Electronic Marketing.* Brochure exploring careers in the fields, including educational requirements, and lists resources such as entry-level recruiters, trade journals, and other publications.

• *Careers in Business-to-Business Direct Marketing.* Brochure on how direct marketing is used to reach businesses. Includes various career options and resources for getting started in the field.

291
DIRECT SELLING ASSOCIATION
1275 Pennsylvania Avenue, NW
Suite 800
Washington, DC 20004
202-347-8866
Fax: 202-347-0055
info@dsa.org
http://www.dsa.org

• *Who's Who in Direct Selling.* (free with SASE) 15 pages. Explains how to become a distributor for DSA-member companies.

Available at the Web site:

• *Careers in Direct Selling.* Includes information about the industry, including the benefits of direct selling and how to get started with a company and product that appeals to you. Includes a list of member companies and contact information.

292
DISTANCE EDUCATION AND TRAINING COUNCIL
1601 18th Street, NW
Washington, DC 20009-2529
202-234-5100
Fax: 202-332-1386
detc@detc.org
http://www.detc.org

• *Directory of Accredited Institutions.* 16 pages. Lists the 70 accredited home-study institutions, as well as the subjects taught by them.

293
DISTRICT OF COLUMBIA DEPARTMENT OF EMPLOYMENT SERVICES
Labor Market Information Research Staff
500 C Street, NW, Suite 201
Washington, DC 20001
202-724-7213
Fax: 202-724-7216
http://does.ci.washington.dc.us

• *Occupational Employment Projections—Year 2005.* 4 pages. Contains occupational employment projections for the District of Columbia to the year 2005.

294
DOW JONES & COMPANY, INC.
Special Services Department
PO Box 7015
Chicopee, MA 01021-0435
800-JOURNAL
Fax: 413-598-2573
education@dowjones.com
http://info.wsj.com/college

All publications are free of charge to students and teachers; $.50 each for the general public.

• *The Wall Street Journal Content Guide.* Explains the columns, charts, and tables available in each section of the *Journal* and gives registration information for wsj.com.

• *The Barron's Educational Edition.*

- *Talk Like a Pro: a Nonprofessional Guide on How to Read Stock Market Quotations.*

295
DOW JONES NEWSPAPER FUND, INC.
PO Box 300
Princeton, NJ 08543-0300
800-DOW-FUND or 609-452-2820
Fax: 609-520-5804
newsfund@wsj.dowjones.com
http://www.dowjones.com/newsfund

- *Journalist's Road to Success: A Career and Scholarship Guide.* ($3) 150 pages. Answers questions about newspaper jobs, describes how to prepare for a journalism career, and provides the latest statistics on beginning salaries. Lists more than 400 colleges and universities that offer majors in print journalism, financial aid available to news-editorial students at those schools, and grants available from newspapers and media organizations.

- *Newspapers, Diversity & You.* 48 pages. Includes an overview of the journalism field, a career and salary report, and material about academic preparation, job hunting, and financial aid programs designated specifically for minority students.

296
EASTERN PARALYZED VETERANS ASSOCIATION
34-39 56th Street
Woodside, NY 11377
800-444-0120
publications@epva.org
http://www.epva.org

The following publications can be ordered at the Association's Web site:

- *Understanding the Americans with Disabilities Act.*

- *The ADA: Help Wanted, Equal Job Opportunities*

- *The ADA: Small Business Fact Sheet.* English, Spanish, Korean, and French versions available.

- *The ADA: Resource Information Guide.*

297
ECOLOGICAL SOCIETY OF AMERICA
1707 H Street, NW, Suite 400
Washington, DC 20006
202-833-8773
Fax: 202-833-8775
http://esa.sdsc.edu

- *Careers in Ecology.* (Specify high school or undergraduate version) A brochure providing information on types of jobs and employers, background needed, job outlook, ways to gain experience while still in school, internship and job searching contacts, and other information on the field of ecology.

- *What Does Ecology Have to do with Me?* Brochure introducing the science of ecology and its role in society.

- *What Do Ecologists Do?* A publication examining the field of ecology and the crucial role of ecologists.

298
EDITOR & PUBLISHER
770 Broadway
New York, NY 10003-9595

646-654-5270
Fax: 646-654-5370
edpub@editorandpublisher.com
http://www.mediainfo.com

- *Editor & Publisher Journalism Awards and Fellowships Directory.* ($8) Published annually in December. Lists hundreds of scholarships, fellowships, grants, and journalism awards and contests.

299
EDITOR'S ASSOCIATION OF CANADA
National Office
35 Spadina Road
Toronto, Ontario M5R 2S9, Canada
416-975-1379
Fax: 416-975-1839
eacinfo@web.net
http://www.web.net/eac-acr

Available by mail or at the Web site:

- *So You Want to Be an Editor?* Informative guide covering editing as a career choice, the range of work available, an editor's career path, freelancing versus in-house editing, rewards and drawbacks of the job, education and training required, and other sources of information about editing.

300
EDUCATION DEVELOPMENT CENTER, INC.
PO Box 1020
Sewickley, PA 15146-1020
800-793-5076
Fax: 412-741-0609
http://www.edc.org

- *Bioscience Education and Training Program Directory.* ($10) 112 pages. Provides information on more than 80 high school, college, and industry-based programs nationwide for those interested in technical positions in biotechnology and pharmaceuticals.

301
EDUCATIONAL THEATRE ASSOCIATION
2343 Auburn Avenue
Cincinnati, OH 45219-3900
513-421-3900
Fax: 513-421-7077
http://www.etassoc.org

- *Dramatics Magazine.* ($4) An educational theatre magazine which is primarily geared toward high school theatre students and teachers.

- *Dramatics Magazine College Theatre Directory.* ($4) Updated annually.

- *Dramatics Magazine Summer Internship Directory.* ($4) Updated annually.

302
ELECTROCHEMICAL SOCIETY, INC.
65 South Main Street
Pennington, NJ 08534-2839
609-737-1902
Fax: 609-737-2743
ecs@electrochem.org
http://www.electrochem.com

- *What is Electrochemistry? Electrochemistry and Solid State Science in the Electrochemical Society.* 46 pages. Contains a series of essays on the work involved in such fields as corrosion, electrodeposition, energy technology, industrial electrolysis, electrochemical engineering, organic and biological electrochemistry, and physical electrochemistry.

303
EMPLOYMENT SITUATION INFORMATION LINE

U.S. Department of Labor
202-691-5200

- *Employment Statistics Information Line.* A recorded message offering current information on the unemployment rate in a number of fields.

304
ENTOMOLOGICAL SOCIETY OF AMERICA

Public Affairs Department
9301 Annapolis Road
Lanham, MD 20706-3115
301-731-4535
Fax: 301-731-4538
http://www.entsoc.org

- *Discover Entomology.* 12 pages. Describes entomology (the study of insects), provides reasons for insect research, and contains advice on how to prepare for the field.

305
ENTREPRENEUR MAGAZINE

2445 McCabe Way
Irvine, CA 92614
949-261-2325
Fax: 949-261-0234
http://www.entrepreneur.com

- *Business Development Catalog.* 64 pages. Lists more than 150 guides to starting your own business.

306
EQUAL OPPORTUNITY PUBLICATIONS, INC.

Circulation Department
1160 East Jericho Turnpike, Suite 200
Huntington, NY 11743
631-421-9421
Fax: 631-421-0359
info@eop.com
http://www.eop.com

- *Minority Engineer.* Free magazine subscription to minority engineering, computer science, or information technology professionals or college students.

- *Woman Engineer.* Free subscription to qualified women engineers and students.

- *Equal Opportunity.* Free subscription to minority college students.

- *Workforce Diversity for Engineering and IT Professionals.* Free magazine subscription for the professional and diversified workforce.

307
ERIC CLEARINGHOUSE ON ADULT, CAREER, AND VOCATIONAL EDUCATION

Ohio State University
Center on Education and Training for Employment
1900 Kenny Road
Columbus, OH 43210-1090
614-292-8625
Fax: 614-292-1260
ericacve@postbox.acs.ohio-state.edu
http://ericacve.org

Visit the ERIC/ACVE Web site for full text of many of the *ERIC Digests, Trends and Issues Alerts,* and other publications or for links to a variety of Web sites related to adult, career, and vocational education and training. Write for a complete listing of ERIC/ACVE publications, updated regularly.

308
ERIC CLEARINGHOUSE ON DISABILITIES AND GIFTED EDUCATION

The Council for Exceptional Children
1920 Association Drive
Reston, VA 20191
800-328-0272
ericec@cec.sped.org
http://ericec.org

Available at the Web site:

* *ERIC EC Digests.* Some titles include:

* *Addressing Diversity in Special Education.* (E561)

* *Bilingual Special Education.* (E496)

* *ADHD and Children Who Are Gifted.* (E522)

* *College Planning for Gifted and Talented Youth.* (E490)

* *Nurturing Giftedness in Young Children.* (E487)

* *Should Gifted Students be Grade-Advanced?* (E526)

* *Coping with Stress in the Special Education Classroom: Can Individual Teachers More Effectively Manage Stress?* (E545)

* *National and State Perspectives on Performance Assessment.* (E532)

309
ERIC CLEARINGHOUSE ON INFORMATION AND TECHNOLOGY

Syracuse University
621 Skytop Road, Suite 160
Syracuse, NY 13244-5290
800-464-9107 or 315-443-3640
Fax: 315-443-5448
eric@ericir.syr.edu
http://ericir.syr.edu

ERIC Digests are free reports giving an overview of topics of current interest and suggesting literature for other reading. Digests can be viewed online or ordered through the mail. Titles include:

* *Internet Basics: Update 1996.*

* *Computer Skills for Information Problem Solving: Learning and Teaching Technology in Context.*

* *Trends in Educational Technology: Update 1995.*

* *The School Librarian's Role in the Electronic Age.*

* *Bread & Butter of the Internet.*

* *Field of Educational Technology: Update 1997.*

* *Evaluation of World Wide Web Sites: Bibliography.*

* *Internet Resources for K-8 Students.*

* *E-Rate: A Resource Guide for Educators.*

* *Internet Resources for K-12 Educators: Information Resources, Part I, Update 1999.*

* *Internet Resources for K-12 Educators: Question Answering, Discussion Groups, Part II, Update 1999.*

* *Using the Web to Access Online Education Periodicals.*

• *AskERIC Brochure.*

Contact ERIC via the Web, e-mail, phone, or mail for a catalog listing other digests and publications.

310
ERIC CLEARINGHOUSE ON TEACHING AND TEACHER EDUCATION
1307 New York Avenue, NW, Suite 300
Washington, DC 20005-4701
800-822-9229
Fax: 202-457-8095
query@aacte.org
http://www.ericsp.org

ERIC Digests, InfoCards, Internet Bookmarks, and other materials are available by mail or online. Contact ERIC via e-mail, phone, or mail for a complete listing of their publications and materials. *ERIC Digests* are online overviews with bibliographies of topics of current interest in education. Titles include:

• *Alternative Career Paths in Physical Education: Fitness and Exercise.* (92-1)

• *Alternative Career Paths in Physical Education: Sport Management.* (93-1)

• *Coaching Certification.* (88-10)

• *Comprehensive School Health Education.* (92-2)

• *Demand and Supply of Minority Teachers.* (88-12)

• *Prekindergarten Teacher Licensure.* (90-6)

• *Preparation of Middle School Teachers.* (90-1)

• *Senior Citizens as School Volunteers: New Resources for the Future.* (93-4)

• *Status of Dance in Education.* (91-5)

• *Teacher-as-Researcher.* (92-7)

InfoCards give concise information on specific topics for those considering a career in elementary or secondary education. Titles include:

• *International Teaching Opportunities.* (#1)

• *Alternative Routes to Teacher Certification.* (#2)

• *Financial Aid for Teacher Education Students.* (#3)

• *Specialized Interests in Teaching.* (#4)

• *Choosing a Teacher Education College/ University.* (#5)

• *Finding a Teaching Position.* (#6)

• *What is the ERIC Clearinghouse on Teaching and Teacher Education?* (#7)

• *What You Should Know about HIV/AIDS Education.* (#8)

• *Teaching in Elementary/Secondary Schools.* (#9)

Internet Bookmarks are laminated, colorful bookmarks for students or adults and are helpful when searching the Internet. Topics include:

• *General Education.*

• *Student-Oriented.*

• *Physical Education, Sports, Kinesiology.*

• *Health Education.*

311
FAIRTEST
342 Broadway
Cambridge, MA 02139
617-864-4810
Fax: 617-497-2224

info@fairtest.org
http://www.fairtest.org

- *SAT Fact Packet.* ($5.50) Includes news articles and fact sheets on SAT bias and abuse, and includes listing of schools where test scores are optional for admissions.

- *Schools in Which SAT/ACT Scores Are Not Used in Admission Decisions for Bachelor Degree Programs.* Online listing by state.

312
FEDERAL ACQUISITION INSTITUTE
General Services Administration
18th and F Streets, NW, Room 4017
Washington, DC 20405
202-501-0964
gladys.poindexter@gsa.gov
http://www.gsa.gov/staff/v/
training.htm

- *Federal Contracting Careers.* 9 pages.

313
FEDERAL AVIATION ADMINISTRATION
Mike Monroney Aeronautical Center
PO Box 25082
Oklahoma City, OK 73125
405-954-4657 or 405-954-4508
http://jobs.faa.gov

- *Remote Electronic Vacancy Announcements Merit Promotion (REVAMP).* Lists FAA vacancies nationwide. Available by fax or by visiting the Web site.

314
FEDERAL AVIATION ADMINISTRATION
Government Printing Office
Superintendent of Documents
PO Box 371954
Pittsburgh, PA 15250-7954
202-512-1800
Fax: 202-512-2250
orders@gpo.gov
http://www.faa.gov

The following brochures from the FAA Aviation Career Series may be obtained by writing to the United States Government Printing Office.

- *Women in Aviation and Space.* 21 pages. Profiles 46 women involved in various aviation and space careers including general flight, federal government, space education/training, engineering, airport management, aircraft maintenance/air traffic control, business/manufacturing, and the arts in aviation.

- *TNAAA/Curriculum Guide for Secondary Level.* This guide for grades 6-12 presents lessons and activities for social studies, mathematics, language arts, and science classes and includes additional career education materials.

- *Teacher's Guide to Aviation Education.* A bibliography of printed and audio-visual materials related to aviation education.

- *Teacher's Guide to Aviation Education, Grades 2-6.* Contains information on aviation as it relates to social studies, communications, arts, health, career education, and science classes.

- *Aviation Education Resource Centers.* Booklet containing information about FAA aviation education resource centers.

- *This is the FAA.* Booklet providing an overview of the mission and responsibilities of the Federal Aviation Administration.

- *A Flying Start.* Booklet providing an overview of how to get started in flying airplanes.

- *A Guide to Aviation Education Resources.* Guide listing information about organizations involved in aviation education.

- *FAA and HACU, Colleges and Universities.* Describes a wide array of FAA/Hispanic Association of College and University Programs that serve as excellent starting points for Hispanic-serving institutions wishing to pursue aviation research and development opportunities, or participate in aviation education programs.

The following are available online at the FAA Web site:

- *Aviation Academies and Universities.* Listing of academies and universities.

- *Career as an Air Traffic Control Specialist.* Read job descriptions and see online pictures of the job.

- *Careers in Transportation: Moving Everyone and Everything, Everywhere.* New DOT career resource available online.

- *Federal Aviation Administration.* Listing of job descriptions, including Air Traffic Control Specialist, Airspace System Inspection Pilot, Aviation Safety Inspector, Electronics Technician, Engineer, Flight Test Pilot, Maintenance Mechanic, and other professional positions.

315
FEDERAL CONSUMER INFORMATION CENTER
U.S. General Services Administration
Pueblo, CO 81109
888-8-PUEBLO (888-878-3256)
Fax: 719-948-9724
catalog.pueblo@gsa.gov
http://www.pueblo.gsa.gov

The following free and low-cost federal publications are listed in the free quarterly *Consumer Information Catalog* and on the Web site. Publications include:

- *Nontraditional Education.* ($1.75) Get high school or college credit through the GED program, the National External Diploma program, correspondence and distance study, and standardized tests.

- *Planning for College.* (free) 10 pages. Strategies to help you plan for tuition and fees along with helpful charts for estimating future costs.

- *Help Wanted—Finding a Job.* ($.50) 8 pages. Describes both private companies and government agencies that offer help in finding a job. Lists precautions to take when contacting an employment service firm.

- *Here Today, Jobs of Tomorrow: Opportunities in Information Technology.* ($1.75) 13 pages. This booklet can help you learn about the high demand for informational technology workers and if this field is right for you.

• *High Earning Workers Who Don't Have a Bachelor's Degree.* ($1) 8 pages. Identifies 50 occupations requiring less than a bachelor's degree.

• *Matching Yourself With the World of Work.* ($2) 19 pages. Don't fall into a job that might not be a perfect fit for you. Find out what to look for in your ideal job with this guide.

• *Occupational Outlook Quarterly.* ($9.50) One year subscription of four issues. Reviews new occupations, salaries, job trends, and much more.

• *Resumes, Applications and Cover Letters.* ($1.50) 15 pages. Prospective employers spend as little as 30 seconds considering a resume. Use this guide's samples to format a winning cover letter and resume, and learn how new technology can help.

• *Tips for Finding the Right Job.* ($1.75) 27 pages. Learn how to assess your skills and interests, prepare a resume, write cover letters, and interview for a job.

• *Tomorrow's Jobs.* ($2.25) 19 pages. Discusses changes and trends in the economy, labor force, occupational growth, education and training requirements, and much more.

Note: Prices and stock availability are subject to change at any time.

316
FEDERAL RESERVE SYSTEM
Publications Services, MS-127
Board of Governors of the Federal
Reserve System
Washington, DC 20551

202-452-3244
Fax: 202-728-5886
http://www.federalreserve.gov

Available by mail or accessible online:

• *A Guide to Business Credit for Women, Minorities, and Small Business.* Describes the application process for small business loans and steps to take if denied. Includes information on the Equal Credit Opportunity Act and lists sources for application assistance.

317
FEDERAL STUDENT AID INFORMATION CENTER
U.S. Department of Education
PO Box 84
Washington, DC 20044
800-4-FED-AID

• *2000-2001 Financial Aid: The Student Guide.* 28 pages. Available by mail or accessible on the Web site. Describes the federal student aid programs and provides general information about eligibility criteria, application procedures, and award levels. Also includes important deadlines and telephone numbers.

• *Funding Your Education.* Available by mail or accessible on the Web site. Outlines the Student Financial Assistance Programs available and how to apply for aid.

• *Tax Cuts for Education.* Online guide to tax cuts that can help you save money while in school.

• *Looking for Student Aid.* General online information about sources of student aid.

318

FEDERAL TRADE COMMISSION
Career Information
CRC-240
Washington, DC 20580
877-FTC-HELP
http://www.ftc.gov

Available at the Web site:

- *Help Wanted...Finding a Job.* Contains facts for consumers on types of employment service firms and other information.

- *Choosing a Career or Vocational School.* Describes some deceptive practices found by the FTC; recommends some precautions to take before enrolling in a career or vocational school; and suggests questions to ask school representatives in an early interview.

- *Get Rich Quick and Self-Employment Schemes Campaign.*

- *Scholarship Scams Campaign.*

- *Federal and Postal Jobs Scams: Tip-offs to Rip-offs Alert.*

- *Negative Credit Can Squeeze a Job Search.*

- *A Business Guide to the Federal Trade Commission's Mail or Telephone Order Merchandise Rule.* 16 pages. A helpful guide to planning and operating a business. Explains the merchandise rule's requirements and includes a question and answer section about the rule and full text of the rule.

319

FEDERAL TRADE COMMISSION
Franchise Information

CRC-240
Washington, DC 20580
877-FTC-HELP
http://www.ftc.gov

Available at the Web site:

- *Franchise and Business Opportunities.* Contains consumer facts about the FTC Franchise Rule, information about buying a business, and other important information.

- *Consumer Guide to Buying a Franchise.* Discusses the benefits and responsibilities of owning a franchise, selecting a franchise, investigating franchise offerings, and additional sources of information.

- *Net Based Business Opportunities: Are Some Flop-portunities?*

- *Franchise Rule Text.*

320

FEDERATION OF AMERICAN SOCIETIES FOR EXPERIMENTAL BIOLOGY
Genetics Society of America
9650 Rockville Pike
Bethesda, MD 20814-3998
301-571-1825
Fax: 301-530-7079
society@genetics.faseb.org
http://www.faseb.org/genetics

Available at the Web site:

- *Solving the Puzzle: Careers in Genetics.* Discusses various genetics careers and the training required.

321
FERRIS STATE UNIVERSITY
HVACR Programs
605 South Warren Avenue
Big Rapids, MI 49307-2287
231-591-2351
Fax: 231-591-2492
feutzm@ferris.edu
http://www.ferris.edu

• *Careers in Heating, Ventilation, Air Conditioning, and Refrigeration.* Booklet describing the HVACR industry and the program available at Ferris State University. Also includes spotlights on past graduates who have graduated with a HVACR degree and are now working in the industry.

322
FINANCIAL PLANNING ASSOCIATION
3801 East Florida Avenue, Suite 708
Denver, CO 80210-2544

• *Your Career in Financial Planning.* Describes the work of financial planners and how to prepare for the field.

323
FINANCIAL PUBLISHING COMPANY
PO Box 570
South Bend, IN 46628-9752
800-247-3214
Fax: 617-720-7106
dhickey@carletoninc.com
http://www.financial-publishing.com

• *College 'Scope National College Directory.* ($6.95) 64 pages. Updated annually. Lists accredited colleges and universities, as well as scholarships, fields of study, entrance tests required, tuition costs, student body size, room and board costs, deadlines, and more.

324
FIVE COLLEGE PROGRAMS IN PEACE AND WORLD SECURITY STUDIES
Hampshire College
Amherst, MA 01002
413-559-5367
Fax: 413-559-5611
pawss@hampshire.edu
http://pawss.hampshire.edu

• *Guide to Careers, Internships, and Graduate Education in Peace Studies.* ($6) Describes career options in the field, lists related organizations and agencies, and examines internships, fellowships, and graduate programs worldwide.

325
FLOOR COVERING INSTALLATION BOARD
310 Holiday Avenue
Dalton, GA 30720
706-278-FCIB (3242)

• *Contractors Certification Program.* 6 pages.

326
FLORIDA DEPARTMENT OF LABOR AND EMPLOYMENT SECURITY
Office of Labor Market Statistics
Hartman Building
2012 Capital Circle, SE, Suite 200
Tallahassee, FL 32399-2151
850-488-1048

Fax: 850-414-6210
http://lmi.floridajobs.org

Contact for a *Labor Market Information Directory,* which includes the following materials and more:

• *Florida's WEB.* A newsletter published semiannually and featuring occupational, educational, and career information of statewide and national importance.

• *Florida LMI NET.* 6 pages. Contains information on how to access LMI NET, a computer-based bulletin board system that links data users with Florida's Bureau of Labor Market Information data and resources.

• *Florida Industry and Occupational Employment Projections, 1994-2005.* Published annually. Includes a ranking of the growing and declining occupations.

Also available:

• *Florida Labor Market Trends.* Published monthly. Contains nonagricultural employment by industry and unemployment rates. Available from the Economic Analysis Unit.

327
FOOD AND AGRICULTURAL CAREERS FOR TOMORROW
1140 Agricultural Administration Building
Purdue University
West Lafayette, IN 47907-1140
765-494-8473
Fax: 765-494-8477
adg@admin.agad.purdue.edu

• *Employment Opportunities for College Graduates in the Food and Agricultural Sciences: Agriculture, Natural Resources,*

and Veterinary Medicine. 20 pages. Identifies major trends in professional employment opportunities for recent college graduates.

• Living Science Poster Sets. ($4 per set) Each set contains 40 (11" x 17") posters, which depict various food, agricultural, and natural resources careers.

328
FOOD MARKETING INSTITUTE
Publications Sales
655 15th Street, NW, Suite 700
Washington, DC 20005
202-452-8444
Fax: 202-220-0879
pubsales@fmi.org
http://www.fmi.org

• *New Opportunities—The Supermarket Industry and YOU!* ($.50)

• *Super Careers in Supermarketing.* ($3) 24 pages. Includes detailed job descriptions and career options, as well as a comprehensive list of schools offering programs related to supermarketing.

• *Looking for a Career.* ($1.50) Brochure designed to recruit young associates by displaying the opportunities available in the supermarket industry.

• *Supermarkets & Pharmacies: Winning Combinations, Rewarding Careers.* ($.50) Brochure useful for acquainting pharmacy employees, students, and other audiences with supermarket pharmacy and its varied career opportunities.

329
FORENSIC SCIENCES FOUNDATION, INC.
PO Box 669
Colorado Springs, CO 80901-0669
719-636-1100
Fax: 719-636-1993
membship@aafs.org
http://www.aafs.org

• *Career Brochure.* 32 pages. Describes various employment opportunities in the forensics field.

• *List of Schools.* 11 pages. Lists graduate and undergraduate schools that offer forensic science programs.

330
FOUNDATION FOR INTERIOR DESIGN EDUCATION RESEARCH
60 Monroe Center, NW, Suite 300
Grand Rapids, MI 49503-2920
616-458-0400
Fax: 616-458-0460
fider@fider.org
http://www.fider.org

• *Directory of Interior Design Programs Accredited by FIDER.* Contains a list of FIDER accredited programs. Also available on FIDER's Web site.

331
FUTURE FARMERS OF AMERICA
National FFA Organization
PO Box 68960
Indianapolis, IN 46268-0960
888-332-2668
Fax: 800-366-6556
aboutffa@ffa.org
http://www.ffa.org

• *FFA Student Handbook.* ($3.50) Provides background information regarding FFA activities, benefits, and opportunities of interest to students.

• *Discover World Class Opportunities in FFA.* ($.35) Outlines FFA membership benefits for students.

• *Open a Promising Future.* ($.85) Summarizes the components and benefits of agricultural education. Great tool for students, parents, school officials, counselors, and industry leaders.

• *Agriculture: An Industry Too Big to Ignore.* ($1.50) Describes the numerous career opportunities in agriculture available to youth.

• *Discovering an Agricultural Biotechnology Career That May Be for You.* ($1) Discusses necessary skills for a career in agricultural biotechnology.

• *Open Door.* ($1.40) Discusses agricultural career opportunities.

• *Think about It.* ($.50) Highlights more than 200 agricultural careers.

332
GENERAL AVIATION MANUFACTURERS ASSOCIATION
1400 K Street, NW, Suite 801
Washington, DC 20005
202-393-1500
Fax: 202-842-4063
http://www.generalaviation.org

• *General Aviation Is....* (First 25 copies free or $.20/each) Tool designed to educate the public on the many different uses for general aviation and the lives it affects.

- *Face to Face.* ($1.50) 24 pages. Captures the experiences and benefits of business aviation through different case studies.

- *Learn to Fly.* (First 25 copies free or $.20/each) Brief synopsis of the levels of pilot certificates available, training required, and basic questions and answers about flight and becoming a pilot.

- *NCAE: A Guide to Aviation Education Resources.* Free resource representing 32 industry and labor organizations. Includes facts about the aviation industry, contact information, and other services.

- *Take Off for Opportunities.* ($12) 11-minute video providing information on future opportunities available to young people interested in aeronautical or aero-space engineering, maintenance, and avionics repair.

- *Making the Difference.* ($10) 14-minute video documenting six situations typically found within the aviation industry. Stories range from common tasks involving photography, agriculture, or business and corporate flying to more critical tasks such as air ambulance flight or crucial aviation training.

333
GENERAL BOARD OF HIGHER EDUCATION AND MINISTRY
The United Methodist Church
Section of Deacons and Diaconal Ministries
PO Box 340007
Nashville, TN 37203-0007
615-340-7406
http://www.gbhem.org

- *Steps Into Certification.* Leaflet.

- *Steps Into Ordained Ministry.* Leaflet.

- *Why I Am A....* 6 pages each. A series of brochures containing career information on particular fields from a personal perspective. Available for the following career disciplines: pastoral counselor, air force chaplain, navy chaplain, national guard chaplain, prison chaplain, nursing home chaplain, mental health chaplain, and hospital chaplain.

- *Serving in Extension Ministries: Chaplains and Pastoral Counselors.* 8 pages. Discusses chaplains and their responsibilities in different settings.

- *United Methodist Pastors and the Armed Forces Reserve/Guard Program.* 6 pages. Questions and answers about pastors in the armed forces.

- *Pastoral Care/Counseling/Education.* 2 pages. Lists organizations offering education for, information about, and certification for pastoral care in specialized settings.

The following are available from Cokesbury Publications, 800-672-1789:

- *God's Call and Your Vocation: A Leader's Guide.* (#818757) ($1)

- *God's Call and Your Vocation: The Book.* (#735446) ($5)

- *College Bound.* (#850520) 28 pages. Features valuable information about choosing a college; a listing of United Methodist colleges and universities; and information about loans and scholarships.

• *School, Colleges, and Universities of The United Methodist Church, U.S.A.* (#740476) A complete listing of higher education institutions related to the General Board of Higher Education and Ministry. Includes a map of their locations.

• *Handbook of the United Methodist-Related Schools, Colleges, Universities and Theological Schools with a Guide to United Methodist Loans and Scholarships.* (#740534) ($7) 338 pages. Designed as a resource for students, families, and pastors. Describes educational opportunities available through United Methodist-related educational institutions and includes information about selecting a college, financing a college education, and United Methodist loans and scholarships programs.

• *The Christian as a Minister.* (#804294) ($4) 104 pages. Chapters include "Servant Ministry," "The Settings for Servant Leadership," and "Steps into Servant Ministries." Contains an index of United Methodist schools for theology.

• *United Methodist Schools of Theology.* (#806910) 27 pages. Lists and describes the 13 United Methodist seminaries.

• *Steps into Ordained Ministry.* (#741436) 4 pages. Describes seven steps for ordination as a deacon or an elder in the United Methodist Church.

• *Are You Ready?* (#789847) ($.50) 8 pages. Information on ordained ministry. Serves as a recruitment piece for young audiences.

334
GEOLOGICAL SOCIETY OF AMERICA
3300 Penrose Place
PO Box 9140
Boulder, CO 80301-9140
800-472-1988 or 303-447-2020
Fax: 303-447-1133
member@geosociety.org
http://www.geosociety.org

• *Careers in the Geosciences.* 12 pages. Describes the work of the geoscientist, job and salary outlook, and other topics.

335
GEORGETOWN UNIVERSITY
Division of Interpretation and Translation
School of Languages and Linguistics
Washington, DC 20057-0993
202-687-5848
vasiliep@gunet.georgetown.edu
http://www.georgetown.edu/departments/translation

• *The Jerome Quarterly.* ($15 for 12 issues)

336
GERMAN STUDIES INFORMATION, LTD.
Monatshefte/Max Kade Institute
Directory of German Studies
818 Van Hise Hall
1220 Linden Drive
Madison, WI 53706
608-262-3008
Fax: 608-262-7949
office@monatshefte.org
http://www.monatshefte.org

• *DAAD/Monatshefte Directory of German Studies.* ($5) Contains a list of German departments, programs, and faculties at four-year colleges and universities in the United States and Canada.

337
GRADUATE MANAGEMENT ADMISSION COUNCIL

1750 Tysons Boulevard, Suite 1100
McLean, VA 22102
703-749-0131
Fax: 703-749-0169
gmacmail@gmac.com
http://www.gmat.org

• *Exploring the MBA.* Discusses MBA degrees and admissions and provides useful information for prospective business school candidates' self assessment and planning, researching program types, and identifying schools which most closely match both professional and academic goals.

• *GMAT Information Bulletin.* 37 pages. Contains detailed information concerning registration, test content and preparation, what to expect on test day, and GMAT(r) scores as well as GMAT(r) test center locations and school codes.

Available on the Web site.

• *MBA Explorer.* Includes general and specific information regarding the pusuit of an MBA degree (including costs and financial aid), careers, MBA programs with a searchable database of over 500 schools, downloadable publications, and additional information about GMAC's products and services.

338
GRAPHIC COMMUNICATIONS COUNCIL

1899 Preston White Drive
Reston, VA 20191-4367
703-648-1768
Fax: 703-620-0994

• *A Counselor's Guide: Careers in Graphic Communications.* 13 pages.

• *Directory of Technical Schools, Colleges & Universities Offering Courses in Graphic Communications.* 90 pages. Spans all degree levels for technology, management, and education.

• *Scholarships.* 7 pages.

• *Guide to Audio/Visual Materials.* 21 pages.

339
GRAPHICS SYSTEMS, INCORPORATED

6400 Shelby View Drive, Suite 114
Memphis, TN 38134
800-854-3212 or 901-843-8395
Fax: 901-373-8411

All career resources are available for $4.95 each plus shipping:

• *Focus on the Future.* Participant manual and leader's guide.

• *Development and You.* Video and brochure.

• *Your Performance and Development Road Map: How to Guides.*

• *Building a Successful Profile.* Brochure.

• *Setting Objectives.* Brochure.

340
GREATER WASHINGTON SOCIETY OF ASSOCIATION EXECUTIVES
Association Career Services Center
1426 21st Street, NW
Washington, DC 20036-5901
202-429-7162
Fax: 202-429-7160
http://www.gwsae.org

• *A Guide to Association Careers.* 24 pages.
Discusses one-on-one counseling, career
workshops, salaries, and where to look
for an association job, such as JOBSmart,
the online marketplace for association
careers in the greater Washington, DC,
area.

341
GUILD OF NATURAL SCIENCE ILLUSTRATORS
PO Box 652
Ben Franklin Station
Washington, DC 20044-0652
301-309-1514 (credit card purchases)
http://www.gnsi.org

• *Careers in Scientific Illustration.* ($2) 10
pages. Describes the profession and its
educational and training requirements.

• *Scientific Illustration Courses and Books.*
($8) A description of known scientific
illustration courses and programs by
state and country. Also includes a bibliography of books on science illustration.

342
HARNESS HORSE YOUTH FOUNDATION
14950 Greyhound Court, Suite 210
Carmel, IN 46032

317-848-5132
http://www.hhyf.org

• *Equine School and College Directory.* ($8)
101 pages. Lists equine degree programs, farrier schools, veterinary
schools, veterinary technical programs,
and related scholarships.

• *Careers in Harness Racing.* 28 pages. A
brief description of various horse-related
career opportunities.

343
HEALTH RESOURCES AND SERVICES ADMINISTRATION
Division of Student Assistance
5600 Fishers Lane
Rockville, MD 20857
http://www.hrsa.dhhs.gov/bhpr/dsa

Available at the Web site:

• *Student Assistance for Various Disciplines.*
Information about the financial aid programs available for the following fields:
allied health, behavioral and mental
health, chiropractic, dentistry, medicine,
nursing, optometry, pharmacy, physician
assistant, podiatry, public health, and
veterinary medicine.

344
HEATH RESOURCE CENTER
American Council on Education
One Dupont Circle, NW, Suite 800
Washington, DC 20036-1193
202-939-9320
Fax: 202-833-5696
health@ace.nche.edu
http://www.heath-resource-center.org

Prior to ordering, contact the HRC about the availability of publications.

• *Career Planning and Employment Strategies for Postsecondary Students with Disabilities.* ($2) 8 pages.

• *Distance Learning and Adults with Disabilities.* ($2) 6 pages. Describes the learning opportunities available via computer conferencing, cable television, and videocassette.

• *Financial Aid for Students with Disabilities.* ($2) 12 pages.

• *How to Choose a College: Guide for the Student with a Disability.* ($1) 17 pages.

• *National Clearinghouse on Postsecondary Education for Individuals with Disabilities Resource Directory.* ($5) 39 pages.

• *Vocational Rehabilitation Services: A Postsecondary Student Consumer's Guide.* ($2) 4 pages.

345
HOBART INSTITUTE OF WELDING TECHNOLOGY
400 Trade Square East
Troy, OH 45373
800-332-9448 or 937-332-5300
Fax: 937-332-5200
hiwt@welding.org
http://www.welding.org

• *Course Catalog.* 35 pages. Provides a description of skill and tech classes, lists costs, and includes an application form. Portions of the catalog are available at the Web site.

Available to order on the Web site:

• *Training Materials Catalog.* 23 pages. Provides a description of materials and publications available for purchase.

346
HOWARD HUGHES MEDICAL INSTITUTE
4000 Jones Bridge Road
Chevy Chase, MD 20815-6789
301-215-8500
http://www.hhmi.org

• *Beyond Bio 101.* 88 pages. Describes opportunities in biology, reports on changes in teaching methods, includes research done by innovative students, and how institutions are attempting to recruit more women into the field. Available free in print form or accessible online.

347
HUMAN FACTORS AND ERGONOMICS SOCIETY
PO Box 1369
Santa Monica, CA 90406-1369
310-394-1811
Fax: 310-394-2410
hfes@compuserve.com
http://hfes.org

• *Career Opportunities in Human Factors/ Ergonomics.* 8 pages. Discusses career options in the field, educational require-ments, employment areas, salaries, and related professions.

• *Human Factors & Ergonomics ... Designing for Human Use.* 6 pages. Describes the history of ergonomics, areas of work, and more.

- *Preparing for a Career in Human Factors/Ergonomics.* ($10 plus $5 shipping and handling) 60 pages. Reprints of articles of interest to those entering the field or transitioning from another field.

348
I-SHIPS
PO Box 368
Cardiff, CA 92007
http://www.chamber4us.org

- *Internships: Rocket Into a Career You Choose.* ($4.50) Popular career columnist, Joyce Lain Kennedy, shares useful information about how to make internships work for you. Includes a list of the major directories which cite thousands of internship opportunities. Make check payable to SFI, and include a $.55 self addressed, stamped envelope.

349
IDAHO DEPARTMENT OF LABOR
317 Main Street
Boise, ID 83735-0600
208-334-6252
Fax: 208-334-6455
http://www.labor.state.id.us

- *Basic Economic Data.* Lists information on nonagricultural wage and salary workers by industry, for each county.

- *Distribution of Wages Paid to Covered Workers in Idaho, by Industry.*

- *Economic Profiles.* Economic overviews in various areas, including income, housing, employment, health care, education, and tax rates. Specify county.

- *Idaho Employment Newsletter.* Contains data on employment, unemployment, and economic trends and indicators.

- *Idaho Occupational Wage Survey.* Covers over 750 occupations in more than 8,500 businesses around the state.

- *Occupational Employment Statistics.* Includes information on occupations and employment within specific industries in the state and for the state as a whole.

350
ILLINOIS ASSOCIATION OF CHAMBER OF COMMERCE EXECUTIVES
215 East Adams Street
Springfield, IL 62701
217-522-5512
Fax: 217-522-5518

- *Is a Career in Chamber of Commerce Management Right for You?* 6 pages. Defines the role of the chamber of commerce and its staff and discusses compensation and other topics.

351
INDEPENDENT INSURANCE AGENTS OF AMERICA, INC.
127 South Peyton Street
Alexandria, VA 22314
800-221-7917 or 703-683-4422
Fax: 703-683-7556
info@iiaa.org
http://www.independent agent.com

- *Take This "I" Test First.* 6 pages. Contains questions for career-bound students and a discussion about the answers.

• *What Do You Want to Be When You Grow Up?* 4 pages. Describes the insurance field and available opportunities.

352
INDUSTRIAL DESIGNERS SOCIETY OF AMERICA
1142 Walker Road
Great Falls, VA 22066
703-759-0100
Fax: 703-759-7679
idsa@erols.com
http://www.idsa.org

Available by mail or on the Web:

• *Getting an Industrial Design Job.* Information on landing the first job in industrial design, including tips on using the Internet to tap into hidden resources.

• *The ID Career Brochure: Straight Answers About Industrial Design.* Highlights products designed by industrial designers everyday and answers commonly asked questions about the field.

• *College and Graduate ID Programs.* Online directory of colleges and universities nationwide that offer programs in industrial design.

353
INDUSTRIAL RELATIONS RESEARCH ASSOCIATION
121 LIR, University of Illinois
504 East Armory Avenue
Champaign, IL 61820
217-333-0072
Fax: 217-265-5130
irra@uiuc.edu
http://www.irra.uiuc.edu

• *Industrial Relations Degree Programs in the United States, Canada, and Australia.* 4 pages. Contains descriptions of degree programs in industrial/labor relations and human resources.

354
INDUSTRIAL TRUCK ASSOCIATION
1750 K Street, NW, Suite 460
Washington, DC 20006
202-296-9880
Fax: 202-296-9884
indtrk@indtrk.org
http://www.indtrk.org

• *Truck Operator, Industrial.* Summarizes career opportunities in the trucking industry.

355
INSTITUTE FOR OPERATIONS RESEARCH AND THE MANAGEMENT SCIENCES
Customer Service
901 Elkridge Landing Road, Suite 400
Linthicum, MD 21090-2909
800-446-3676
Fax: 410-684-2963
informs@informs.org
http://www.informs.org

• *Is a Career in Operations Research/ Management Science Right for You?* 21 pages. Contains 12 questions to help people decide if the career is for them.

• *Career Information in the Mathematical Sciences: A Resource Guide.* 29 pages. Lists mathematical career materials and sources for a variety of audiences.

• *Educational Programs in Operations Research and the Management Sciences*. 85 pages. Contains descriptions of 123 degree programs supporting operations research and the management sciences at institutions in the United States and abroad.

356
INSTITUTE OF ELECTRICAL AND ELECTRONICS ENGINEERS, INC.
1828 L Street, NW, Suite 1202
Washington, DC 20036
202-785-0017
Fax: 202-785-0835
http://www.ieeeusa.org

Available at the Web site:

• *Your Career in the Electrical, Electronics, and Computer Engineering Fields.* Contains information on specific careers in the field. Also includes a sample high school and college curriculum.

357
INSTITUTE OF FOOD TECHNOLOGISTS
Scholarship Department
221 North LaSalle Street
Chicago, IL 60601
312-782-8424
Fax: 312-782-8348

• *Food Scientists*. 4 pages. Discusses food scientists and the work they perform, education and training required, employment outlook, and more.

• *Food Technology Career Booklet*. 16 pages. Sections include "Your Future," "Your Mission," "Your Job," "Your Boss," "Your Reward," and "Your First Step."

• *IFT Administered Fellowship/Scholarship Program.* 17 pages. Contains program descriptions and application procedures. In the 1999-00 year, the IFT administered 39 graduate fellowships and more than 110 undergraduate scholarships.

358
INSTITUTE OF INDUSTRIAL ENGINEERS
25 Technology Park-Atlanta
Norcross, GA 30092
800-494-0460 or 770-449-0460
Fax: 770-441-3295
cs@www.iienet.org
http://www.iienet.org

Available at the Web site:

• *Industrial Engineering: The Career of Choice.* Includes the following: professional highlights; definition of the career; typical responsibilities, locations, and salaries of industrial engineers; recommended routes towards a career in the field; and sources of additional information.

359
INSTITUTE OF INTERNAL AUDITORS
International Headquarters
249 Maitland Avenue
Altamonte Springs, FL 32701-4201
407-830-7600
Fax: 407-831-5171
http://www.theiia.org

• *Get on the Road to Success as an Internal Auditor.* Includes information on internal auditing, job descriptions, the training and educational requirements, means to certification, internship opportunities, and more.

• *They Outnumber You 25,000 to 1.* Brochure about the importance of becoming a certified internal auditor (CIA). Includes information on the exam and eligibility requirements.

• *Internal Auditing: All in a Day's Work.* 10 pages. Booklet of the varied roles of internal auditors.

• *Certified Internal Auditor Program Information for Candidates.* 26 pages. Contents include the following: eligibility requirements; examination format, schedules, locations, and fees; performance awards; registration information; CIA application forms; and more.

• *The Learning Center, 1999-2000.* 96 pages. Includes information on the following: core curriculum seminars; customized seminars; internal control curriculum seminars; information technology curriculum seminars; conferences; IIA Bookstore products; and other important information.

360
INSTITUTE OF INTERNATIONAL EDUCATION
PO Box 371
Annapolis Junction, MD 20701-0371
800-445-0443
Fax: 301-953-2838
iiebooks@pmds.com
http://www.iie.org

• *Basic Facts on Study Abroad in the 21st Century.* 24 pages. Brochure outlining important information you should know before going abroad. Contains sections on defining goals, making a plan, financ-

ing tips, and includes additional resources for students and advisors.

• *Study Abroad: A Guide for Women.* 32 pages. Focuses on many questions targeted specifically for women interested in studying abroad.

361
INSTITUTE OF MANAGEMENT ACCOUNTANTS
10 Paragon Drive
Montvale, NJ 07645-1718
800-638-4427 or 201-573-9000
Fax: 201-573-0559
ima@imanet.org
http://www.imanet.org

Available at the Web site:

• *IMA Student Campus.* Includes the following article links:

• *How Do I Start My Career in Financial Management?*

• *What They Didn't Teach You in Accounting Class.*

• *What Can You Expect as an Entry-Level Accountant?*

• *Motivation: The Key to Professional Success.*

• *How We Passed the CMA Exam.*

362
INSTITUTE OF PACKAGING PROFESSIONALS
481 Carlisle Drive
Herndon, VA 20170-4823
800-432-4085 or 703-318-8974
Fax: 703-814-4961
iopp@pkgmatters.com
http://www.iopages.org

Available online or by mail:

• *Information on The Certified Professional in Training Program (CPIT).* Includes information on the importance of certification, the steps to earning your CPIT designation, and application form.

363
INSTITUTE OF REAL ESTATE MANAGEMENT
Customer Services Department
430 North Michigan Avenue
Chicago, IL 60611
800-837-0706, ext. 4650
Fax: 800-338-4736
http://www.irem.org

• *Careers in Real Estate Management.* ($5) 12 pages. Introduction to the wide array of career opportunities that exist today in the field of real estate management. Includes information on how to get started, how much you can expect to earn, and how to overcome challenges on the road to professional success.

364
INSTITUTE OF TRANSPORTATION ENGINEERS
525 School Street, SW, Suite 410
Washington, DC 20024
202-554-8050
Fax: 202-863-5486
http://www.ite.org

Available at the Web site:

• *The Transportation Profession.* Highlights the wide variety of projects that are available in planning, designing, and operating streets and highways, transit systems, airports, railroad, and ports and harbors. Includes sources for additional information.

Available by mail:

• *Careers in Transportation Engineering.* Describes the opportunities and challenges of a career in transportation engineering.

365
INTERNATIONAL SOCIETY OF WOMEN AIRLINE PILOTS
2250 East Tropicana Avenue
Suite 19-395
Las Vegas, NV 89119-6594
http://www.iswap.org

Available at the Web site:

• *Tips on Becoming an Airline Pilot in the United States.*

366
INTEREXCHANGE
161 Sixth Avenue
New York, NY 10013
212-924-0446
Fax: 212-924-0575
info@interexchange.org
http://www.interexchange.org

Available by mail or accessible online:

• *Working Abroad.* Describes a number of work programs and au pair programs offered in Europe. Outlines eligibility, visas, and other important issues.

367

INTERNATIONAL ASSOCIATION OF ADMINISTRATIVE PROFESSIONALS

10502 Northwest Ambassador Drive
PO Box 20404
Kansas City, MO 64195-0404
816-891-6600
Fax: 816-891-9118
service@iaap-hq.org
http://www.iaap-hq.org

The following short articles are available at the Web site:

• *The 21st Century Administrative Professional.*

• *Skills Most in Demand.*

• *Glossary of Job Descriptions.*

• *Average Salaries.*

• *How to Obtain the Proper Training.*

• *Should You Go Back to School?*

• *Future Technology Trends.*

• *Office of the Future: 2005.*

• *Workplace 2000.*

• *Administrative Trends.*

• *Tips on Staying Ahead in a Changing Workplace.*

368

INTERNATIONAL ASSOCIATION OF BUSINESS COMMUNICATORS

One Hallidie Plaza, Suite 600
San Francisco, CA 94102
415-544-4700
Fax: 415-544-4747
http://www.iabc.com

• *IABC Communication Bank Career Packet.* 31 pages. Contains background information on business communication and resource tips for career development.

369

INTERNATIONAL ASSOCIATION OF FISH AND WILDLIFE AGENCIES

444 North Capitol Street, NW, Suite 544
Washington, DC 20001
202-624-7890
Fax: 202-624-7891
http://www.sso.org/iafwa

The following is available on the Association's Web site:

• *Planning a Career in Fish and Wildlife Management and Related Fields of Natural Resource Conservation.* Outlines ways to prepare for a career in the field during high school, college, and beyond. Includes recommended course work, tips on planning your major, and graduate work possibilities. Lists sources of additional information, and lists job opportunities in state, federal, and private organizations.

370

INTERNATIONAL BROTHERHOOD OF PAINTERS AND ALLIED TRADES JOINT APPRENTICESHIP TRAINING FUND

1750 New York Avenue, NW, 8th Floor
Washington, DC 20006
800-276-7289 or 202-637-0740
Fax: 202-628-4897

• *Reach Out for Tomorrow.* Newsletter about the benefits of apprenticeship training in painting, decorating, and drywall finishing.

371
INTERNATIONAL CHIROPRACTORS ASSOCIATION
1110 North Glebe Road, Suite 1000
Arlington, VA 22201-5722
703-528-5000
Fax: 703-528-5023
chiro@chiropractic.org
http://www.chiropractic.org

• *Information about Chiropractic Education Career Kit.* 6 pages. Includes information on undergraduate requirements, admission, licensure, and financial aid and scholarships. Lists CCE-accredited colleges and universities.

372
INTERNATIONAL FACILITY MANAGEMENT ASSOCIATION
One East Greenway Plaza, Suite 1100
Houston, TX 77046-0194
713-623-4362
Fax: 713-623-6124
ifmahq@ifma.org
http://www.ifma.org

Available at the Web site:

• *Recognized Programs of Education.* Information on educational institutions offering degrees or course work in or related to facility management.

373
INTERNATIONAL INSTITUTE OF MUNICIPAL CLERKS
1212 North San Dimas Canyon Road
San Dimas, CA 91773-1223
909-592-4462
Fax: 909-592-1555
hq@iimc.com
http://www.iimc.com

Available at the Web site:

• *Clerk Institutes Directory.* Lists certification and master's programs in the United States and Canada recognized by the IIMC. Each listing contains the name of the sponsoring university and association.

374
INTERNATIONAL MASONRY INSTITUTE
The James Brice House
42 East Street
Annapolis, MD 21401
800-IMI-0988 or 202-383-3911
http://www.imiweb.org

• *Get a Grip on Your Future.* 6 pages. Contains answers to questions about the trowel trades.

• *IMI Today.* Bi-monthly newsletter covering the latest trends and news in the masonry field.

• *Building Your Future.* 10-minute video highlighting the many ways women are contributing to the masonry work force throughout the U.S.

• *Stone Training.* 11-minute video about the National Stone Training Program.

375

INTERNATIONAL PERSONNEL MANAGEMENT ASSOCIATION
1617 Duke Street
Alexandria, VA 22314
703-549-7100
Fax: 703-684-0948
ipma@ipma-hr.org
http://www.ipma-hr.org

Available at the Web site:

• *Student Center.* Includes information on HR careers, including job descriptions, educational/training requirements, career outlook, advice on how best to land HR jobs, and links to additional helpful information.

376

INTERNATIONAL SOCIETY OF CERTIFIED ELECTRONICS TECHNICIANS
2708 West Berry Street
Fort Worth, TX 76109-2356
817-921-9101
Fax: 817-921-3741
iscet@flash.net
http://www.iscet.org

• *Careers in the Electronics Industry.* 13 pages. Discusses the nature of the work, training and qualifications, employment outlook, earnings, and working conditions for a variety of jobs in the field.

377

INTERNATIONAL TECHNOLOGY EDUCATION ASSOCIATION
1914 Association Drive, Suite 201
Reston, VA 20191-1539
703-860-2100

Fax: 703-860-0353
ite@iris.org
http://www.iteawww.org

Available at the Web site:

• *Directory of ITEA Institutional Members.* List of institutions aiding individuals who are considering pursuing undergraduate or graduate degrees in technology education. Includes degrees offered and financial aid available.

378

INTERNATIONAL TRADEMARK ASSOCIATION
1133 Avenue of the Americas
New York, NY 10036
212-768-9887
Fax: 212-768-7796
publications@inta.org
http://www.inta.org

• *A Guide to Proper Trademark Use.* ($3) Concise guide illustrating the basic guidelines for proper use of trademarks for clients and emloyees.

• *Trademark Basics: A Guide for Business.* ($6) Brochure introducing the fundamentals of trademark selection, registration, amd maintenance.

• *Fame or Misfortune.* ($3) Offers practical suggestions on how to protect the well-known trademarks of market leaders.

379

INTERNATIONAL TRAINING INSTITUTE FOR THE SHEET METAL AND AIR CONDITIONING INDUSTRY
601 North Fairfax Street, Suite 240
Alexandria, VA 22314

703-739-7200
Fax: 703-683-7461
http://www.sheetmetal-iti.org

- *Careers in Sheet Metal.* 24 pages. Can be ordered online or by mail.

380

INTERSOCIETY COMMITTEE ON PATHOLOGY INFORMATION

9650 Rockville Pike
Bethesda, MD 20814-3993
301-571-1880
Fax: 301-571-1879
icpi@pathol.faseb.org
http://www.pathologytraining.org

- *Pathology as a Career in Medicine.* 12 pages. Describes the pathologist in patient care, as a teacher, and in research. Includes information on graduate medical education and career options.

- *Directory of Pathology Training Programs.* 650 pages. Published annually, the directory includes geographically arranged descriptions of the training facilities, residencies, remuneration, application requirements, and faculty at nearly all the approved programs for anatomic and clinical pathology training in the United States and more than half of the approved programs in Canada. Also includes listings describing the requirements, stipends, and application information for fellowships and other postgraduate opportunities for training in the certifiable specialized areas of pathology.

381

IOWA WORKFORCE DEVELOPMENT

Policy and Information Division
1000 East Grand Avenue
Des Moines, IA 50319-0209
800-562-4692 or 515-281-6642
Fax: 515-281-8203
http://www.iowaworkforce.org

- *Merchandising Your Job Talents.* 16 pages. Offers tips for those just out of school— or those looking for a new position after years of experience—on carrying out a well-planned job search.

- *Condition of Employment.* Analyzes Iowa's labor market and includes an occupational and industry outlook with wage and income information.

- *Iowa Licensed Occupations.* 97 pages. Provides career counselors and others with information concerning occupations in Iowa that require a license, certificate, or commission issued at the state level. Includes brief job descriptions for each listed occupation.

- *Iowa WorkNet.* A quarterly publication that analyzes the state's current economic condition.

- *Iowa Job Outlook.*

- *Iowa Wage Survey.*

- *Job Insurance Benefits.* Tables, prepared monthly, showing the unemployment insurance benefits paid in each county in the state.

- *Labor Force Summary Tables.* Data outlining employment and unemployment statewide and for every county in Iowa, as well as the employment by industry. Prepared monthly.

• *Employment and Wages Covered by Unemployment Insurance.*

382

ISA

67 Alexander Drive
PO Box 12277
Research Triangle Park, NC 27709
919-549-8411
Fax: 919-549-8411
info@isa.org
http://www.isa.org

• *Measurement and Control Careers: A Design for Your Future.* 6 pages. Describes the careers, the educational requirements, and personal qualifications.

383

J.L. SCOTT MARINE EDUCATION CENTER AND AQUARIUM

PO Box 7000
Ocean Springs, MS 39564-7000
228-374-5550
Fax: 228-374-5559
scott.aquarium@usm.edu
http://www.aquarium.usm.edu

• *Marine Education: A Bibliography of Education Materials Available from the Nation's Sea Grant College Programs.* ($2)

384

JETS INC.

1420 King Street, Suite 405
Alexandria, VA 22314-2794
703-548-5387
Fax: 703-548-0769

jets@nae.edu
http://www.jets.org

• *Engineering Specialty Brochures.* (GF-04 + discipline) ($10 per 100 copies) Suitable for middle and high school students, these single-panel brochures describe specific engineering disciplines. Subjects include: *Aerospace Engineering; Agricultural Engineering; Audio Engineering; Automotive Engineering; Environmental Engineering; Industrial Engineering; Mechanical Engineering; Nuclear Engineering; Optical Engineering; Safety Engineering;* and more. Visit the Web site for a complete list of titles.

• *Engineering Is For You!* (GB-02) ($15 per 100 copies) Two-panel motivational brochure clarifying what engineers do and how middle school students can prepare for this career.

• *Engineering Technologists and Technicians.* (GB-03) ($15 per 100 copies) Two-panel brochure describing the roles and functions of the fields. Suitable for high school students.

385

JEWELERS OF AMERICA, INC.

1185 Avenue of the Americas, 30th Floor
New York, NY 10036
212-768-8777
Fax: 212-768-8087
contactus@jewelers.org
http://www.jewelers.org

• *Careers in Jewelry: Sales, Craftsmanship, Management.* 10 pages. Covers the working conditions, career opportunities, educational requirements, skills and personal qualifications, employment outlook, and how to get started in a jewelry career.

386
JIST PUBLISHING
8902 Otis Avenue
Indianapolis, IN 46216-1033
317-613-4200
Fax: 317-613-4309
general@jist.com
http://www.jist.com

- *Dream Catchers: Developing Career and Educational Awareness.* ($4.95) 74 pages. Workbook for students in grades 4-7 that teaches basic career concepts. Teacher's guide and reproducible activities also available.

- *Pathfinder: Exploring Career and Educational Paths.* ($6.95) 112 pages. Workbook for students in grades 7-10 to help design an Individual Career Plan (ICP) and career paths through high school and into post-secondary training. Teacher's guide and six-panel portfolio also available.

- *Getting the Job You Really Want.* ($12.95) 208 pages. Workbook that covers all essential job search topics for students in high school or college, or adults in employment/training programs. Instructor's guide also available.

- *La Busqueda Rapida de Trabajo (The Spanish Quick Job Search).* ($7.95) 60 pages. A booklet that covers job search essentials with English and Spanish text on facing pages.

- *Effective Strategies for Career Success.* ($9.95) 160 pages. A workbook designed for adults to help them prepare for, find, and succeed on the job. Gives overview of training options and how to apply and focus on study skills, time management, positive thinking, and assertiveness.

387
JOCKEYS' GUILD, INC.
250 West Main Street, Suite 1820
Lexington, KY 40507
606-259-3211
Fax: 606-252-0938
http://www.jockeysguild.com

- *So You Want to Be a Jockey....* 6 pages. Covers the qualifications, training, and expenses.

388
JOINT COMMISSION ON ALLIED HEALTH PERSONNEL IN OPHTHALMOLOGY
2025 Woodlane Drive
St. Paul, MN 55125-2995
888-284-3937 or 651-731-2944
Fax: 651-731-0410
jcapho@jcapho.org
http://www.jcapho.org

Available at the Web site:

- *What is Ophthalmic Medical Assisting?* Explains who ophthalmic medical personnel are, what they do, what their qualifications are, what education is required, and why they must be certified.

- *Certification—Why and How.* Describes certification levels and exam.

- *CE Program Listings: Regional and Nationwide.* Online listing of schools and universities offering continued education in the field.

389

JOINT REVIEW COMMITTEE ON EDUCATION IN CARDIOVASCULAR TECHNOLOGY
3525 Ellicott Mills Drive, Suite N
Ellicott City, MD 21043-4547
410-418-4800
Fax: 410-418-4805
cynthia@assochq.com

• *Accredited Cardiovascular Technology Programs.* 4 pages.

• *Essentials and Guidelines of an Accredited Educational Program for the Cardiovascular Technologist.* 18 pages.

390

KANSAS LABOR MARKET INFORMATION
401 Topeka Boulevard, SW
Topeka, KS 66603
785-296-5058
Fax: 785-296-5286
laborstats@hr.state.ks.us
http://laborstats.hr.state.ks.us

The following publications are available free in print form or accessible online:

• *Labor Market Information 2000 Catalog.* Lists career-related resources available from federal agencies, Kansas state offices, colleges and universities in Kansas, and private sources.

• *Kansas Monthly Employment Review.* Monthly newsletter of labor and economic data for Kansas and metropolitan areas. Includes labor force estimates, nonfarm wage and salary employment, hours and earnings estimates, unemployment insurance data, and consumer price information.

• *Lawrence Labor Market Review.* Summary of labor data for the Lawrence, Kansas, area.

• *Topeka Labor Market Review.* Summary of labor data for the Topeka, Kansas, area.

• *Wichita Labor Market Review.* Summary of labor data for the Wichita, Kansas, area.

• *Kansas Labor Force Estimates.* Estimates of the civilian labor force, unemployment, and employment levels. Includes data for Kansas, metropolitan areas, counties, and selected cities.

• *Kansas Wage Survey, 1999.* Occupational wage information for the state and metropolitan areas.

• *Occupational Outlook 2005.* Occupational projections for the state and regions.

• *Job Opportunities in Kansas.* Information on 45 well-paying occupations that do not require a college degree.

• *Kansas Annual Employment and Wages, 1998.* Industry employment and wage information for counties, state, and metropolitan areas.

391

KANSAS STATE UNIVERSITY
Department of Grain Science and Industry
201 Shellenberger Hall
Manhattan, KS 66506-2201

913-532-6161
http://www.oznet.ksu.edu/dp_grsi/

- *Information Sheets.* 2 pages each. Available disciplines: bakery science; feed science and management; grain science and industry; and milling science and management.

392
KENTUCKY CABINET FOR WORKFORCE DEVELOPMENT
Department for Employment Services Research and Statistics,
CHR Building 2W
Frankfort, KY 40621-0001
502-564-7976
Fax: 502-564-2937
des.labor@mail.stste.ky.us
http://www.state.ky.us/agencies/wforce/index.htm

- *Kentucky Occupational Wage Data.*

- *Kentucky Career Outlook and Job Opportunities Guide.*

- *Kentucky Occupational Outlook to 2006 (Statewide).*

- *Kentucky Occupational Outlook to 2005 (Local Areas).*

393
LAW SCHOOL ADMISSIONS COUNCIL
215-968-1001
Fax: 215-968-1119
lsacinfo@lsac.org
http://www.lsac.org

Available at the Web site:

- *Thinking about Law School.* Guide for those considering a law career. Includes information on the application process, surviving law school, and choosing a career path.

- *Minorities Interested in Legal Education.* Covers preparing for the LSAT, academic advising, frequently asked questions and links to minority legal organizations.

394
LEARNING DISABILITIES ASSOCIATION OF AMERICA
4156 Library Road
Pittsburgh, PA 15234-1349
412-341-1515
Fax: 412-344-0224
http://www.ldanatl.org

- *College Students with Learning Disabilities.* 8 pages.

- *Colleges/Universities That Accept Students with Learning Disabilities.* ($5) 50 pages.

- *Helping Adolescents with Learning Disabilities Achieve Independence.* 6 pages.

- *A Learning Disabilities Digest for Literacy Providers.* ($3) 24 pages.

- *You Can Open a Door ....* 8 pages.

395
LIFE SKILLS EDUCATION
314 Washington Street
Northfield, MN 55057-2025
800-783-6743, Department 199
Fax: 507-645-2995
http://www.lifeskillsed.com

• Life Skills Education publishes 20-page pamphlets on employment and training issues. Pamphlets are $1 each with a minimum order of $50. Visit the Web site for complete descriptions of all titles. Topics covered include: the first job; the job search; letters and resumes; applying and interviewing; keeping the right attitude; networking and resources; adjusting to challenges; financial management; improving performance; and balancing work/family life.

396
LINGUISTIC SOCIETY OF AMERICA
1325 18th Street, NW, Suite 211
Washington, DC 20036-6501
202-835-1714
Fax: 202-835-1717
lsa@lsadc.org
http://www.lsadc.org

• *The Field of Linguistics.* Available at LSA's Web site.

397
LOUISIANA STATE UNIVERSITY SEA GRANT COLLEGE PROGRAM
Communications Office
Wetland Resources Building
Baton Rouge, LA 70803-7507
504-388-6710
Fax: 504-388-6331

• *Marine Science Careers: A Guide to Ocean Opportunities.* 40 pages. An introduction to a wide range of marine career fields and to people working in those fields.

398
MAGAZINE PUBLISHERS OF AMERICA
919 Third Avenue
New York, NY 10022
212-872-3700
Fax: 212-888-4217
http://www.magazine.org

Available at the Web site:

• *Magazine Internship Programs.* Updated annually, includes contact information.

• *Glossary of Magazine Research Terminology.* Defines commonly used terms in the magazine industry.

399
MARINE TECHNOLOGY SOCIETY
1828 L Street, NW, Suite 906
Washington, DC 20036-5104
202-775-5966
Fax: 202-429-9417
mtspubs@aol.com
http://www.mtsociety.org

• *University Curricula in Oceanography and Related Fields.* ($6) 204 pages. Presents data (facilities, programs offered, faculty, student support, and contact information) on 266 colleges and universities, as well as 44 technical schools and institutions.

• *Ocean Opportunities: A Guide to What the Oceans Have to Offer.* ($3)

400
MATHEMATICAL ASSOCIATION OF AMERICA
Service Center
PO Box 90973
Washington, DC 20090

800-331-1622 or 301-617-7800
Fax: 301-206-9787
maahq@maa.org
http://www.maa.org

• *Careers in the Mathematical Sciences.* 8 pages. A discussion by professionals from diverse mathematical settings about their workday, challenges they encounter, and how mathematics directed them toward their careers.

• *More Careers in the Mathematical Sciences.* 8 pages. A discussion by professionals in the field about the variety of occupations open to those with bachelor's or master's degrees in mathematics.

• *Mathematical Scientists at Work.* ($3) 16 pages. Describes the work of the mathematical scientist.

401
MEDICAL LIBRARY ASSOCIATION
65 East Wacker Place, Suite 1900
Chicago, IL 60602-4805
312-419-9094
Fax: 312-419-8950
http://www.mlanet.org

Single copies of the following publications are available free of charge:

• *Careers in Health Sciences Information: The Health Sciences Library Technician.* Describes the work involved, work environment, required education, salary, and employment opportunities.

• *Library Technicians and Assistants.*

Available at the Web site:

• *Library Schools.* Listing of colleges and universities offering courses in health sciences information. Includes course numbers, title, instructor, and scheduled class offerings.

402
MEET THE COMPOSER PUBLICATIONS
2112 Broadway, Suite 505
New York, NY 10023
212-787-3601
http://www.meetthecomposer.org

• *Commissioning Music: A Basic Guide.* 7 pages. Available by mail or online. Defines the term, "commissioning music" and outlines the steps and general fees when commisioning music for a specific purpose or event.

403
MERION PUBLICATIONS, INC.
2900 Horizon Drive
Box 61556
King of Prussia, PA 19406-0956
610-278-1400
otedit@merion.com
http://www.advanceweb.com

Available by mail or accessible on the Web:

• *ADVANCE Publications.* Free to senior students or licensed, registered, or certified practitioners. Available for the following careers: nurses, speech-language pathologists, audiologists, directors of rehabilitation, physical therapists and PT assistants, nurse practitioners, physicians assistants, health information professionals, radiologists, and respiratory care practitioners.

404
MICHIGAN BRICKLAYERS AND ALLIED CRAFTWORKERS TRAINING CENTER
3321 Remy Drive
Lansing, MI 48906
517-886-2221

• *Michigan Bricklayers and Allied Craftworkers Training Center.* Brochure covering the trowel trades, including information on wages and benefits, future outlook, room for advancement, and applying for membership in the Bricklayers and Allied Craftworkers Union.

405
MICHIGAN CHAPTER ASSOCIATED GENERAL CONTRACTORS
2323 North Larch
Lansing, MI 48906
517-371-1550
michigc@ibm.net
http://mi.agc.org

• *2000 Construction Careers Manual.* 69 pages. Apprenticeship and training resource including information on job opportunities, apprenticeship programs, salaries, and job descriptions.

• *Apprenticeship Opportunities in Construction.* Contains contracting job descriptions, including information on work environment, general job tasks, skills and education needed, earnings, outlook, and suggestions for steps to take to enter the field. Also includes self-

assessment guides to help students develop their career path.

• *Build Up! Kit.* Activity worksheets aimed at young students curious about careers in construction and contracting.

• *Michigan Carpenters Apprenticeship and Training Program: Building Futures for Michigan Workers.* Covers entrance requirements, what carpenters do, the advantages to unions, and how to apply for an apprenticeship.

• *You Can Become a Millwright.* Informational brochure about the career, hours and working conditions, pay and benefits, how to become a millwright, and apprenticeship programs available.

• *Career Opportunities: Mechanical Construction.* Developed by the Lansing Mechanical Contractors Association, this brochure covers what it takes to enter the field, career positions available, and lists industry contractors in the Michigan area.

• *Work with the Best.* Information about the Journeyman and Apprentice Training Fund from the Operating Engineers Local 324.

406
MILITARY OPERATIONS RESEARCH SOCIETY
101 South Whiting Street, Suite 202
Alexandria, VA 22304
703-751-7290
Fax: 703-751-8171
morsoffice@aol.com
http://www.mors.org

• *Careers in Military Operations Research.* 8 pages.

407
MINE SAFETY AND HEALTH ADMINISTRATION
Office of Information and Public Affairs
U.S. Department of Labor
4015 Wilson Boulevard, Room 601
Arlington, VA 22203
703-235-1452
Fax: 703-235-4323
http://www.msha.gov

• *Catalog of Training Programs for the Mining Industry.* Discusses cement, mining, and underground coal, among other fields.

408
MINERALS, METALS & MATERIALS SOCIETY, THE
Education Department
184 Thorn Hill Road
Warrendale, PA 15086
724-776-9000
Fax: 724-776-3770
crc@tms.org
http://www.tms.org

• *Materials Science and Engineering: An Exciting Career Field for the Future.* 12 pages. Discusses the future of the field, job opportunities, typical duties, personal qualifications, and education and training. Lists the 80 accredited colleges and universities offering materials/metallurgical engineering programs.

409
MINING AND METALLURGICAL SOCIETY OF AMERICA
Attn: Alan K. Burton
476 Wilson Avenue
Novato, CA 94947
415-924-7441
Fax: 415-924-7463

• *Opportunities for a Career in Mining & Metallurgy.* 304 pages. Discusses the career options in the industry and provides a complete, four-page profile of each educational institution offering a degree in materials/metallurgical engineering.

410
MODERN LANGUAGE ASSOCIATION OF AMERICA
10 Astor Place
New York, NY 10003-6981
212-614-6382
Fax: 212-358-9140
bookorders@mla.org
http://www.mla.org

• *The MLA Guide to the Job Search.* ($10) 156 pages. A handbook for departments, PhDs, and PhD candidates in English and foreign languages.

Available at the Web site:

• *Information for Job Candidates.* Includes a checklist for job seekers, interview advice, and additional sources of information.

411
MUSIC EDUCATORS NATIONAL CONFERENCE
1806 Robert Fulton Drive
Reston, VA 20191-4348

800-336-3768 or 703-860-4000
Fax: 703-860-1531
http://www.menc.org

Available at the Web site:

• *A Career Guide to Music Education.*
Includes information on starting the job
search, locating job openings, tips on
writing resumes, cover letters, and
applications, improving your interview
skills, and selecting and applying to
grad school. Also contains an appendix
of power verbs to improve your resume.

412

MUSIC LIBRARY ASSOCIATION

Bowling Green State University
Jerome Library, Third Floor
Attn: Bonna J. Boettcher
Bowling Green, OH 43403-0179
419-372-9929
Fax: 419-372-7996
bboettc@bgnet.bgsu.edu
http://wwwmusiclibraryassoc.org

• *Directory of Library School Offerings in
Music Librarianship.* Available in print
copies or online.

• *Music Librarianship: Is It For You?* Online
source providing an overview of the
music librarian career, including
employment opportunities, educational
requirements, everyday duties, career
prospects, and sources of additional
information.

413

MUSKEGON COMMUNITY COLLEGE

Education Department
221 South Quarterline Road

Muskegon, MI 49442
231-777-0277
Fax: 231-777-0255

• *Care about Your People? Come Fly with Us
into the World of Early Childhood
Education.*

• *Career Choices in Early Childhood
Education.*

414

MYCOLOGICAL SOCIETY OF
AMERICA

PO Box 19687
New Orleans, LA 70179
504-286-4364
Fax: 504-286-4367
http://www.erin.utoronto.ca/~w3msa

• *What Can You Do with Training in
Mycology?* Poster.

415

NATIONAL ACADEMY OF
OPTICIANRY

8401 Corporate Drive, #605
Landover, MD 20785
800-229-4828 or 301-577-4828
Fax: 301-577-3880
http://www.nao.org/edducal.cfm

The following information is available at
the Web site:

• *Commision on Opticianry Accreditation.*
Directory of accredited programs.

• *National Federation of Opticianry Schools.*
Directory of member schools.

• *State Opticianry Licensing Boards.*

416

NATIONAL ACCREDITING COMMISSION OF COSMETOLOGY ARTS AND SCIENCES
901 North Stuart Street, Suite 900
Arlington, VA 22203-1816
703-527-7600
http://www.naccas.org

The following information can be found at the Web site:

- *List of Accredited Training Schools in Cosmetology Arts.*

- *Where Do I Go From Here?*

417

NATIONAL ACTION COUNCIL FOR MINORITIES IN ENGINEERING, INC.
350 Fifth Avenue, Suite 2212
New York, NY 10118-2299
212-279-2626
Fax: 212-279-1453
http://www.nacme.org

- *Academic Gamesmanship: Becoming a "Master" Engineering Student.* ($1)

- *Design for Excellence: How to Study Smartly.* ($1)

- *Math is Power* Poster. ($10)

- *NACME Research Letters.* ($5)

418

NATIONAL AERONAUTICS AND SPACE ADMINISTRATION
Office of Human Relations and Education
300 E Street, SW
Washington, DC 20546
http://spacelink.nasa.gov

Available on NASA's Web site:

- *Careers in Aerospace Fact Sheet.* Resource for young adults interested in space careers.

- *Careers in Aviation and Aerodynamics.* Career section of NASA's Aeronautics Internet Textbook. Designed for ages K-8.

- *Consider a Career in Aerospace.* Educational poster developed to encourage young women to pursue mathematics, science, engineering, and technology as career possibilities. Provides information about past, present, and future careers in aerospace.

- *Superstars of Modern Aeronautics.* Educational poster designed to encourage students to consider the increased opportunities that education provides as they prepare for future careers.

- *Superstars of Spaceflight.* Poster featuring 15 astronauts who were selected for their unique contributions to the space program.

419

NATIONAL AGRICULTURAL AVIATION ASSOCIATION
1005 E Street, SE
Washington, DC 20003
202-546-5722
Fax: 202-546-5726
information@agaviation.org
http://www.aviation-ag.com

Information packet includes:

- *AG Aviation/AG-Pilot...a Career You Can Grow In.* ($1)

• *Agricultural Aviation Pilot Training.* Listing of organizations offering pilot training courses and schools offering a degree in agricultural aviation.

420

NATIONAL AGRICULTURAL LIBRARY

Alternative Farming Systems
Information Center
U.S. Department of Agriculture
10301 Baltimore Avenue, Room 304
Beltsville, MD 20705-2351
301-504-5724
Fax: 301-504-6409
afsic@nal.usda.gov
http://www.nal.usda.gov/afsic

• *Educational and Training Opportunities in Sustainable Agriculture 2000, 12th edition.* 45 pages. A directory for institutions in the United States and Canada, as well as international opportunities.

Additional resources may be found on the Internet. For on-farm internships, please see http://www.attra.org.

421

NATIONAL AQUARIUM IN BALTIMORE

501 East Pratt Street, Pier 3
Baltimore, MD 21202
410-576-3860
http://www.aqua.org

Available at the Web site:

• *Careers in Aquatic and Marine Science.* Describes general marine-related careers and lists specific job titles found at the National Aquarium in Baltimore. Also includes tips on how to prepare for a

marine-related career and lists sources for additional information.

• *About Marine Mammal Trainers.* Includes information on marine mammals and the methods trainers use to work with them.

422

NATIONAL ARBORIST ASSOCIATION, INC.

3 Perimeter Road, Unit #1
Manchester, NH 03103
800-733-2622 or 603-314-5380
Fax: 603-314-5386
naa@natlarb.com
http://www.natlarb.com

• *Careers in Arboriculture.* 14 pages. Discusses career tracks in arboriculture, career preparation, and employment opportunities.

• *Database of Educational Institutions.* 8 pages. Lists colleges and universities offering arboriculture or related courses.

423

NATIONAL ARCHITECTURAL ACCREDITING BOARD, INC.

1735 New York Avenue, NW
Washington, DC 20006
202-783-2007
Fax: 202-783-2822
info@naab.org
http://www.naab.org

The following information can be found at the Web site:

• *Accredited Programs in Architecture.* Lists accredited programs and indicates program types by identifying the professional degree conferred upon completion of the program.

424
NATIONAL ART EDUCATION ASSOCIATION
1916 Association Drive
Reston, VA 20191-1590
800-299-8321 (Visa/Mastercard orders)
or 703-860-8000
Fax: 703-860-2960
naea@dgs.dgsys.com
http://www.naea-reston.org

• *Teaching Art as a Career.* ($2) Discusses the necessary skills and training to become an art teacher.

• *Your First Job Interview.* ($3.50) 7 pages. Advice for those wanting to teach art at an elementary or secondary school. Covers the application, resume, letters of recommendation, the interview, and more.

425
NATIONAL ASSOCIATION FOR GIRLS AND WOMEN IN SPORT
AAHPERD
PO Box 385
Oxon Hill, MD 20750-0385
800-321-0789 (customer service)
or 800-213-7193 (membership)
Fax: 301-567-9553

• *Leadership Skills for Women in Sport.* ($3)

• *NAGWS Guide to Internship: Climbing the Ladder.* ($5) 52 pages. Lists more than 75 organizations offering sport-related internship programs.

426
NATIONAL ASSOCIATION FOR LAW PLACEMENT
1666 Connecticut Avenue, NW
Suite 325
Washington, DC 20009
202-667-1666
Fax: 202-265-6735
http://www.nalp.org

• *NALP Pro Bono Guide for Law Students.* ($5) 26 pages. Discusses questions to ask prospective employers, the benefits of pro bono work, and related topics.

427
NATIONAL ASSOCIATION FOR THE EDUCATION OF YOUNG CHILDREN
1509 16th Street, NW
Washington, DC 20036-1426
800-424-2460 or 202-232-8777
Fax: 202-328-1846
http://www.naeyc.org/naeyc

• *Careers in Early Childhood Education.* ($.50 each or $12 per 100 copies) Looks at the role of early childhood educators, career options, educational preparation, and personal qualifications.

428
NATIONAL ASSOCIATION OF ADVISORS FOR THE HEALTH PROFESSIONS
PO Box 1518
Champaign, IL 61824-1518
217-355-0063
Fax: 217-355-1287
http://www.naahp.org

- *The Medical School Interview.* ($3) 24 pages. Applicable to anyone interviewing in a professional school admissions system.

- *Write for Success: Preparing a Successful Professional School Application.* ($10) 61 pages. Provides help in writing clearly for tasks related to the health professions application process. Includes suggestions, strategies, and examples.

- *Meeting the Challenge of the MCAT: A Test Preparation Guide.* ($18) 78 pages.

- *Medical Professions Admission Guide: Strategy for Success.* ($19.95) 170 pages.

429

NATIONAL ASSOCIATION OF ANIMAL BREEDERS
401 Bernadette Drive
PO Box 1033
Columbia, MO 65205
573-445-4406
Fax: 573-446-2279
naab-css@naab-css.org
http://www.naab-css.org

- *Exciting Career Opportunities in Artificial Insemination.* 7 pages. Lists various job titles for a number of areas.

430

NATIONAL ASSOCIATION OF BIOLOGY TEACHERS
12030 Sunrise Valley Drive, Suite 110
Reston, VA 20191
703-264-9696
Fax: 703-264-7778
http://www.nabt.org

- *Careers in Biology: An Introduction.* 4 pages. Highlights research, technology, and educational opportunities in the biology profession.

- *Biotechnology—Careers for the 21st Century.* ($10) A videotape for middle and high school students. Explores the career opportunities in the field of biotechnology.

431

NATIONAL ASSOCIATION OF BOARDS OF PHARMACY
Foreign Pharmacy Graduate
Examination Committee
700 Busse Highway
Park Ridge, IL 60068
847-698-6227
http://www.nabp.net

Available at the Web site:

- *FPGEC Certification Program Information Booklet.* 30 pages. Includes general certification information, application and qualifying procedures, and examination specifics. Updated annually.

432

NATIONAL ASSOCIATION OF BROADCASTERS
1771 N Street, NW
Washington, DC 20036-2891
800-214-1328
Fax: 202-429-4199
irc@nab.org
http://www.nab.org

- *Careers in Radio.* ($4)

- *Careers in Television.* ($4) Describes the key jobs found in radio and television, as well as the educational requirements and job-related experience required for each.

433

NATIONAL ASSOCIATION OF CHAIN DRUG STORES

413 North Lee Street
PO Box 1417-D49
Alexandria, VA 22313-1480
703-549-3001
Fax: 703-836-4869
http://www.nacds.org

Available at the Web site:

• *Careers in Pharmacy.* Covers industry statistics, educational and training requirements, work environments, typical locations, salary statistics, and tips on breaking into a career in pharmacy. Includes an online listing of pharmaceutical schools in the United States, listed by state.

434

NATIONAL ASSOCIATION OF COLLEGE ADMISSION COUNSELORS

1631 Prince Street
Alexandria, VA 22314-2818
703-836-2222
Fax: 703-836-8015
http://www.nacac.com

• *A Guide to the College Admission Process.* ($6)

435

NATIONAL ASSOCIATION OF DENTAL ASSISTANTS

900 South Washington Street, Suite G-13
Falls Church, VA 22046
703-237-8616

• *Salary Survey.* ($7) 2 pages. Lists job titles, types of practice, and salaries by state. Home study courses related to dentistry also available.

436

NATIONAL ASSOCIATION OF DENTAL LABORATORIES

8201 Greensboro Drive, Suite 300
McLean, VA 22102
703-610-9035
Fax: 703-610-9005
nadl@nadl.org
http://www.nadl.org

The following are available at the Association's Web site:

• *The Art and Science of Dental Laboratory Technology.* Resource examining the field of dental laboratory technology. Includes information on the art, science, necessary skills, employment outlook, work setting, tips on getting started, earnings, and sources of additional information.

• *Accredited Dental Laboratory Technology Educational Programs.*

437

NATIONAL ASSOCIATION OF ELEMENTARY SCHOOL PRINCIPALS

1615 Duke Street
Alexandria, VA 22314-3483
703-684-3345

• *Principal K-8.* Brochure of information about the principal profession and what abilities and skills are needed for the job. Also includes information on the working conditions, average salary, the demand outlook, how best to prepare for a job in the field, and additional sources of information.

438
NATIONAL ASSOCIATION OF EXECUTIVE SECRETARIES AND ADMINISTRATIVE ASSISTANTS
900 South Washington Street, Suite G-13
Falls Church, VA 22046
703-237-8616
Fax: 703-533-1153
naesaa@erols.com
http://www.naesaa.com

• *Improving Communication in the Workplace.* ($9.50) 54 pages. A how-to book for administrative professionals on improving communication in the workplace.

• *Biennial Salary Survey.* ($7) Lists salaries of executive secretaries and administrative assistants.

• *What's in a Name?* ($6.50)

439
NATIONAL ASSOCIATION OF INDEPENDENT COLLEGES AND UNIVERSITIES
1025 Connecticut Avenue, NW, Suite 700
Washington, DC 20036
202-785-8866
Fax: 202-835-0003
http://www.naicu.edu

• *10 Facts About Tuition at Independent Colleges and Universities*

• *Independent Colleges and Universities: A National Profile.* 19 pages. Contains sections on minority students, family income, college costs, student financial aid, scholarships, degree completion rates, and other topics.

440
NATIONAL ASSOCIATION OF INDEPENDENT SCHOOLS
Assistant to the Director of Career Paths and Gender Equity Services
1620 L Street, NW, 11th Floor
Washington, DC 20036-5605
202-973-9700
Fax: 202-973-9790
http://www.nais.org

• *Teaching Abroad.* A packet containing employment sources for overseas teachers, overview of overseas teaching opportunities, listing of NAIS affiliated schools, and more.

• *Intern and Teaching Fellow Programs in Independent Schools.* 40 pages. List of schools.

The following packet is available in a print and online version:

• *Getting Started.* A packet containing the NAIS guide to finding the right independent school job;

• *Backgrounder: Teachers at Independent Schools;* and

• *NAIS School Leadership Group Resource List for Teacher Candidates*, which lists teacher placement agencies, available directories of schools, and more.

441
NATIONAL ASSOCIATION OF LEGAL ASSISTANTS
1516 South Boston, Suite 200
Tulsa, OK 74119-4013

918-587-6828
Fax: 918-582-6772
nalanet@nala.org
http://www.nala.org

• *What is a Legal Assistant?* 6 pages.
Discusses career and employment
opportunities, education and training,
and certification information.

• *How to Choose a Paralegal Education
Program.* 8 pages. Describes paralegal
education programs and the paralegal
school approval process of the American
Bar Association.

442

NATIONAL ASSOCIATION OF LETTER CARRIERS

Information Center
100 Indiana Avenue, NW
Washington, DC 20001
202-393-4695

• *Carrying the Mail: A Career in Public
Service.* 8 pages. Addresses a carrier's
duties, wages and benefits, and qualifications, as well as how to apply for a
position.

443

NATIONAL ASSOCIATION OF PEDIATRIC NURSE ASSOCIATES AND PRACTITIONERS

1101 Kings Highway North, Suite 206
Cherry Hill, NJ 08034
856-667-1773
Fax: 856-667-7187
info@napnap.org
http://www.napnap.org

• *Pediatric Nurse Practitioner School List.* 17
pages. Lists for each institution programs

and degrees offered, the academic schedule, and the minimum prerequisites.

• *Scope of Practice.* ($2.50) Outlines basic
functions and responsibilities of pediatric nurse associates and practitioners.

444

NATIONAL ASSOCIATION OF PROFESSIONAL BAND INSTRUMENT REPAIR TECHNICIANS

PO Box 51
Normal, IL 61761-0051
309-452-4257
Fax: 309-452-4825
chagler@napbirt.org
http://www.napbirt.org

Information on band instrument repair
and schools is available at the
Association's Web site or by mail or
phone.

• *Survey of Musical Instrument Repair
Schools.*

445

NATIONAL ASSOCIATION OF PROFESSIONAL INSURANCE AGENTS

400 North Washington Street
Alexandria, VA 22314
703-836-9340
Fax: 703-836-1279
piaweb@pianet.org
http://www.pianet.com

• *Straight Talk About Careers in Insurance.* 8
pages. Describes career opportunities in
the property and casualty insurance
industry.

446

NATIONAL ASSOCIATION OF PURCHASING MANAGEMENT

2055 East Centennial Circle
PO Box 22160
Tempe AZ 85285-2160
800-888-6276
Fax: 480-752-2229
http://www.napm.org

The following publications are available at the Association's Web site.

• *Colleges and Universities Offering Purchasing/Supply Management Courses.*

• *Purchasing and Supply Management Careers.* Discusses duties and responsibilities, opportunities for advancement, salary, personal characteristics, and required education and training.

447

NATIONAL ASSOCIATION OF SCHOOLS OF ART AND DESIGN

Publications Department
11250 Roger Bacon Drive, Suite 21
Reston, VA 20190
703-437-0700
Fax: 703-437-6312
info@arts-accredit.org
http://www.arts-accredit.org/
nasad/default.htm

• *Work of Arts Executives in Higher Education.* Covers duties of those who direct arts programs in higher education.

• *Brief Guide to Art and Design Studies.* SASE. Describes opportunities in the art and design field.

448

NATIONAL ASSOCIATION OF SCHOOLS OF DANCE

11250 Roger Bacon Drive, Suite 21
Reston, VA 20190
703-437-0700
Fax: 703-437-6312
info@arts-accredit.org
http://www.arts-accredit.org

• *Directory.* ($5) Lists accredited institutions and dance major programs. Includes contact information for all member institutions.

• *Handbook.* ($10) Includes NASD standards for non-degree granting, baccalaureate, and graduate programs in dance.

Available at the Web site:

• *Frequently Asked Questions.* Includes information about NASD, accreditation procedure, choosing a school, loan and scholarship application, and how best to prepare for a dance major.

• *Listing of Accredited Institutions for Dance.* Listed by name or state.

449

NATIONAL ASSOCIATION OF SCHOOLS OF MUSIC

11250 Roger Bacon Drive, Suite 21
Reston, VA 20190
703-437-0700
Fax: 703-437-6312
info@arts-accredit.org
http://www.arts-accredit.org

Available at the Web site:

• *Frequently Asked Questions.* Includes information on NASM, how schools are ranked, how to choose a school, accreditation procedure, scholarship and grant application, and how best to prepare for a music major.

• *Listing of Accredited Institutions of Music.* Listed by name or state.

450

NATIONAL ASSOCIATION OF SCHOOLS OF PUBLIC AFFAIRS AND ADMINISTRATION
1120 G Street, NW, Suite 730
Washington, DC 20005
202-628-8965
Fax: 202-626-4978
naspaa@naspaa.org
http://www.naspaa.org

• *Annual Roster of Accredited Programs.* 16 pages.

451

NATIONAL ASSOCIATION OF SCHOOLS OF THEATRE
11250 Roger Bacon Drive, Suite 21
Reston, VA 20190
703-437-0700
Fax: 703-437-6312
info@arts-accredit.org
http://www.arts-accredit.org

• *Directory.* ($10) Lists accredited institutions and theatre degree programs. Includes contact information for all member institutions.

• *Handbook.* ($10) Includes NAST standards for non-degree granting, baccalaureate, community/junior college, and graduate programs in theatre.

Available at the Web site:

• *Frequently Asked Questions.* Includes information about NAST, how schools are ranked, accreditation procedures, scholarship and loan application, and how best to prepare for a theatre degree.

• *Listing of Accredited Institutions of Theatre.* Listed by name or state.

452

NATIONAL ASSOCIATION OF SCIENCE WRITERS
PO Box 294
Greenlawn, NY 11740
631-757-5664
Fax: 631-757-0069
http://www.nasw.org

Available at the Web site:

• *Advice for Beginning Science Writers.* Important issues discussed on the NASW mailing list, including tips on how to break into a scientific writing career, training required, how to make job transitions, and the distinction between science journalism and science writing.

453

NATIONAL ASSOCIATION OF SECONDARY SCHOOL PRINCIPALS
1904 Association Drive
Reston, VA 20191-1537
703-860-0200
Fax: 703-476-5432
http://www.nassp.org

• *Tips for Aspiring Principals.*

454

NATIONAL ASSOCIATION OF SOCIAL WORKERS
750 First Street, NE, Suite 700
Washington, DC 20002-4241
800-638-8779 or 202-408-8600
Fax: 202-336-8331
http://www.naswdc.org

Available at the Web site:

• *Choices: Careers in Social Work.* Contains information on educational requirements and social work careers.

455

NATIONAL ASSOCIATION OF SPORT AND PHYSICAL EDUCATION
1900 Association Drive
Reston, VA 20191
703-476-3410
Fax: 703-476-8316
naspe@aahperd.org
http://www.aahperd.org/naspe.html

• *List of NASPE-Approved Schools Offering Degrees in Physical Education, Sports Management, and Coaching.*

• *Careers in Physical Education, Sports and Related Areas.* 5 pages. SASE. Lists various physical education and sport occupations, the education required, the compensation range, and the occupational outlook.

456

NATIONAL ASSOCIATION OF STUDENT PERSONNEL ADMINISTRATORS
1875 Connecticut Avenue, NW, Suite 418
Washington, DC 20009-5728

202-265-7500
Fax: 202-797-1157
office@naspa.org
http://www.naspa.org

• *Consider a Career in College Student Affairs.* ($7) 11 pages. Designed to assist college students in exploring the field of student affairs.

457

NATIONAL ASSOCIATION OF WOMEN IN CONSTRUCTION
327 South Adams Street
Ft. Worth, TX 76104-1081
817-877-5551
Fax: 817-877-0324
nawic@nawic.org
http://www.nawic.org

• *Set Your Sights.* Brochure for women interested in a career in construction. Covers industry outlook, opportunities available in skilled trades, technical areas, and office occupations.

Available at the Web site:

• *NAWIC and the Woman in Construction.* Explains how NAWIC helps women in the construction industry enhance their careers by associating with other women in construction, sharing knowledge and educational opportunities, networking with other organizations, and promoting community involvement.

458

NATIONAL ATHLETIC TRAINERS' ASSOCIATION
2952 Stemmons Freeway, Suite 200
Dallas, TX 75247-6196
214-637-6282

Fax: 214-637-2206
http://www.nata.org

The following publications are available at the Association's Web site:

- *What is an Athletic Trainer?* Discusses education, certification, a typical day in the life of an athletic trainer, and female trainers.

- *Accredited Athletic Training Educaiton Programs.*

459
NATIONAL AUCTIONEERS ASSOCIATION

8880 Ballentine
Overland Park, KS 66214-1985
913-541-8084
Fax: 913-894-5281
naahq@aol.com
http://www.auctioneers.org

- *The Auction Profession.* 4 pages. Discusses the work, necessary personal traits, education and licensing.

460
NATIONAL AUTOMOBILE DEALERS ASSOCIATION

8400 Westpark Drive
McLean, VA 22102-3591
703-821-7000
consumer@nada.org
http://www.nada.org/

The following publication is available in both a print and online version.

- *What's the Deal on Dealerships?* (NCB-030). 12 pages. Explains administrative

service, parts, and sales careers, as well as how to prepare for a job.

461
NATIONAL AUTOMOTIVE TECHNICIANS EDUCATION FOUNDATION, INC.

13505 Dulles Technology Drive, Suite 2
Herndon, VA 20171-3421
703-713-0100
Fax: 703-713-3919

- *Automobile Technician: Realize Your Dream.*

- *Autobody Technician: Realize Your Dream.*

- *Truck Technician: Realize Your Dream.*

- *Parts Specialist: Realize Your Dream.*

- *AFV Technician: Realize Your Dream.*

462
NATIONAL BUSINESS ASSOCIATION

PO Box 700728
Dallas, TX 75370
800-456-0440
Fax: 972-960-9149
admin.asst@nationalbusiness.org
http://www.nationalbusiness.org

Available on diskette only, the following are part of the First Step Software Series..

- *First Step Review.* For PC or Macintosh. Assesses one's chance of receiving a loan backed by the Small Business Association (SBA).

- *First Step Balance Sheet.* ($5) For PCs only. Designed to help prepare balance sheets for general accounting purposes.

• *First Step Projected Profit or Loss Statement.* ($5) For PCs only. Offers an exact duplicate of the SBA Operating Plan Forecast form used by the SBA as part of the loan eligibility process.

• *First Step Cash Flow Analysis.* ($5) For PCs only. Helps estimate the expected profit or loss for the month or year.

• *First Step Business Plan.* ($5) For PCs only.

463

NATIONAL CABLE TELEVISION ASSOCIATION

1724 Massachusetts Avenue, NW
Washington, DC 20036-3695
202-775-3629
Fax: 202-775-1055
http://www.cablecareersnetwork.com

Available on the online Cable Careers Network:

• *Career Center.* Includes links to information on interviewing tips, resume preparation, setting performance expectations, planning your career path, management strategies, self assessment, and communication strategies.

464

NATIONAL CARTOONISTS SOCIETY

Columbus Circle Station
PO Box 20267
New York, NY 10023
http://www.reuben.org/

The Society offers the following online publication:

• *Wanna be a Cartoonist?* Tips on becoming a cartoonist.

465

NATIONAL CENTER FOR EDUCATION STATISTICS

ED Pubs
PO Box 1398
Jessup, MD 20794-1398
877-576-7734
Fax: 301-470-1244
edpubs@inet.ed.gov
http://nces.ed.gov

• *Digest of Education Statistics, 1998.* Single copies available free in print form or accessible online. Summary of the information on education today, including the different levels of learning, federal programs for education and related activities, outcomes of education, international comparisons, and learning resources and technology.

466

NATIONAL CHILD CARE INFORMATION CENTER

243 Church Street, NW, 2nd Floor
Vienna, VA 22180
800-616-2242
Fax: 800-716-2242
http://nccic.org

Available at the Web site:

• *Frequently Asked Questions.* Covers topics such as child care funding, starting a career or child care center, and child care demographics.

467

NATIONAL CLEARINGHOUSE FOR ESL LITERACY EDUCATION
Product Orders
4640 40th Street, NW
Washington, DC 20016-1859
202-362-0700, ext 200
Fax: 202-363-7204
ncle@cal.org
http://www.cal.org/ncle

An organization focusing on literacy education for adults and out-of-school youth learning English as a second language. For a complete publications list and order form, call, write, or send an e-mail request.

• *Learning to Work in a New Land: A Review and Sourcebook for Vocational and Workplace ESL.* ($7) 165 pages.

• *The Vocational Classroom: A Great Place to Learn English.* ($4) 31 pages.

• *ERIC Digest, ERIC Q&A*, and annotated bibliography topics include but are not limited to:

• *Adult ESL Learner Assessment: Purposes and Tools.*

• *English Plus and Official English: Linguistic Diversity in the United States.*

• *Refugees as English Language Learners: Issues and Concerns.*

• *Current Terms in Adult ESL Literacy.*

• *Improving ESL Learners' Listening Skills: At the Workplace and Beyond.*

• *Creating a Professional Workforce in Adult ESL Literacy.*

• *Union Sponsored Workplace ESL Instruction.*

468

NATIONAL CLEARINGHOUSE FOR PROFESSIONS IN SPECIAL EDUCATION
1920 Association Drive
Reston, VA 20191-1589
800-641-7824 or 703-264-9476
Fax: 703-264-1637
ncpse@cec.sped.org
http://www.specialedcareers.org

Available at the Web site:

• *Career Center.* Links to information on financial aid resources, recruiters, professional advice to starting a career in special education, preparation tips, licensing and educational requirements, salary statistics, and state licensing agencies.

469

NATIONAL CLEARINGHOUSE OF REHABILITATION TRAINING MATERIALS
Oklahoma State University
5202 Richmond Hill Drive
Stillwater, OK 74078-4080
800-223-5219 or 405-624-7650
Fax: 405-624-0695
http://www.nchrtm.okstate.edu

The following text is downloadable off the Web site:

• *Careers in Rehabilitation: Rehabilitation Related Professions.*

470

NATIONAL COALITION FOR CHURCH VOCATIONS
5420 South Cornell Avenue, # 105

Chicago, IL 60615-5604
800-671-NCCV
Fax: 312-663-5030
nccv400@aol.com
http://www.nccv-vocations.org

The following 32-page booklets cost $2 each:

- *Brothers.*
- *Diocesan Priests.*
- *Lay Ministers.*
- *Missionaries.*
- *Religious Priests.*
- *Sisters.*

471

NATIONAL COLLEGIATE ATHLETIC ASSOCIATION

PO Box 781046
Indianapolis, IN 46278-8046
800-638-3731
Fax: 317-471-8230
http://www.ncaa.org

- *Guide for the College-Bound Student-Athlete.* (first copy is free; $9.50 for 25 copies) 15 pages. Summarizes the rules and regulations of the game in easy-to-read form. Also addresses academic eligibility, core-course requirements, financial aid, recruiting, professionalism, and other topics.

- *A Career in Professional Athletics.* ($18 for 25 copies) Contains practical and useful information to assist athletes making the transition to a professional sports career.

472

NATIONAL COMMISSION FOR COOPERATIVE EDUCATION

360 Huntington Avenue, 384 CP
Boston, MA 02115
617-373-3770
Fax: 617-373-3463
http://www.co-op.edu

- *Advantages of Cooperative Education.* 6 pages. Lists advantages of cooperative education to the student, society, employers, and educational institutions. Briefly describes cooperative education.

- *Choosing Your College for Today...For the Future...a Student/Parent Guide to Cooperative Education.* 12 pages. Includes a list of 345 colleges with cooperative education programs.

- *Where Do You Plan to Be Five Years after You Graduate From College?* 4 pages. Applicable to college freshmen. Features career success stories from outstanding graduates, as well as information about professional employment opportunities.

473

NATIONAL COMMITTEE ON PAY EQUITY

1126 16th Street, NW, Suite 411
Washington, DC 20036
202-331-7343
Fax: 202-331-7406
fairpay@aol.com
http://feminist.com/fairpay

For a complete publications and materials list and order form, call, write, or send an e-mail request.

• *Background on the Wage Gap.* ($2) 5 pages. Clarifies some common misconceptions about the wage gap and provides information about earnings by age, education, sex, and race/ethnicity.

• *Pay Equity Bibliography and Resource List.* ($4) 16 pages. More than 100 citations of books, articles, and other publications on pay equity.

• *Bargaining for Pay Equity: A Strategy Manual.* ($9) 120 pages. A collection of stories of union struggles for pay equity. Serves as a how-to manual for developing winning pay equity campaigns.

• *Job Evaluation: A Tool for Pay Equity.* ($7) A basic introduction to job evaluations. Includes definitions, brief descriptions of different types of systems, and suggestions on working with consultants.

• *Closing the Wage Gap: An International Perspective.* ($2) 16 pages. An overview of pay equity policies and activity in more than 20 international jurisdictions.

• *Fair Pay Action Kit.* ($10) 48 pages. Contains fact sheets, background information on pay equity, and suggestions for organizing to eliminate sex- and race-based wage discrimination.

The following factsheets (1995-1997) are available:

• *Questions & Answers on Pay Equity.*

• *The Wage Gap: 1995.*

• *Information on the Fair Pay Act.*

• *The Contingent Workforce.*

• *Work & Retirement.*

• *Women, Family, Future Trends: A Selective Research Overview.*

474
NATIONAL COMMUNICATION ASSOCIATION

NCA Publication Center
PO Box 361
Annapolis Junction, MD 20701-0361
301-362-3912
Fax: 301-206-9789
http://www.natcom.org/studies

• *Pathways to Careers in Communication.* ($2) 20 pages. Looks at different fields entered by people with a communication degree, as well as the outlook and salary for a number of positions. (Order #410)

Available online:

• *Competent Communication: K-12 Speaking, Listening and Media Literacy Standards and Competency Standards.* Concentrates on speaking, listening, and media literacy standards; their importance; the criteria for selecting them; and their implementation.

475
NATIONAL CONFERENCE OF EDITORIAL WRITERS

6223 Executive Boulevard
Rockville, MD 20852-3906
301-984-3015
Fax: 301-231-0026
ncewhgs@erols.com
http://www.ncew.org/

• *So You Want to Know about Editorial Writing: Some Questions and Answers....* First five copies are free. Must send a business sized SASE. Describes how to become an editorial writer, what editorial writers do, and how to prepare for an editorial writing career.

476

NATIONAL CONSORTIUM FOR GRADUATE DEGREES FOR MINORITIES IN ENGINEERING AND SCIENCE, INC.

PO Box 537
Notre Dame, IN 46556
219-631-7771
Fax: 219-297-1486
http://www.nd.edu/~gem/

• *Graduate Financial Resources in Engineering and Science.* ($3) Listings on over 200 financial aid sources for minority students pursuing graduate studies in engineering or science disciplines. Eligibility requirements and funding amounts are included.

• *Making the Grade in Graduate School: Survival Strategy 101.* ($5) Meets the informational needs of students desiring to pursue a doctoral degree with an emphasis on the needs of minority students. Also useful for counselors, advisors, mentors, and administrators who are interested in improving the retention and graduation rates of minority graduate students.

• *Minority Student Graduate School Information Kit.* ($8) Includes articles and publications on graduate studies.

• *Successfully Negotiating the Graduate School Process.* ($3) Clarifies the pathways to advanced education.

• *Your Internship Is As Good As You Make It: A Practical Guide.* ($5) Provides an overview of internships in the context of planning a career. Designed to identify the nature of interning from the perspectives of the student intern and the industrial/governmental sponsor. Provides information on how to make the internship experience the catalyst to a career/networking relationship.

477

NATIONAL COUNCIL FOR ACCREDITATION OF TEACHER EDUCATION

2010 Massachusetts Avenue, NW
Suite 500
Washington, DC 20036-1023
202-466-7496
Fax: 202-296-6620
ncate@ncate.org
http://www.ncate.org

• *List of Professionally Accredited Schools, Colleges, and Departments of Education.* 4 pages. Contains the names of institutions whose professional education units (schools, departments, or colleges of education) or programs have been accredited by NCATE.

• *Professionally Accredited Non-Traditional Routes to Teaching.* 8 pages. Lists accredited schools of education that offer teacher training to students with a bachelor's degree.

• *Quality Assurance for the Teaching Profession.* 16 pages. Describes the NCATE, necessary skills for teaching, and professional accreditation, and other topics.

478
NATIONAL COUNCIL OF CHURCHES
Professional Church Leadership
475 Riverside Drive, Room 812
New York, NY 10115
212-870-2298
Fax: 212-870-2030
news@ncccusa.org
http://www.ncccusa.org

• *Ministry Options.* 8 pages. Lists church-related vocations, applicable personality types, and work-setting preferences.

• *What Are You Going to Do with the Rest of Your Life?* 8 pages. Discusses how to choose your life work, illustrates the life of a church leader, and includes sources for additional information.

479
NATIONAL COUNCIL OF LA RAZA
Distribution Center
PO Box 291
Anapolis Junction, MD 20701-0291
301-604-7983
Fax: 301-604-0158
http://www.nclr.org

• *Hispanics in the Workforce, Part I.* (H36) ($5) 35 pages. Examines the labor market statistics of Hispanics, including demographics affecting employment levels. Includes information on employment patterns, unemployment, average earnings, and policy implications.

• *Hispanics in the Workforce, Part II: Hispanic Women.* (H37) ($5) 26 pages. Analyzes the experiences of Hispanic women in the labor market, including their employment levels, occupations, earnings, and unemployment statistics.

Also includes information on fertility rates, poverty levels, education, occupational distribution, policy implications, and other labor market factors.

• *Hispanics in the Workforce, Part III: Hispanic Youth.* (H38) ($5) 23 pages. Examines population trends, educational levels, and poverty rates as a background for understanding the labor market performance of Hispanic youth. Includes labor market status, obstacles, reviews federal responses, and policy implications.

• *Hispanics in the Labor Force: A Chart Book.* ($5) 25 pages. Illustrates Hispanic representation in 13 occupational categories. Shows current status and projected outlook for the next few decades.

480
NATIONAL COUNCIL OF TEACHERS OF ENGLISH
1111 West Kenyon Road
Urbana, IL 61801-1096
800-369-6283 or 217-278-3634
Fax: 217-278-3760
mdavis@ncte.org
http://www.ncte.org

NCTE's *Career Packet* includes:

• *The Average Teacher's Salary in 1996-1997.* Lists salaries by state.

• *The College Board: Guide to 150 Popular College Majors.* Discusses preparation programs, postgraduate certification, opportunities in teaching, and exploration of teaching.

• *Don't Leave Teaching: Examine Other Teaching-Related Careers.* Suggestions for teaching careers outside the typical classroom.

- *ECS Gets Teacher Grant.* Discusses the Education Commission's plan.

- *Notes to My Daughter, The New English Teacher.* Tips from an experienced English teacher to his daughter just starting out.

- *SLATE Starter Sheet: Easing the Transition from College to Classroom.* Examines what it was like to go from college to the classroom, comparing experiences in 1964 and today.

- *Suggested Bibliography.* Annotated bibliography of NCTE publications concerning careers along with a list of other sources for teaching and other English-related careers.

- *Teacher Shortage.* Discusses PBS' productions about the teacher shortage in America.

- *Tips for the Beginning Teacher.*

- *U.S. Enrollment Surge Shifts to High Schools.* Depicts the all-time high enrollment rates in America's schools.

- *What Can You Do With an English Major?* Discusses the connection between majoring in English and working in the "real world" from several perspectives.

481
NATIONAL COUNCIL OF TEACHERS OF MATHEMATICS
1906 Association Drive
Reston, VA 20191
800-235-7566 (orders only)
or 703-620-9840
Fax: 703-476-2970
nctm@nctm.org
http://www.nctm.org

Contents of the *Career Information Packet:*

- *Cover Letter.* 1 page.

- *Resources for Mathematical Science Careers.* 2 pages.

- *Certification of Mathematics and Science Teachers, Grades 9-12.* 1 page.

- *Certification of Mathematics and Science Teachers, Grades 7-8.* 1 page.

- *Percent of Mathematics and Science Teachers with Major or Minor, Grades 7-12.* 1 page.

- *Mathematics or Science Teachers with Major in Assigned Field, Grades 7-12.* 1 page.

- *State Licensing Agencies.* 1 page.

- *Going the Alternative Route.* 1 page.

- *Jobs Online.* 4 pages.

- *Invest in Yourself: NCTM Membership Brochure.*

- *NCTM Educational Materials and Products Catalog.*

- *Shape the Future.* Brochure.

- *NCTM Beliefs Statement.* 1 page.

- *Recruiting New Teachers, Inc.* 2 pages.

482
NATIONAL COURT REPORTERS ASSOCIATION
8224 Old Courthouse Road
Vienna, VA 22182-3808
800-272-6272 or 703-556-6572
Fax: 703-556-6291
msic@ncrahq.org
http://www.verbatimreporters.com
or http://www.bestfutures.com

• *Court Reporting as a Career.* 8 pages. Includes general information on the field such as future outlook, skills required, and employment options.

• *NCRA List of Approved Court Reporter Training Programs.* Lists programs by state.

483

NATIONAL ENERGY INFORMATION CENTER

United States Department of Energy
1000 Independence Avenue, SW
Washington, DC 37831
202-586-8800
Fax: 202-586-0727
infoctr@eia.doe.gov
http://www.eia.doe.gov

• *Energy Education Resources: Kindergarten Through 12th Grade.* Provides free or low-cost energy-related educational materials to kindergarten through 12th grade students and educators.

484

NATIONAL FEDERATION OF LICENSED PRACTICAL NURSES, INC.

893 West Highway 70, Suite 202
Garner, NC 27529
919-779-0046
Fax: 919-779-5642
http://www.nflpn.org

• *A Profile of Practical Nursing.* 6 pages. Describes what LPNs actually do, where they work, and what they earn. Also discusses the education required, school selection, licensure, continuing education, and general information about NFLPN.

485

NATIONAL FEDERATION OF PARALEGAL ASSOCIATIONS

PO Box 33108
Kansas City, MO 64114
816-941-4000
Fax: 816-941-2725
info@paralegals.org
http://www.paralegals.org

The following are available on the Federation's Web site:

• *Directory of Paralegal Education Programs.* Lists educational institutions that offer paralegal training and includes "How to Choose a Paralegal Education Program."

• *What is a Paralegal?* Defines paralegal and legal assistants by discussing job responsibilities, salaries, office locations, and typical background training.

• *How to Choose a Paralegal Education Program.* Outlines methods for evaluating paralegal education programs.

486

NATIONAL FUNERAL DIRECTORS ASSOCIATION

13625 Bishop's Drive
Brookfield, WI 53005
800-228-6332 or 262-789-1880
Fax: 262-789-6977
nfda@nfda.org
http://www.nfda.org

The following is available at the Web site:

• *Are You Interested in a Career in Funeral Service?* Describes the duties and responsibilities, educational requirements, and career opportunities of a funeral service professional. Includes a list of mortuary science programs.

• *Schools of Mortuary Science.* Lists of ABSFE accredited mortuary colleges and programs.

• *State Funeral Service Boards and Licensing Requirements.* Lists by state the type of license required, educational and apprenticeship requirements, and state board addresses.

• *Funeral Service Scholarships.* Lists scholarships available for funeral service students.

487
NATIONAL HEALTH COUNCIL
1730 M Street, NW, Suite 500
Washington, DC 20036-4505
202-785-3910
Fax: 202-785-5923
http://www.nhcouncil.org

• *270 Ways to Put Your Talent to Work in the Health Field.* ($15) Lists job descriptions and educational requirements for health professions ranging from art therapists and clinical chemists to nurse practioners and physicians. Also lists sources of information on training schools and financial aid programs for health professions.

488
NATIONAL HOME STUDY COUNCIL
1601 18th Street, NW
Washington, DC 20009
202-234-5100

• *Accredited Home-Study Schools.*

489
NATIONAL MANAGEMENT ASSOCIATION
2210 Arbor Boulevard
Dayton OH 45439-1580
937-294-0421
Fax: 937-294-2374
http://www.nma1.org

• *Management As a Career.* 6 pages. Describes the roles and duties of managers, careers in the field, and keys to success.

490
NATIONAL MUSEUM OF NATURAL HISTORY
Smithsonian Institution
10th Street and Constitution Avenue, NW
Washington, DC 20560-0166
202-357-4548
Fax: 202-786-2563
http://www.nmnh.si.edu

Available at the Web site:

• *Research Training Program.* Opportunities for undergraduate students to actively participate in the research investigations of prominent museum scientists. Includes program summary, application instructions, FAQs, and online application form.

• *Summer Fieldwork Opportunities in Anthropology.* Suggests ways teachers, students, and the general public can become personally involved in the field of anthropology through field schools and research organizations.

• *Sources for Information on Careers in Biology, Conservation, and Oceanography.* 15 pages.

491
NATIONAL PARALEGAL ASSOCIATION
PO Box 406
Solebury, PA 18963
215-297-8333
Fax: 215-297-8358
admin@nationalparalegal.org
http://www.nationalparalegal.org

• *Local Paralegal Club Directory.* ($5) Lists over 200 local paralegal clubs.

• *Paralegal Career Guide.* ($8) Contains information about the profession including, type of work involved, educational requirements, salary ranges, working conditions, and more.

• *Paralegal Schools: State Listings.* ($2.50 each; $3.50 each for schools in NY, PA, TX, and CA) Each state listing includes universities, vocational schools, proprietary institutions, community colleges, and correspondence schools; ABA-approved programs are earmarked.

• *Paralegal Information Packet.* (Free with SASE with $.55 postage) Contains details about membership in the National Paralegal Association, information about the profession, and includes a list of publications available from the organization.

• *Paralegal Employment Network.* (Free with SASE) Information about employment opportunities available to paralegals of all levels. Includes application and more details.

492
NATIONAL PARK SERVICE
1849 C Street, NW
Washington, DC 20240
202-208-6843
http://www.nps.gov

Available at the Web site:

• *National Park Service Careers.* Contains information about the National Park Service; describes career opportunities in the field; covers employment benefits and the application and hiring process; and lists federal job information.

493
NATIONAL PEST MANAGEMENT ASSOCIATION
Resource Center
8100 Oak Street
Dunn Loring, VA 22027
800-678-6722 or 703-573-8330
Fax: 703-573-4116
http://www.pestworld.org

• *Multilingual Sanitation Card.* ($10) Laminated posters for use in the hospitality industry to educate employees about pest prevention and guide sanitation. Available in seven different languages: Cambodian, Chinese, Japanese, Korean, English, Spanish, and Vietnamese.

• *Sanitation Guidelines for the Pest Control Operator.* ($10) Handbook prepared to aid pest control workers pass sanitation inspections.

494

NATIONAL PRESS PHOTOGRAPHERS ASSOCIATION, INC.
3200 Croasdaile Drive, Suite 306
Durham, NC 27705
919-383-7246
Fax: 919-383-7261
nppa@mindspring.com
http://www.nppa.org

Specify request for scholarship, career, or membership information. Enclose a SASE for scholarship information.

• *Careers in Photojournalism.* 4 pages. Addresses the necessary skills, personal attributes, required education, employment opportunities, and employment outlook.

• *National Press Photographers Association.* Describes NPPA, member benefits, activities, and education and student programs.

• *NPPA Membership Application.*

• *Scholarships in Photojournalism.* 6 pages. Lists scholarships and awards available and includes an application form.

495

NATIONAL RECREATION AND PARK ASSOCIATION
NRPA Book Center
22377 Belmont Ridge Road
Ashburn, VA 20148
703-858-0784
Fax: 703-858-0794
jhoward@nrpa.org
http://www.activeparks.org

• *Preparing for a Career in Therapeutic Recreation.* ($7.50) 21 pages. Describes the continuum of service within thera-

peutic recreation and standards for certification. Lists colleges and universities offering therapeutic recreation programs, including those accredited by the NRPA/AALR Council on Accreditation.

• *Recreation: A Medical Viewpoint.* ($12) Explores play, fun, and recreation and their relationship to psychiatry and medicine.

• *Therapeutic Recreation: A Comprehensive Approach to a Continuum of Care.* ($12 for 50) Brochure describing the continuum of services in therapeutic recreation practice.

Available online:

• *Teen Career Central.* Includes tips to becoming a recreation professional, information on field organizations, and certification information.

496

NATIONAL REHABILITATION COUNSELING ASSOCIATION
8807 Sudley Road, Suite 102
Manassas, VA 20110-4719
Fax: 703-361-2489
nrcaoffice@aol.com
http://www.nrca-net.org/

• *The Growing Profession of Rehabilitation Counseling.* 13 pages. Analyzes the demand for rehabilitation counseling services, as well as the roles and responsibilities, the scope of services, academic preparation, financial assistance, certification and licensure, salary, and career and employment opportunities.

497
NATIONAL RESEARCH COUNCIL
Fellowship Office
2101 Constitution Avenue, NW
Washington, DC 20418
202-334-2872
Fax: 202-334-3419
infofell@nas.edu
http://national-academies.org/osep/fo

- *Ford Foundation Postdoctoral Fellowships for Minorities.* 4 pages.

- *Ford Foundation Predoctoral Fellowships for Minorities.* 6 pages.

- *Ford Foundation Dissertation Fellowships for Minorities.* 6 pages.

- *Predoctoral Fellowships in Biological Sciences 2000.* 15 pages.

- *United States Department of Energy OERI Visiting Scholars Fellowships.* 4 pages.

- *NASA Administrators Fellowship Program.* 6 pages.

498
NATIONAL RESTAURANT ASSOCIATION
Educational Foundation
250 South Wacker Drive, Suite 1400
Chicago, IL 60606-5834
800-765-2122 or 312-715-1010
Fax: 312-715-0807
http://www.restaurant.org

- *Fork in the Road.* Free copy of the association's magazine to students interested in a culinary profession.

Available at the Web site:

- *The Real Deal: Unravel the Mysteries of Job Searches, Job Interviews, and School Choices.* Tips on how to break into the food service industry.

- *Career Paths.* Lists the different job options within the large food industry, from corporate to specialty positions. Includes contacts for more information.

- *Scholarships.* Includes information on scholarships and grants available to those who are eligible.

499
NATIONAL RETAIL FEDERATION
325 7th Street, Suite 1100
Washington, DC 20004
800-NRF-HOW2 or 202-783-7971
Fax: 202-737-2849
mancek@nrf.com
http://www.nrf.com

- *Careers in Retailing.* 11 pages. Covers many retailing topics, including opportunities available and career preparation. Also lists colleges and universities offering degrees in retailing, retail management, retail merchandising, retail marketing, retail sales, and fashion/apparel merchandising.

500
NATIONAL SAFETY COUNCIL
1121 Spring Lake Drive
Itasca, IL 60143-3201
800-621-7619 or 630-285-1121
Fax: 630-285-1315
http://www.nsc.org

- *Emergency First Aid Guide.* ($2.50) 32 pages. Handbook ideal for first aid kits and for employee distribution.

• *Good Samaritan: Helping in an Emergency.* ($2.50) 34 pages. Information on the basics of emergency care. Covers recognizing emergencies, getting help, and how to handle common emergencies.

• *Informational Booklets.* ($1 each) Titles include:

• *Cumulative Trauma.*

• *Working Safely on Your Computer.*

• *Accident Investigation.*

• *Job Safety Analysis.*

• *High-Rise Office Safety and Security.*

• *Safety Orientation.*

• *On the Job Posters.* Educational safety posters in different sizes: 17"x 23" ($2.80 each) or 8.5"x 11" ($1.75 each). Includes: *Don't Be the Fall Guy; Don't Overextend; Juggling Too Much; Good Housekeeping; Report All Near Misses; Select the Right Wardrobe; Stay Calm;* and *Take Time Out.* Can be ordered online or by mail.

501

NATIONAL SCHOOL TRANSPORTATION ASSOCIATION

625 Slaters Lane, Suite 205
Alexandria, VA 22314-1176
703-684-3200
Fax: 703-684-3212
http://www.schooltrans.com

• *Career Information Packet.*

502

NATIONAL SCIENCE FOUNDATION

Forms and Publications Unit
4201 Wilson Boulevard
Arlington, VA 22230

703-306-1234
info@nsf.gov
http://www.nsf.gov/

The following publications are available in print and online:

• *Shaping the Future: New Expectations for Undergraduate Education in Science, Mathematics, Engineering, and Technology.*

• *Gaining the Competitive Edge.* Addresses critical issues in science and engineering technician education.

503

NATIONAL SCIENCE TEACHERS ASSOCIATION

1840 Wilson Boulevard
Arlington, VA 22201-3000
703-243-7100
http://www. nsta.org

Online only:

• *You Can Teach Science.* Available in an elementary version and an adult version. Highlights the teaching profession, salaries, and related topics.

504

NATIONAL SOCIETY OF ACCOUNTANTS

1010 North Fairfax Street
Alexandria, VA 22314-1574
703-549-6400
Fax: 703-549-2984
http://www.nsacct.org

Career Information Packet includes:

• *A Special Opportunity in Accounting for You.* 6 pages. Includes information on small business practice and entering the field.

• *THE NSPA Annual Scholarship Awards.* 6 pages. Describes eligibility, how to apply, and how scholarship recipients are selected.

• *Accountants and Auditors.* 2 pages. Reprint from the *Occupational Outlook Handbook.* Fact sheet about careers in accounting and auditing. Includes information on the general nature of the work, working conditions, types of employment, training or educational requirements, future outlook for the careers, average earnings, related occupations, and sources of additional information.

• *Accreditation: A Standard for Excellence, A Commitment to Professional Development, Your Competitive Edge.* Discusses the importance and means of accreditation for accounting and taxation professionals.

505
NATIONAL SOCIETY OF GENETIC COUNSELORS, INC.
233 Canterbury Drive
Wallingford, PA 19086-6617
610-872-7608; Press # 1
nsgclistq@aol.com
http://www.nsgc.org

• *Is a Career in Genetic Counseling in Your Future?*

506
NATIONAL SPELEOLOGICAL SOCIETY
2813 Cave Avenue
Huntsville, AL 35810-4431

256-852-1300
Fax: 256-851-9241
nss@caves.org
http://www.caves.org

• *Caving Basics.* ($11) 50 pages. Covers the basics of caving and the equipment required.

507
NATIONAL STUDENT NURSES' ASSOCIATION, INC.
555 West 57th Street, Suite 1327
New York, NY 10019
212-581-2211
nsna@nsna.org
http://www.nsna.org

Available at the Web site:

• *Nursing: The Ultimate Adventure.* Designed for junior and high school students. Includes information on nursing opportunities, educational pathways, and how to apply to a nursing school.

• *Is Nursing For You?* Describes the various specialties, accreditation, how to choose a degree program, and personal requirements.

508
NATIONAL THERAPEUTIC RECREATION SOCIETY
22377 Belmont Ridge Road
Ashburn, VA 20148
703-858-2151
Fax: 703-858-0794
ntrsnrpa@aol.com
http://www.nrpa.org

• *About Therapeutic Recreation.* 16 pages.

• *Consider a Career in Therapeutic Recreation.* 6 pages. Discusses various settings and career opportunities.

• *Prep for a Career in Therapeutic Recreation.* ($7.50) Describes therapeutic recreation careeers.

509
NATIONAL TOURISM FOUNDATION
546 East Main Street
Lexington, KY 40508
800-682-8886, ext 4251
Fax: 606-226-4437
http://www.ntaonline.com

• *Internship List.* 41 pages. Free listing by state of tour operator, tour supplier, and destination marketing organization internship programs.

• *Schools List.* 75 pages. Free booklet containing more than 600 colleges and universities nationwide that offer tourism education, including certificate programs and programs offering associate, bachelor's, master's, or doctorate degrees.

Available only on the Web site:

• *National Tourism Foundation 2000 Scholarship Awards.* Guide to the scholarship opportunities offered by the NTF. Includes rules and application.

510
NATIONAL TRAPPERS ASSOCIATION
PO Box 3667
Bloomington, IL 61702
309-829-2422
Fax: 309-829-7615
trappers@aol.com
http://www.nationaltrappers.com

• *NTA Trapping Handbook.* ($8 plus shipping) 206 pages. Contains an introduction to trapping in the United States and covers furbearer management objectives, laws, responsibilities, harvesting, and safety. Special rate available for libraries.

511
NATURE CONSERVANCY, THE
4245 Fairfax Drive, Suite 100
Arlington, VA 22203-1606
800-628-6860
http://www.tnc.org

The following is available at the Web site:

• *Job Opportunities by State.* Discusses career areas and how to apply for employment opportunities.

• *The Nature Conservancy Intern and Volunteer Opportunities.* Lists by state the typical internships and short-term positions that are available annually.

• *The Nature Conservancy Educational Packets.* ($3.70 for elementary-aged children; $3.70 for teenagers) Designed for young people, this packet provides information about the importance of preservation efforts. Describes the threats to our ecosystems and suggests ways young people can get involved to improve the environment. Two versions of the packet are available for different age groups: elementary-age children and teens.

512
NELLIE MAE
50 Braintree Hill Office Park, Suite 300
Braintree, MA 02184

800-FOR-TUITION
Fax: 800-931-2200
http://www.nelliemae.com

The following are available free in print form; excerpts can be accessed from the Web site:

• *Steps to Success.* Nellie Mae is the largest nonprofit provider of student loan funds in the country. This guide provides helpful financial aid guidelines and timelines for students and their parents. Includes information on types of financial aid available and uselful phone numbers for more information.

• *Meet the Challenge.* Addresses the concerns of junior and senior high school students as they prepare to pay for college. Includes tips on wise borrowing and debt management to make the transition from high school to college an easier one.

• *Reach for the Stars.* Early college planning guide including information on saving for tuition, academic and social preparation, how to choose the college right for you, and the financial aid programs available to help pay for it.

513
NEW HAMPSHIRE DEPARTMENT OF EMPLOYMENT SECURITY

Economic and Labor Market
Information Bureau
32 South Main Street
Concord, NH 03301-4857
603-228-4124
Fax: 603-228-4172
http://www.nhes.state.nh.us

• *How to Look for a Job.* 12 pages. Includes a checklist and information on time management for job searching.

• *Job Search Letters.* 12 pages. Offers tips on writing cover letters and letters of application.

• *Job Interviewing Techniques.* 16 pages. Suggests how to organize and prepare for an interview and effectively present yourself and your skills.

• *Job Applications.* 14 pages. Includes tips for completing a job application, information on state applications, and sample application forms.

• *Preparing a Resume.* 16 pages. Helpful tips on resumes.

• *Economic Conditions in New Hampshire.* 8 pages. A monthly report discussing economic conditions in New Hampshire.

• *New Hampshire Employment Projections by Industry and Occupation 1996 to 2006.* 48 pages. Includes the results of a long-term forecast of employment in New Hampshire in the year 2006.

• *New Hampshire Job Outlook and Locator Occupation by Industry: Base Year 1996 to Projected Year 2006.* 189 pages. Lists the primary industries providing employment for occupational categories in New Hampshire.

• *A User's Guide to Labor Market Information.* 33 pages. Provides labor market information and lists available publications.

514

NEW JERSEY DEPARTMENT OF LABOR

Workforce New Jersey Public
Information Network
rmartine@dol.state.nj.us
http://www.wnjpin.state.nj.us

Available online:

• *Workforce New Jersey Public Information Network.* Links to information for job seekers and students, including job fair listings, career guidance aides, job search tools, career descriptions, NJ college listing, graduate school information, and study abroad facts.

• *Labor Market Information.* Includes demographic data, economic and demographic projections for the future, sources of additional information, labor market press releases, worker safety statistics, economic data, and other labor program data.

515

NEW JERSEY OCCUPATIONAL INFORMATION COORDINATING COMMITTEE

Labor and Industry Building
PO Box 057, 5th Floor
Trenton, NJ 08625-0057
609-292-2682
Fax: 609-292-6692
lseidel@dol.state.nj.us
http://www.wnjpin.state.nj.us/
onestopcareercenter/soicc

• *A Guide to Labor Demand Occupations.* ($5) 64 pages.

516

NEW MEXICO DEPARTMENT OF LABOR

Economic Research and Analysis Bureau
PO Box 1928
Albuquerque, NM 87103
505-841-8711
http://www3.state.nm.us/dol

• *Jobs for Graduates.* Provides short-term hiring plans of 140 major state employers for college and vocational school graduates. Includes hiring rates, salaries, personnel office addresses, and other information.

• *New Mexico Job Outlook—in Brief.* 3 pages. Presents information about the New Mexico job market and economy now entering the next century. Contains graphs and tables detailing the industries and occupations that will have an impact on the state's economic outlook through the year 2006.

The following are available by mail or on the Web:

• *New Mexico Occupational Wage Survey.* 38 pages. Annual mail survey measuring occupational employment and wage rates for wage and salary workers in nonfarm establishments, by industry.

• *New Mexico 2006 Employment Projections.* 62 pages. Designed to meet the needs of students, counselors, job seekers, and public and private planning groups interested in the industrial patterns and career opportunities in New Mexico. Includes information on nearly 600 occupations and incorporates information on major economic, political, and social changes at the national and local levels.

- *Large Employers in New Mexico by County.* Lists contact information for employers of 25 or more workers by county, excluding Bernalillo County.

- *Large Employers in the Albuquerque Area.* Lists contact information for employers of 50 or more workers in the Bernalillo County (the Albuquerque area).

- *Job Hunter's Guide.* Basic information on education, job sources, resumes, interviews, and employers.

- *Prospects: A Job Hunter's Guide.* Career publication providing a wide variety of economic, occupational, and educational information intended to help high school students and recent graduates make career decisions and prepare for job entry.

517
NEW YORK SEA GRANT INSTITUTE
121 Discovery Hall
SUNY at Stony Brook
Stony Brook, NY 11794-5001
516-632-6905
nyseagrant@ccmail.sunysb.edu

- *Marine-Related Occupations: A Primer for High School Students.* 16 pages. Publication to assist high school students to better understand the scope of job opportunities in marine fields, including scientific, technical, and professional jobs.

518
NEW YORK STATE DEPARTMENT OF LABOR
Division of Research Statistics
Publications Unit, Room 401
State Campus, Building 12
Albany, NY 12240
518-457-1130
Fax: 518-457-3652
http://www.labor.state.ny.us

- *Is Your Resume a Dinosaur?* Describes how to reformat the traditional resume in order to make it compatible with the types of resume scanning software increasingly used by employers.

- *Vision, a Teenager's Guide to Career Development.* Introduces the subject of career exploration and discusses adjusting to a work environment and understanding the role work plays in a society.

- *What Next? The Road to a New Job.* Aims to assist unemployed workers by outlining job search strategies, offering advice on handling financial difficulties, and suggesting methods to reduce stress and improve mental and physical health. Not intended for youth.

- *Your Writing Edge.* Provides tips on how to prepare a resume; includes sample resumes.

- *LMI, A Tool for Making Sense of the World.* Explains what labor market information is and how it can be used to accomplish job and career-related goals.

- *A Better Way.* Guides novice job seekers through an action plan to help them focus on their job-search efforts.

- *CareerZone Bookmark.* Information about an award-winning career exploration tool.

• *Directory of Labor Market Information.* Publications, statistical series, and contact for labor-related topics.

• *Knowledge, Information, Tools for Understanding the Job Market, Welfare to Work.* Brochure describing the products and services useful to those who help public assistance clients search for work.

• *Occupations Licensed or Certified by New York State.* Describes occupations requiring a license or certificate from New York State agencies. Includes job description, and requirements for licensure or certification, including fees, education/training needed, and examination information.

Other career-related information and region-specific publications are available. Call or write for a publications order form. Many of the publications listed above are already available online.

519
NEWSLETTER & ELECTRONICS PUBLISHERS ASSOCIATION
1501 Wilson Boulevard, Suite 509
Arlington, VA 22209
703-527-2333
Fax: 703-841-0629
nepa@newsletters.org
http://www.newsletters.org

• *Newsletter Career Guide.* 8 pages.

520
NEWSPAPER ASSOCIATION OF AMERICA
Diversity Department
1921 Gallows Road, Suite 600
Vienna, VA 22182-3900

703-902-1600
Fax: 703-902-1735
dukem@naa.org
http://www.naa.org

• *Newspaper Career Guide: Where Do You Fit In?* (single copy is free) 33 pages. Booklet showing the vast and diverse career opportunities available in the newspaper industry. Written with a young perspective, this booklet disproves the myth that newspapers are part of a "lost world." Includes individuals' stories of their job in different cutting-edge areas of the industry.

Also available in text form and at the Web site:

• *Facts About Newspapers.* (single copy is free) Brochure overviewing the newspaper field, focusing on key indicators of the industry's healthy future outlook. Combines graphics, surveys, industry statistics, and trends making for a very useful resource tool.

521
NEWSPAPER GUILD-CWA
501 Third Street, NW, Suite 250
Washington, DC 20001-2797
202-434-7177
Fax: 202-434-1472
guild@cwa-union.org
http://www.newsguild.org

• *Professional Specialty Occupations.* 11 pages. Covers the nature of the work, working conditions, training, job outlook, and earnings for a number of occupations in the field, including reporters.

- *The Voice for Media Workers.* 1 page. Describes The Newspaper Guild-CWA.

522
NORTH AMERICAN ASSOCIATION FOR ENVIRONMENTAL EDUCATION
Member Services Office
410 Tarvin Road
Rock Spring, GA 37039
706-764-2926
Fax: 706-764-2094
csmith409@aol.com
http://www.naaee.org

- *List of Colleges and Univerities with Programs Related to EE.* ($6 plus $3.95 shipping) 35 pages. Lists by state the names and addresses of colleges and universities offering environmental education programs.

523
NORTH AMERICAN STUDENTS OF COOPERATION
PO Box 7715
Ann Arbor, MI 48107
734-663-0889
Fax: 734-663-5072
txgr@umich.edu
http://www.umich.edu/~nasco

Available at the Web site:

- *What is a Co-op?* Includes information on campus cooperatives, the history of student cooperatives, and the future of the cooperative movement.

- *Organizer's Handbook.* (also available by mail for a fee) Explains the cooperative movement, how to get organized, addresses housing challenges, and com-

pares the past, present, and future of cooperatives.

524
NORTHEASTERN STATE UNIVERSITY
Center for Tribal Studies
Tahlequah, OK 74464
800-722-9614 or 918-456-5511
Fax: 918-458-2326
http://www.nsuok.edu

- *Scholarships for American Indian Students.* ($10) 76 pages. Lists scholarships available to American Indians and contact information by subject matter (e.g., education, medicine/health-related fields, art/literature/library/liberal arts, science/math/engineering/computer science).

525
NUCLEAR ENERGY INSTITUTE
1776 I Street, NW, Suite 400
Washington, DC 20006-3708
202-739-8000
http://www.nei.org

The following is available at the Institute's Web site:

- *Careers and Education: Your Bright Future in Nuclear Energy and Technology.* Includes sections: "Nuclear Professions: An Introduction," reviews the areas of study, practical applications, career fields, and suggestions for your career search; "Nuclear Energy," discusses the industry's future outlook, jobs involved in running a nuclear power plant, scholarships and fellowships available, and related Web sites; "Nuclear Medicine," covers the use of nuclear technology in medicine, careers available, and the required study; and "Nuclear Industrial Applications," lists the many industrial applications of radiation, career opportunites, and training and education necessary to enter the field.

526
OCTAMERON ASSOCIATES
PO Box 2748
Alexandria, VA 22301
703-836-5480
Fax: 703-836-5650
sales@octameron.com
http://www.octameron.com

For the following publications, postage equals five percent of the total order and handling is $3. Write for a catalog.

• *College.Edu: On-Line Resources for the Cyber-Savvy Student.* ($8) 132 pages. Provides an overview of Internet basics and useful sites on financial aid and admission, including bulletin boards and newsgroups.

• *Campus Daze: Easing the Transition from High School to College.* ($6) 64 pages. Contains anecdotes and practical advice. Describes what to expect and how to minimize any difficulties.

• *The Winning Edge: The Student Athlete's Guide to College Sports.* ($5) 96 pages. For all students interested in college athletics. Shows students how to use their athletic skills to increase their chances for financial aid and admission at the schools of their choice. Practical advice from coaches, information on scholarship opportunities, and a summary of NCAA rules and regulations.

• *College Opportunities for Students with Learning Differences.* ($5) 40 pages. Advises LD students on what questions to ask when selecting a school, how to prepare for a more rigorous academic schedule, and how and when to get special assistance. This book does not deal with physical handicaps, nor does it describe specific LD programs.

• *Don't Miss Out: The Ambitious Student's Guide to Financial Aid.* ($9) 208 pages. A how-to guide for parents and students. Explains how to lower their expected contribution to college costs; get the most money possible from federal, state, and collegiate sources; and develop short- and long-range planning strategies.

• *The A's and B's of Academic Scholarships.* ($9) 208 pages. Lists about 100,000 scholarships at 1,200 schools in the United States. Includes the names of awards, amounts, eligibility criteria, renewability options, and application deadlines.

• *Loans and Grants From Uncle Sam: Am I Eligible and for How Much?* ($6) 64 pages. Contains simple explanations and handy worksheets to help readers determine amount of federal student aid, the difference between lenders, and repayment options.

• *SAT Savvy: Last Minute Tips and Strategies.* ($6) 96 pages. Helps students build their test-taking confidence, brush up on math and verbal skills, and refine logic and reasoning techniques.

• *College Match: A Blueprint for Choosing the Best School for You!* ($8) 132 pages. Combines easy-to-use worksheets with loads of practical advice to give students control over the entire college admission process.

- *Do-It Write: How to Prepare a Great College Application.* ($6) 64 pages. Shows students how to get started and gives hints for writing essays. Answers questions about the rest of the application process.

- *Campus Pursuit: Making the Most of Your Visit and Interview.* ($5) 32 pages. Discusses what to look for during campus visits and how to survive interviews.

- *Our Counseling Service.* Describes a range of services helpful in finding money for college, selecting a college, and applying to college.

527
OFFICE OF STATEWIDE HEALTH PLANNING AND DEVELOPMENT
Health Professions Career Opportunity Program
1600 Ninth Street, Room 441
Sacramento, CA 95814
916-654-2102
http://www.oshpd.state.ca.us

Available at the Web site:

- *Health Pathways.* A quarterly newsletter containing timely information on health professional schools, admissions, post-baccalaureate and summer enrichment programs, financial aid, health careers, student health organizations, and health issues.

Available by mail:

- *Financial Advice for Minority Students Seeking an Education in the Health*

Professions. Discusses financial aid basics—costs, eligibility, availability, and resources.

- *The Physician Assistant: A Guide for Minority Students.* Covers career preparation, entry requirements, admissions procedures, financial aid, curriculum, training, and certification. Describes the physician assistant role, available opportunities, and employment outlook.

- *Minorities and Public Health Careers.* Highlights public health careers, how to apply to graduate school, and specific public health curricula.

- *The Many Roles of Nursing.* Includes information on career preparation, entry requirements, admission procedures, financial aid, and training.

- *Minorities in Medicine: A Guide for Premedical Students.* Contains descriptions of medical careers, information on how to prepare for them, and a list of sources.

- *Educational Survival Skills Study Guide.* Offers techniques for developing study skills and improving chances of academic success.

- *Time Management for Students.* Geared toward medical and other graduate students. Includes techniques for improving time usage.

- *Minority Public Health Student Contact List.* A list of individuals to contact for support, information, and networking. Designed for new or prospective public health students.

• *Minority Medical Student Contact List.* Lists persons to contact for support, information, and networking. Designed for new or prospective medical students.

• *Third World Student Organizations and Health Groups Directory.* A list of under-graduate minority student health science clubs and associations in California.

528

OFFICE TEAM

800-804-8367
http://www.officeteam.com

The following publications can be ordered online:

• *How to Succeed in Administrative Fields.* Offers tips on resume writing, interview-ing, excelling on the job, and enhancing your marketability.

• *Career Resource Guide.* Provides an overview of administrative trends and advice for achieving career success, such as keeping up with technology, polish-ing communication skills, and becoming more efficient.

• *2000 Salary Guide.* Annual survey of use-ful fact and information, including com-pensation levels and hiring trends for administrative positions.

Available at the Web site:

• *Resume Tips: Do's and Don'ts.*

• *Interview Dynamics.* Includes informa-tion on researching employers, questions to expect and ask, do's and don'ts, and suggestions for closing the interview.

529

OHIO SEA GRANT COLLEGE PROGRAM PUBLICATIONS

Ohio State University
1314 Kinnear Road
Columbus, OH 43212-1194
800-306-9941
Fax: 614-292-4364
cruickshank.3@osu.edu
http://www.sg.ohio-state.edu

The following is available in print form and accessible on the Web site:

• *Is Aquaculture for You?* (FS-039) 2 pages. Describes aquaculture and includes a checklist to help determine whether an aquaculture career is for you.

• *Marine-Related Careers: Options and Resources.* (FS-012) 2 pages. Lists marine career categories and job titles and other contact sources.

530

OKLAHOMA DEPARTMENT OF VOCATIONAL AND TECHNICAL EDUCATION

1500 West Seventh Avenue
Stillwater, OK 74074
405-743-5108
Fax: 405-743-5541
http://www.okvotech.org

• *Career Stuff.* Catalog of counseling and teaching materials.

• *Through the Jungle: A Job Search Guide.* ($6) Covers interviewing, resume prepa-ration, and other important topics.

Available at the Web site:

• *Student Resources.* Includes links to information on America's 50 hottest jobs, finding your career interest, high school graduation requirements, and more.

531
OKLAHOMA EMPLOYMENT SECURITY COMMISSION
Directory of Labor Market Publications
Economic Research and Analysis Division
Will Rogers Memorial Office Building
Labor Market Informational Unit
PO Box 52003
Oklahoma City, OK 73152-2003
405-557-5401
Fax: 405-525-0139
lmi@oesc.state.ok.us
http://www.oesc.state.ok.us

Available only on the Web site:

• *Career Videos.* 92 career videos ranging in occupations, downloadable to your computer.

The following publications are available by mail or on the Commission's Web site:

• *Workforce Oklahoma Occupational Outlook 2006.* Presents occupational employment, projected growth, and average openings for more than 500 occupations. Includes charts, graphs, and tables to visually reveal the occupational outlook.

• *Oklahoma Labor Force Data.* Includes civilian labor force data and the county, and metropolitan, state, and national employment statistical data. Published monthly and revised yearly.

• *County Employment and Wage Data.* Contains county employment and pay-roll totals, average covered employment and weekly earnings for each county in Oklahoma, and by major industry division for workers covered by unemployment insurance.

• *Current Employment Statistics.* Contains historical data about nonagricultural employment and selected industries in Oklahoma. Also includes hours and earnings data.

• *Oklahoma State Employment Service Job Openings and Applicants.* An annual publication detailing job openings most frequently listed with the Employment Service. Openings are listed by industry and by occupation and includes the number of applicants, openings, and average wage offered.

• *Oklahoma Wage Report, 1999.* Contains results of wage surveys by occupation and labor market area. Descriptions of each occupation are included.

• *Oklahoma Labor Market Information Monthly Newsletters.* Contains monthly descriptions and tables of the current employment, hours, and earnings for the state and the four MSAs. Also includes articles regarding agency programs and other topics of interest.

• *Your Guide to Oklahoma Labor Market Information.* Loaded with answers to FAQs about labor market information. Helpful to jobseekers, employment/guidance counselors, educators, or students who want to make informed decisions.

• *The Oklahoma Labor Market Information Annual Summary.* Provides information on the state's economic and employment health. Data is organized by type and geographic area, and presented at sub-state, statewide, and national levels.

• *Oklahoma Labor Market Information Fact Cards.* Pocket-sized cards providing employment rates of the civilian labor force and the unemployment rates for the state and the nation. Provides quick and easy reference to information about the labor market.

• *A World of Information at Your Fingertips.* 54 pages. Booklet designed to help Internet users in job searching, career exploration, and labor market analysis. Includes a list of Web sites to aid in the job search, and sources of career development information.

532
OREGON STATE UNIVERSITY
Indian Education Office
Snell Hall, Room 330
Corvalis, OR 97331-1634
541-737-4383
indimed@ccmail.orst.edu
http://www.orst.edu/dept/indianed

• *Financial Aid Resource Guide.* Information on scholarships provided for Native American students at Oregon State University, as well as federal and national corporate scholarships.

533
ORGANIZATION FOR EQUAL EDUCATION OF THE SEXES, INC.
PO Box 438
Blue Hill, ME 04614-0438
207-374-2489

Fax: 207-374-5350
oees@acadia.net

• *Women at Work.* (posters each $4) 11" x 17" career-related posters. 25 posters in all, including:

• *Money, Jobs & Women;*

• *Science Jobs; Women in the Trades;*

• *Who Says There Are No Women Firefighters; and*

• *Dentistry.*

• *Stay in School.* ($4) 11" x 17" posters encouraging young women to handle adversity and stay in school. Twenty titles in all, including:

• *Peer Pressure;*

• *Family Problems;*

• *Meeting Challenges; and*

• *Why Finish School?*

534
ORGANIZATION OF AMERICAN HISTORIANS
112 North Bryan Street
Bloomington, IN 47408-4199
812-855-7311
Fax: 812-855-0696
oah@oah.org
http://www.indiana.edu/~oah

• *Careers for Graduates in History.* A one page chart depicting career opportunities for history graduates in the nonprofit, private, and public sectors.

• *Career Information Source List.* 1 page. Lists historical organizations that provide information about jobs for historians.

535
OUTWARD BOUND U.S.A.
National Headquarters
Route 9D, R2 Box 280
Garrison, NY 10524-9757
800-243-8520 or 914-424-4000
http://www.outwardbound.org

- *Outward Bound National Course Catalog.*
  46 pages. Describes Outward Bound and
  provides information on instructors, the
  various programs, courses for young
  teens, international courses, tuition,
  enrollment, and financial aid.

536
PEACE CORPS OF THE UNITED STATES OF AMERICA
1111 20th Street, NW
Washington, DC 20526
800-424-8580
http://www.peacecorps.gov

Peace Corps information is available by
phone or at the Web site.

537
PEDORTHIC FOOTWEAR ASSOCIATION
7150 Columbia Gateway Drive, #G
Columbia, MD 21046-1151
800-673-8447 or 410-381-7278
Fax: 410-381-1167
http://www.pedorthics.org

- *Pedorthics: Foot Care Through Proper
  Footwear.* Send first class SASE to PFA.
  Brochure provides information on
  pedorthics and the professionals (certified pedorthists) who provide it.

538
PENNSYLVANIA DEPARTMENT OF LABOR AND INDUSTRY
Center for Workforce Information and
Analysis
Labor and Industry Building, Room 220
7th and Forster Streets
Harrisburg, PA 17121
717-787-6466
Fax: 717-772-2168
info-lmi@dli.state.pa.us
http://www.lmi.state.pa.us

- *Employment Outlook in Pennsylvania
  Industries and Occupations.* 50 pages.
  Compares employment in Pennsylvania
  in 1994 with employment projections for
  the year 2005. Includes industry employment tables and occupational data as
  well as data on the average annual number of job openings for approximately
  700 occupations.

- *Pennsylvania Workforce 2005.* Contains
  concise analytical texts, summary tables
  and charts on population, labor force,
  and industrial and occupational
  employment.

539
PETERSON'S
Princeton Pike Corporate Center
2000 Lenox Drive
Lawrenceville, NJ 08648
800-338-3282 or 609-896-1800
Fax: 800-772-2465
info@petersons.com
http://www.petersons.com

Free resources available at the Web site:

- *Program Search.* Online directories to
  graduate and undergraduate programs

in business, culinary arts, visual communications, information technology, and paralegal training.

- *Test Preparation Help.* Hot tips and sample questions for the SAT, ACT, GRE, and GMAT.

- "The Financial Aid Story." Article outlining various ways available to help pay for college.

- *How Colleges Evaluate Applications.* Helpful information illuminating the mystery behind college application review.

The following can be ordered online or by phone:

- *College and University Almanac 2000.* ($7.96) 581 pages. Facts about college selection, application, and funding your tuition.

- *USA Today: Getting Into College.* ($7.16) 160 pages. Tips on how to select a school and maximize campus visits.

- *USA Today: Financial Aid for College.* ($7.16) 160 pages. Information on financial aid applications, requirements, and details of how, when, and where to apply.

- *Writing a Winning College Application Essay.* ($7.96) 120 pages. Handbook includes great examples of essays that attract and hold the attention of the admissions office.

- *The Ultimate New Employee Survival Guide.* ($11.96) 254 pages. Information on how to make the transition from school to work and get on the right track to success.

- *Scholarship Almanac 2000.* ($7.96) 522 pages. Reference book of the 500 major undergraduate scholarships, awards, and prizes available from private sources.

- *Job Seeker's Almanac.* ($7.96) 906 pages. Includes resume and interviewing tips, employment outlooks, and contact information for more than 3,000 growing companies in 175 industries.

- *Virtual College.* ($7.96) 156 pages. Information about online college courses, frequently asked questions, and tips from students and teachers.

- *Careers Without College Series.* ($7.96 each) Career titles include: *Cars, Computers, Health Care,* and *Fashion.*

540
PHOTO MARKETING ASSOCIATION INTERNATIONAL
3000 Picture Place
Jackson, MI 49201-8898
517-788-8100
Fax: 517-788-8371

- *Photo Industry Careers: A Lifelong Commitment to Excellence and Creativity.* 4 pages. Discusses job availability, salaries, benefits, career opportunities, and schools offering a photofinishing curriculum.

541
PLUMBING-HEATING-COOLING CONTRACTORS ASSOCIATION
180 South Washington Street
PO Box 6808
Falls Church, VA 22040
800-533-7694

Fax: 703-237-7442
http://www.naphcc.org

• *Your Pipeline to Hot Careers and Cold Cash: Careers in the Plumbing and HVAC Industry.* ($5.25. Extra booklets available for $.35 each.) 10-minute video and 16-page booklet for those interested in the plumbing, heating, and cooling industry. Experts respond to high school students' questions about opportunities in the field, illuminated by visual examples of hands-on work typical of the career.

542
POPULATION ASSOCIATION OF AMERICA
721 Ellsworth Drive, Suite 303
Silver Spring, MD 20910
301-565-6710
Fax: 301-565-7850
info@popassoc.org
http://www.popassoc.org

• *Careers in Population.* 16 pages. Topics covered include "Why the Study of Population Matters," "What the Study of Population Involves," "Where Population Specialists Work," and "Training to Be a Population Specialist." Also includes a list of other contact resources.

543
PRECISION MACHINED PRODUCTS ASSOCIATION
6700 West Snowville Road
Brecksville, OH 44141-3292
216-526-0300
Fax: 216-526-5803
http://www.pmpa.org

• *Focus on Your Future in the Precision Machined Products Industry.* 6 pages. Describes career opportunities, skills required, future outlook and earnings.

• *Focus on Your Future.* 10-minute video aimed at high school graduates with basic shop and math background. Describes excellent entry-level jobs and career opportunities in the machined products industry. For more career information and companies in your area, check out the Web site.

544
PRESBYTERIAN CHURCH (USA)
Office of Financial Aid for Studies
100 Witherspoon Street
Louisville, KY 40202-1396
502-569-5745
Fax: 502-569-8766
http://www.pcusa.org/highered

• *Programs for Higher Education.* 12 pages.

545
PRESIDENT'S COMMITTEE ON EMPLOYMENT OF PEOPLE WITH DISABILITIES
1331 F Street, NW, Suite 300
Washington, DC 20004-1107
202-376-6200 or 202-376-6205 (TDD)
info@pcepd.gov
http://www.pcedp.gov

• *Career and Business Information.* Available at the Web site (see Publications and Business Focus) or by mail. Several fact sheets and brochures are available. Titles include:

- *Employment Checklist for Hiring People with Disabilities: Practical Suggestions;*

- *Essential Elements of an Effective Job Search;*

- *Preparing for and Conducting a Job Interview;*

- *Interviewing Tips for the Job Applicant;*

- *High School/High Tech: Promoting Science, Engineering; and*

- *Technology Careers for Students with Disabilities.*

546
PRIESTS OF THE SACRED HEART
SCJ Vocation Office
PO Box 206
Hales Corner, WI 53130-0206
414-529-4255
Fax: 414-529-3377
jackkures@compuserve.com
http://www.sintunum.org

Call or write for a complete vocation resource catalogue.

- *A Student's Guide: Priest, Brother, Sister.* (#1601) ($.25) For teachers, parents, and pastors. Provides answers to the questions children ask about the priesthood and religious life.

- *A Parent's Guide: Priest, Brother, or Sister.* (#1608) ($.25 each) Brochures addressing questions parents may have about their child's pursuit of a vocation to the priesthood or religious life.

- *Religious Life: A Life of Prayer and Shared Service in Community.* (#1602)

- *The Brother: A Life of Sevice, Community and Prayer.* (#1603)

- *Today's Sister: Living a Life of Loving Service.* (#1604)

- *The Priest: Called to Serve and Proclaim.* (#1605)

- *The Contemplative Life.* (#1606)

- *The Deacon: A Ministry of Service in the Church.* (#1607)

547
PRINT AND GRAPHICS SCHOLARSHIP FOUNDATION
200 Deer Run Road
Sewickley, PA 15143
412-741-6860
Fax: 412-741-2311
kwinkowski@gatf.org
http://www.gatf.org

- *Directory of Technical Schools, Colleges, and Universities Offering Courses in Graphic Communications.* 90 pages. Spans all degree levels for technology, management, and education.

- *A Counselor's Guide: Careers in Graphic Communications.* 13 pages.

- *Scholarship Application For National Scholarship Trust Fund.* Suitable for graphics arts students.

548
PRO-PAK, INC.
527 Dundee Road
Northbrook, IL 60062
847-272-0408
Fax: 847-272-4943

propak@interacess.com
http://www.propakinc.com

- *Off to College.* SASE. 2 pages. Includes a "What to Take to College" checklist.

549
PROFESSIONAL BASEBALL UMPIRE CORP.
PO Box A
St. Petersburg, FL 33731
727-822-6937, ext. 3138
Fax: 727-821-5819
pbuc@minorleaguebaseball.com
http://www.minorleaguebaseball.com/pbuc/

- *Making the Call: Becoming a Profesional Baseball Umpire.* 6 pages. Describes the training, work, and compensation of professional baseball umpires.

550
PROFESSIONAL BOWLERS ASSOCIATION
1720 Merriman Road
PO Box 5118
Akron, OH 44334-0118
330-836-5568
Fax: 330-836-2107
http://www.pbatour.com

- *PBA Tour: Guidelines to a Professional Image.* 6 pages. Answers what it means to be a professional bowler, how to deal with the media, and how to promote yourself.

551
PROFESSIONAL GROUNDS MANAGEMENT SOCIETY
720 Light Street
Baltimore, MD 21230
800-609-7467
Fax: 410-752-8295
pgms@assnhqtrs.com
http://www.pgms.org

- *The Professional Grounds Manager.* 4 pages. Briefly describes what a grounds manager is, duties and expertise, and suggested educational requirements.

552
PROFESSIONAL LAWN CARE ASSOCIATION OF AMERICA
1000 Johnson Ferry Road, NE
Suite C-135
Marietta, GA 30068-2112
770-977-5222
Fax: 770-578-6071
plcaa@plcaa.org
http://www.plcaa.org

The following is available on the association's Web site:

- *Career Paths in the Green Industry: Focus on Lawn Technicians and Sales Representatives.* Describes typical entry-level positions in lawn care service, average compensation, and educational requirements.

- *Career Paths in the Green Industry: Focus on Management.* Information on getting started in the industry and moving up to management positions. Includes skill requirements and average compensation amounts.

553

PROFESSIONAL TRUCK DRIVER INSTITUTE
2200 Mill Road
Alexandria, VA 22314
703-838-8842
Fax: 703-836-6610
ptdi@truckload.org
http://www.ptdi.org

• *Careers in Trucking.* A recruitment magazine for anyone interested in working for the trucking industry. Contains information about types of truck driving, compensation, qualifications to become a truck driver, truck driver training, and how to find the right training school. Also contains a list of truck driver training schools that have been certified to PTDI standards.

• *Schools With PDTI Certified Courses Listed by State.* 6 pages.

554

PROTOTYPE CAREER PRESS
1086 West 7th Street
St. Paul, MN 55102
800-368-3197
Fax: 651-224-5526
http://prototypecareerservice.com

The Pocket Job Series. ($2.95 each) Must be ordered in a set of these seven titles:

• *Cracking the Hidden Job Market.* Offers advice about tapping the unadvertised job market which comprises nearly 95 percent of all jobs. Provides sample cold-calls, follow-up letters, and contact sheets.

• *Financial Survival Between Jobs.* Offers information on budgeting, dealing with creditors, and maintaining an upbeat attitude.

• *Five Steps to Your Next Job.* Offers tips for success in today's competitive job market.

• *Job Interviews: 10 Steps to Success.* Offers tips on salary negotiation, six types of interview styles, the four basic parts of an interview, and follow-up strategy.

• *Job Search Over 40: Selling to Your Strengths.* Offers tips to combat age descrimination and includes facts and myths about workers over age 40.

• *Job Search Problem-Solving Companion.* Addresses issues job seekers face daily such as overcoming rejection, targeting a job search, and seeking out support groups.

• *Resumes Etc.* Offers instructions for four different styles of resumes, cover letters, follow-up letters, and applications.

555

PUBLIC RELATIONS SOCIETY OF AMERICA, INC.
Educational Affairs Department
33 Irving Place, 3rd Floor
New York, NY 10003-2376
212-995-2230
hq@prsa.org
http://www.prsa.org

Available online:

• *Careers in Public Relations.* Discusses the field today, salaries, types of duties public relations professionals perform, personal qualifications, academic preparation, and employment opportunities.

556
PUBLIC/PRIVATE VENTURES
Communications Department
One Commerce Square
2005 Market Street, Suite 900
Philadelphia, PA 19103
215-557-4400
Fax: 215-557-4469
geninfo@ppv.org
http://www.ppv.org

Call or write for a complete catalog.
Prepayment is required by check or
money order to cover printing and
postage costs.

- *Skills, Standards and Entry-Level Work:
  Elements of a Strategy for Youth
  Employability Development.* ($6) 74 pages.

- *Replication: A Strategy to Improve the
  Delivery of Education and Job Training
  Programs.* ($7) 50 pages.

- *YouthSources: An Employment Training
  Bibliography.* ($8.50) 96 pages.

- *College Students as Mentors for At-Risk
  Youth: A Study of Six Campus Partners in
  Learning Programs.* ($6) 56 pages.

- *Finding One's Way: Career Guidance for
  Disadvantaged Youth.* ($2) 63 pages.

- *Seniors in National and Community
  Service: A Report Prepared for the
  Commonwealth Fund's American Over 55
  at Work Program.* ($6) 79 pages.

- *Youth and the Workplace: Second Chance
  Programs and the Hard-to-Employ.* ($6) 55
  pages.

557
RADIO-TELEVISION NEWS
DIRECTORS ASSOCIATION
1000 Connecticut Avenue, NW, Suite 615
Washington, DC 20036-5302
202-659-6510
Fax: 202-223-4007
http://www.rtnda.org

Available online:

- *Minority Recruitment Directory.* Provides
  resources and associations that will be of
  use to minorities interested in a career in
  broadcasting.

Available by mail:

- *Professional Field Guide for Television
  News.* ($10) A guide that is aimed at
  accelerating the professional growth of
  young and experienced reporters.

- *Careers in Radio and Television News.* ($5)
  24 pages. Discusses qualifications,
  responsibilities, and how to prepare
  yourself and get a job.

558
RADIOLOGICAL SOCIETY OF NORTH
AMERICA
820 Jorie Boulevard
Oak Brook, IL 60523
630-571-2670
Fax: 630-571-7837
http://www.rsna.org

Written request on letterhead required to
obtain the following materials.

- *Career Encounters: Radiology.* 28-minute
  video offering a detailed look at support careers in major subspecialties of
  radiology.

• *Medicine's New Vision.* 178 pages. Provides career information on major subspecialties in radiology.

559
RANDOM HOUSE, INC.
1540 Broadway
New York, NY 10036
212-782-9000
Fax: 212-302-7985
http://www.randomhouse.com/catalog/

Available to order through Random House's Web site:

• *Pocket Guide to Colleges, 2000 Edition.* ($9.95) Compact resource that is detailed and informative, containing all the essential college information available in larger guides. Includes complete profiles of 1500 U.S. colleges and universities, admissions data, financial information, academic features, student body information, and much more.

• *Job Notes: Resumes.* ($4.95) Portable book for easy reference about how to build a resume from scratch.

• *Job Notes: Networking.* ($4.95) Explores how and where to network to discover contacts in unlikely places.

• *Job Notes: Interviews.* ($4.95) Explains the straight facts about talking yourself right into a job. Includes information on what to wear, what to bring, what to say (and not say), questions to ask, and much more.

• *Job Notes: Cover Letters.* ($4.95) Compact resource on how to write cover letters that customize to each potential employer.

560
RECRUITING NEW TEACHERS, INC.
385 Concord Avenue, Suite 103
Belmont, MA 02478
800-45-TEACH or 617-489-6407
Fax: 617-489-6005
rnt@rnt.org
http://www.rnt.org/

Call or write for a complete RNT Educational Materials and Products list.

• *Careers in Teaching Handbook.* ($12.95) 122 pages. A comprehensive guide to pursuing a career in teaching. Provides information, resources, and advice to aspiring and novice teachers from all educational and professional backgrounds and experience (including college students, GED recipients, and business and technical professionals). Identifies topics of primary concern to would-be teachers, such as finding the right teacher education program, making a career transition, and funding.

561
RITTNERS FLORAL SCHOOL
345 Marlborough Street
Boston, MA 02115
617-267-3824
stevrt@tiac.net
http://www.tiac.net/users/stevrt/index.html

The following publication is available online:

• *Floral Designing: The Now Profession.* Covers working conditions, pay, preparation, and job outlook.

562
ROBERT HALF INTERNATIONAL
565 Fifth Avenue
New York, NY 10017
212-983-1800 or 212-687-7878
http://www.roberthalf.com

• *How to Get Ahead in Accounting, Finance and Banking.* 5 pages. Contains numerous tips on resume preparation and interviewing.

• *Salary Guide.* 28 pages. Annual source for reliable hiring and compensation data. Provides an in-depth look at employment factors affecting each geographic region of the United States, as well as cost-of-living variances for major cities.

563
ROMAC INTERNATIONAL
120 West Hyde Park Place, Suite 150
Tampa, FL 33606
813-251-1700
http://www.experienceondemand.com

• *1999 Salary Surveys and Career Navigators.* Available by mail or online. Highlights the latest trends and provides detailed compensation data for 11 major industries.

Resources available at Romac International's Web site:

• *Interview Tips.* Outlines typical interviewing questions and suggests intelligent ways to answer; lists important

questions the interviewer should ask about the company or job; and includes proper interviewing etiquette.

• *Cover Letter and Resume Builder.* Tips on how to make the written part of you as impressive as the physical part of you.

564
SALES AND MARKETING EXECUTIVES INTERNATIONAL
5500 Interstate North Parkway, Suite 545
Atlanta, GA 30328
770-661-8500
Fax: 770-661-8512
smeihq@smei.org
http://www.smei.org

Available at the Web site:

• *Opportunities in the Sales & Marketing Profession.* Describes the duties of different types of salespeople, personal characteristics, and education and training.

565
SCIENCE SERVICE, INC.
1719 N Street, NW
Washington, DC 20036
202-785-2255
Fax: 202-785-1243
sciedu@sciserv.org
http://www.sciserv.org

• *Directory of Student Science Training Programs for Teachers and Students.* Now available in print and on the Web, the directory lists over 400 science training programs for pre-college students and teachers. Lists training programs that cover a wide variety of scientific disciplines and take place throughout the year at a variety of institutions—predominantly at colleges and universities. Many of the programs listed specifically target members of groups traditionally under-represented in the sciences.

566
SCIENTIST, THE
3600 Market Street, Suite 450
Philadelphia, PA 19104-2645
215-386-9601
Fax: 215-387-7542
info@the-scientist.com
http://www.the-scientist.com

• *The Scientist: The News Journal for the Life Scientist.* Provides information on issues in research, technology, employment, funding, policy, and other subjects important to the life scientist. Archived issues available on the Web site.

567
SCREEN ACTORS GUILD
Publications Cashier
5757 Wiltshire Boulevard
Los Angeles, CA 90046
213-549-6755
http://www.sag.org

• *AFTRA-SAG Young Performers Handbook.* ($5 for print version) Available by mail or accessible online. Includes useful information including the importance of unions, parents' role and responsibilites, tools of the trade, what to know and where to find crucial information, frequently asked questions, appendix of specific contract language, and a listing of child labor provisions listed by state.

568
SCREEN ACTORS GUILD
IATSE Local 884
Betterment of Sevice Chairman
PO Box 461467
Los Angeles, CA 90046
http://www.sag.org

• *The Blue Book: Employment of Minors in the Entertainment Industry.* ($5) Compilation of all relevant federal, state, and local laws and codes relating to working minors in California.

569
SEA GRANT COMMUNICATIONS
Kingman Farm
University of New Hampshire
Durham, NH 03824-3512
603-749-1565

• *Marine Science Careers: A Sea Grant Guide to Ocean Opportunities.* ($5) 40 pages. Compilation of interviews with 38 people who work in the marine sciences in a variety of occupations.

570
SEAWORLD ADVENTURE PARK
Education Department/Book Orders
7007 SeaWorld Drive
Orlando, FL 32821-8097
407-363-2380
Fax: 407-363-2399
education@seaworld.org
http://www.seaworld.org

• SeaWorld's Education Department offers more than 75 marine science educational resources (booklets and teacher's guides) designed for K-12 students and teachers. Write for a complete list and order form.

571
SELF HELP FOR HARD OF HEARING PEOPLE, INC.
Publications
7910 Woodmont Avenue, Suite 1200
Bethesda, MD 20814
301-657-2248 or 301-657-2249 (TTY)
Fax: 301-913-9413
National@shhh.org
http://www.shhh.org

For the following publications, add $.75 in postage and handling for orders up to $2 or $1.75 for orders of $2.01 to $5. Call, write, or visit the Web site for a publications catalog.

- *College-Bound Students.* ($2.25)

- *Employment Discrimination: How to Recognize It and What to Do about It.* ($2)

- *Getting Help with a Job: Exploring Vocational Rehabilitation.* ($2)

- *Putting You in the Successful Employment Picture (Series).* ($6.50)

- *What Employers Want to Know about Assistive Technology in the Workplace.* ($2.25)

572
SMITHSONIAN INSTITUTION
Smithsonian Center for Education and Museum Studies
Washington, DC 20560-0427
202-357-3102
Fax: 202-357-3346

siintern@soe.si.edu
http://www.si.edu/cms

- *Internship Opportunities at the Smithsonian Institution.* ($5) 129 pages. A guide to the work of the Smithsonian Institution and where to fit in as an intern. Describes projects to participate in, skills necessary, and how to apply for internships. Includes quotes from former Smithsonian interns as well as information on the Smithsonian Minority Internship Program and the Native American Internship Program.

- *The Internships and Fellowships Brochure.* Lists Smithsonian museums and offices that offer internships.

573
SOCIAL SECURITY ADMINISTRATION
Attn: Muriel Kelly
U.S. Department of Health and Human Services
Room G-122, West High Rise
6401 Security Boulevard
Baltimore, MD 21235
410-965-8186
Fax: 410-966-6413
http://www.ssa.gov

- *Disability.* (05-10029) 17 pages. Discusses the various kinds of disability benefits available, as well as who is eligible and how to apply.

- *If You Are Blind: How Social Security and SSI Can Help.* (05-10052) 1 page.

- *Medicare.* (05-10043) 20 pages.

- *Retirement.* (05-10035) 17 pages.

- *SSI.* (05-11000) 1 page. Explains the Supplemental Security Income program, which provides a basic income to people with limited resources who are 65 or older, disabled, or blind.

- *Survivors.* (05-10084) 12 pages. Outlines the benefits available when a family breadwinner dies.

- *Understanding Social Security.* (05-10024) 40 pages.

- *When You Get Social Security Disability Benefits: What You Need to Know.* (05-10153) 24 pages.

- *When You Get Social Security Retirement or Survivors Benefits: What You Need to Know.* (05-10077) 27 pages.

- *When You Get SSI: What You Need to Know.* (05-11011) 1 page.

- *Working While Disabled: We Can Help.* (05-10095) 1 page.

Write or call for other available materials.

574
SOCIETY FOR AMERICAN ARCHAEOLOGY
900 Second Street, NE, Suite 12
Washington, DC 20002-3557
202-789-8200
Fax: 202-789-0284
info@saa.org
http://www.saa.org

The following is available on the Society's Web site:

- *Archaeology & You.* Provides an overview of the current states of American archaeology and clearly defines the role of archaeologists. Also includes information about the importance of perserving archaeological sites and concerns of Native Americans.

- *Archaeology and Public Education.* Back issues of the newsletter of the SAA Public Education Committee.

- *Academic Programs.* A listing of four-year educational institutions in Canada, Latin America, and the United States that have at least one archaeologist on the faculty.

- *Survey of Ph.D. Programs.* Experts in the field define the most important characteristics of an outstanding graduate program and rate which schools offer the best or most improved programs.

575
SOCIETY FOR ETHNOMUSICOLOGY, INC.
Morrison Hall 005
Indiana University
Bloomington, IN 47405-2501
812-855-6672
Fax: 812-855-6673
sem@indiana.edu
http://www.indiana.edu/~ethmusic

- *Guide to Programs in Ethnomusicology in the United States and Canada.* ($4 plus $2 shipping) 74 pages. Provides information about a variety of academic programs in ethnomusicology. Lists undergraduate and graduate programs.

576

SOCIETY FOR HISTORICAL ARCHAEOLOGY

PO Box 30446
Tucson, AZ 85751-0446
520-886-8006
Fax: 520-886-0182
sha@azstarnet.com
http://www.sha.org/

- *Mapping Out a Career in Historical Archaeology.* Lists background information on colleges and universities that offer training in historical archaeology.

- *Guide to Higher Education in Historical and Underwater Archaeology.*

- *Careers in Historical Archaeology.* 8 pages. (Excerpts available at the SHA Web site)

577

SOCIETY FOR HUMAN RESOURCE MANAGEMENT

1800 Duke Street
Alexandria, VA 22314
703-548-3440
Fax: 703-836-0367
shrm@shrm.org
http://www.shrm.org

The following publication is available in print and at the Society's Web site:

- *Careers in Human Resource Management.* 8 pages. Covers the many career options and specializations, required educational background and experience, personal characteristics, and salaries.

578

SOCIETY FOR INDUSTRIAL AND APPLIED MATHEMATICS

3600 University City Science Center
Philadelphia, PA 19104-2688
800-447-7426 or 215-382-9800
Fax: 215-386-7999
service@siam.org
http://www.siam.org

The following publication is available in print and at the Society's Web site:

- *Careers in Applied Mathematics & Computational Science.*

579

SOCIETY FOR INTEGRATIVE AND COMPARATIVE BIOLOGY

1313 Dolley Madison Boulevard
Suite 402
McLean, VA 22101-3926
703-790-1745
Fax: 703-790-2672
sicb@burkinc.com
http://www.sicb.org

- *Careers in Animal Biology.* 21 pages. Discusses opportunities in academic fields, fields of special interest, opportunities in health-related fields and other nonacademic fields, financing your education, and sources of information.

580

SOCIETY FOR MARINE MAMMOLOGY

Association Manager
PO Box 1897
Lawrence, KS 66044
800-627-0629
Fax: 785-843-1274

sfmm@allenpress.com
http://www.pegasus.cc.ucf.edu/~smm

Available at the Web site:

• *Strategies for Pursuing a Career in Marine Mammal Science.* Defines the field, the jobs available, the education/training required, and sources of additional information about careers in marine mammal science.

581
SOCIETY FOR MINING, METALLURGY, AND EXPLORATION, INC.
8307 Shaffer Parkway
Littleton, CO 80127
800-763-3132 or 303-973-9550
Fax: 303-973-3845
smenet@aol.com
http://www.smenet.org

• *Careers in the Minerals Industry.* 13 pages. Describes the duties and responsibilities for a number of career options, employment opportunities, and accredited programs in minerals fields leading to degrees in engineering or engineering technology.

• *Career Planning Workshops.* ($5) Contains presentations made at annual career planning workshops.

582
SOCIETY FOR RANGE MANAGEMENT
445 Union Boulevard, Suite 230
Lakewood, CO 80228
303-986-3309
Fax: 303-986-3892
srmden@ix.netcom.com
http://srm.org

• *Careers in Range Science and Range Management.* Discusses career and employment opportunities and educational preparation. Lists schools offering programs in management or range science in the United States and Canada.

583
SOCIETY FOR TECHNICAL COMMUNICATION
901 North Stuart Street, Suite 904
Arlington, VA 22203-1854
703-522-4114
Fax: 703-522-2075
stc@stc-va.org
http://www.stc-va.org

• *Careers in Technical Communication.* Describes career opportunities and education requirements. Also lists Web sites of colleges and universities offering programs in technical communication.

• *Technical Communication Salary Survey.* An annual salary and benefits survey is available on the Web site.

584
SOCIETY OF ACTUARIES
475 North Martingale Road, Suite 800
Schaumburg, IL 60173
847-706-3500
Fax: 847-706-3599
http://www.soa.org

• *Actuaries Make a Difference.* 22 pages. Explains what actuaries do and where they work by highlighting several real-life actuaries who describe how they became an actuary, what they do on the job, and what they most enjoy.

• *Actuarial Training Programs.* 29 pages. Lists programs in the United States and Canada, as well as contact information, salary range, types of employment, employment requirements, and general program information.

• *Associateship and Fellowship Catalog.* 114 pages. Includes general information; lists requirements for admission, a schedule for examinations, and course descriptions; and provides order forms and applications for exams.

• *Canadian and U.S Schools Offering Actuarial Science Courses Including Actuarial Mathematics.* 2 pages. Lists schools in Canada and the United States that offer actuarial science courses, including regularly scheduled classes covering substantially all the topics in the Society of Actuaries (SOA) Course 150, Actuarial Mathematics.

• *Canadian and United States Schools Offering a Pre-Actuarial Curriculum.* 8 pages. Lists schools in Canada and the United States that offer an actuarial related curriculum.

585
SOCIETY OF AMERICAN ARCHIVISTS
527 South Wells Street, 5th Floor
Chicago, IL 60607-1452
312-922-0140
Fax: 312-347-1452
http://www.archivists.org

• *The Image of Archivists: Resource Allocators' Perceptions.* ($12) 62 pages. Study highlighting how research allocators perceive and characterize archivists. Includes interviews with experts from government, universities, historical societies, museums, private businesses, and social organizations.

• *Planning for the Archival Profession.* ($8) 46 pages. Report to challenge and assist members of the archival profession in charting their own future course. Designed to respond to the changing needs of the occupation as it strives to preserve our documentary heritage.

The following resources are available free on the Society's Web site:

• *Directory of Archival Education in the United States and Canada.* Describes the archival profession and archival education; contains guidelines for the development of a curriculum for a master of archival studies degree; and lists archival education programs grouped geographically.

• *Directory of Student Chapters.* Explains the history of student chapters of the Society of American Archivists and provides a current listing of chapters, including faculty advisors, addresses, phone and fax numbers, e-mail, and Web site information.

• *So You Want to Be an Archivist: An Overview of the Archival Profession.* Defines archives, the work of archivists, and archival repositories. Lists qualifications for employment, and average salaries and benefits offered.

586
SOCIETY OF AMERICAN FLORISTS
1601 Duke Street
Alexandria, VA 22314

800-336-4743 or 703-836-8700
http://www.aboutflowers.com

- *Careers in Floriculture.* Describes the field and lists certificate programs and colleges that offer education in floriculture.

587
SOCIETY OF AMERICAN FORESTERS
5400 Grosvenor Lane
Bethesda, MD 20814-2198
301-897-8720
Fax: 301-897-3690
http://www.safnet.org

- *So You Want to Be in Forestry.* SASE, 9" x 12" envelope. 16 pages. Explains the roles and duties of foresters, their education and training, career opportunities, and related fields.

The following publications are in the *Forestry Career Packet.* SASE, 9" x 12" envelope.

- *Accredited Professional Forestry Degree Programs.* 3 pages. Lists institutions with SAF-accredited curricula and SAF-recognized curricula in the United States and Canada.

- *Forestry Career Information Question and Answer Sheet.* 2 pages. Contains the most frequently asked questions about the profession of forestry.

- *Job Seekers' Guide.* 2 pages. Lists contact information of forestry employers.

588
SOCIETY OF AUTOMOTIVE ENGINEERS, INC.
400 Commonwealth Drive
Warrendale, PA 15096-0001

724-776-4841
http://www.sae.org

- *Automotive Engineering: A Moving Career.* 6 pages. Describes the field and educational requirements and provides information on schools.

- *SAE Collegiate Chapters.* 27 pages. Lists student chapters and contact information.

589
SOCIETY OF COSMETIC CHEMISTS
120 Wall Street, Suite 2400
New York, NY 10005-4088
212-668-1500
Fax: 212-668-1504
scc@scconline.org
http://www.scconline.org

- *Career Opportunities in Cosmetic Science.* 14 pages.

590
SOCIETY OF DIAGNOSTIC MEDICAL SONOGRAPHERS
12770 Coit Road, Suite 708
Dallas, TX 75251
972-239-7367
Fax: 972-239-7378
info@sdms.org
http://www.sdms.org

The following publication is available in print and at the Society's Web site:

- *Diagnostic Medical Sonography Career Information.* 6 pages. Discusses the various specialties in the field, as well as duties, education, advancement, and salary.

591

SOCIETY OF EXPLORATION GEOPHYSICISTS

PO Box 702740
Tulsa, OK 74170-2740
918-493-3516
Fax: 918-497-5557
http://www.seg.org

• *Catch the Wavelet: 21st Century Careers in Exploration Geophysics.* 6 pages. Briefly describes geophysics, how to prepare for a career in the field, and scholarship opportunities.

592

SOCIETY OF FIRE PROTECTION ENGINEERS

7315 Wisconsin Avenue
Suite 1225 W
Bethesda, MD 20814
301-718-2910
Fax: 301-718-2242
sfpehqtrs@sfpe.org
http://www.sfpe.org/careers.html

• *Careers in Fire Protection Engineering.* A comprehensive guide to careers and resources for students interested in entering the profession. Contact e-mail address listed for a complimentary copy.

Visit the Web site for more information on universities that offer programs in fire protection engineering.

593

SOCIETY OF NAVAL ARCHITECTS AND MARINE ENGINEERS

601 Pavonia Avenue
Jersey City, NJ 07306
800-798-4800

Fax: 201-798-4975
eromanelli@sname.org
http://www.sname.org

• *Careers in the Maritime Industry: Naval Architecture, Marine Engineering, Ocean Engineering.* 24 pages. Discusses the future of the maritime industry; the roles of naval architects, marine engineers, and ocean engineers; and employers. Lists accredited institutions offering bachelor's degrees in engineering or engineering technology and provides scholarship information.

594

SOCIETY OF NUCLEAR MEDICINE

1850 Samual Morse Drive
Reston, VA 20190-5316
703-708-9000
Fax: 703-708-9013
m.ferg@snm.org
http://www.snm.org

• *Joint Review Committee on Educational Programs in Nuclear Medicine Technology: Accredited Programs.* 18 pages.

• *Nuclear Medicine Technology: A High-Tech Career for Today and Tomorrow.* Takes a look at the technologist's role and responsibilities, employment outlook and opportunities, salary, career alternatives, educational programs, and certification.

595

SOCIETY OF PETROLEUM ENGINEERS

Customer Service/Books
PO Box 833836
Richardson, TX 75083-3836
972-952-9393, ext. 261

Fax: 972-952-9435
books@spe.org
http://www.spe.org

- *Explore a World of Unlimited Opportunities: Careers in Petroleum Engineering.* 12 pages. Describes various careers in the field. More information available on the Web site.

596
SOCIETY OF PLASTICS ENGINEERS
14 Fairfield Drive
Brookfield, CT 06804-0403
203-775-0471
Fax: 203-775-8490
http://www.4spe.org

The following is accessible on the Web site:

- *Careers in Plastics Injection Molding.* Lists and describes different job titles of the field of plastics injection molding and where to find more information.

597
SOCIETY OF THE PLASTICS INDUSTRY, INC.
1801 K Street, NW, Suite 600K
Washington, DC 20006
202-974-5200
Fax: 202-296-7005
http://www.plasticsindustry.org

- *Careers in Plastics Brochure.* (#AB144) Single copies are available free of charge.

598
SOCIETY OF TOXICOLOGY
1767 Business Center Drive, Suite 302
Reston, VA 20190-5332

703-438-3115
Fax: 703-438-3113
http://www.toxicology.org

- *Resource Guide to Careers in Toxicology.* 147 pages. Discusses duties and responsibilities, employment opportunities, regional distribution of toxicology jobs, salaries, preparation, and profiles schools offering toxicology programs.

599
SOCIETY OF WOMEN ENGINEERS
120 Wall Street, 11th Floor
New York, NY 10005-3902
212-509-9577
Fax: 212-509-0224
http://www.swe.org

- *A Guide to Engineering Majors.*

- *FAQs.* Overview of engineering disciplines, requirements, curriculum, and ways of exploring careers for high school students.

- *Engineering May Be For You.* Covers engineering specialties, salaries, and lists potential employers.

- *Guide for the High School Women on Becoming an Engineer.* Covers skills, training, career paths, and gender issues related to women in engineering.

- *Is Engineering for You?* Explains college entrance requirements and what women engineers do.

600
SOCIETY OF WOOD SCIENCE AND TECHNOLOGY
One Gifford Pinchot Drive

Madison, WI 53705
608-231-9347
Fax: 608-231-9592
vicki@swst.org
http://www.swst.org

• *Careers in Wood Science and Technology: The Material Science of the Forest Products Industry.* (single copy free) Discusses background information about careers in the field and also includes educational requirements.

• *Directory of North American Schools Offering Baccalaureate and Graduate Programs of Study in Wood Science and Technology.*

601
SOIL AND WATER CONSERVATION SOCIETY
7515 Northeast Ankeny Road
Ankeny, IA 50021-9764
515-289-2331
Fax: 515-289-1227
pubs@swcs.org
http://www.swcs.org

• *Fact Sheet: Careers for the Future.* 1 page. Describes what careers are available in the Natural Resources Conservation Service.

602
SOLAR ENERGY INDUSTRIES ASSOCIATION
1111 North 19th Street, Suite 260
Arlington, VA 22209
703-248-0707
Fax: 703-248-0714
http://www.seia.org

• *Solar Jobs For Today and Tomorrow.* A brief overview of career opportunities in the solar industry.

• *Renewable Energy.* 12 pages. Discusses the field and its various specialties. Defines each specialty and lists its applications and potential.

603
SPECIAL LIBRARIES ASSOCIATION
1700 18th Street, NW
Washington, DC 20009-2514
202-234-4700
Fax: 202-265-9317
irc@sla.org
http://www.sla.org

• *Careers in Special Libraries.*

604
SPIE—THE INTERNATIONAL SOCIETY FOR OPTICAL ENGINEERING
PO Box 10
1000 20th Street
Bellingham, WA 98227-0010
360-676-3290
Fax: 360-647-1445
spie@spie.org
http://www.spie.org/

The following publication is available in print and at the Society's Web site:

• *Optics Education: SPIE's Annual Guide to Optics Programs Worldwide.* 135 pages. Includes a detailed entry for each program. Lists contact information, degrees granted, number of students specializing in optics or related fields, academic and research specialties, research facilities, continuing education, and industry/university cooperative programs, tuition, application deadline and admission requirements, financial assistance information, and a description of the department/program.

605
SPORTING GOODS MANUFACTURERS ASSOCIATION
200 Castlewood Drive
North Palm Beach, FL 33418
561-842-4100
Fax: 561-863-8984
sgma@ix.netcom.com
http://www.sportlink.com

The following publication is available in print and at the Association's Web site:

• *Gaining Ground: A Progress Report on Women in Sports.* 24 pages.

606
STUDENT CONSERVATION ASSOCIATION, INC.
Urban and Diversity Programs
1800 North Kent Street, Suite 1260
Arlington, VA 22209-2104
703-524-2441
Fax: 703-524-2451
internships@sca-inc.org
http://www.sca-inc.org/vol/ccdc/ccdc.htm

Available on the SCA Web site:

• *Conservation Career Advice from Green at Work.* Answers questions for anyone interested in environmental careers. Includes information on resume writing, internships, choosing the right career field, and more.

607
SUBURBAN NEWSPAPERS OF AMERICA
401 North Michigan Avenue
Chicago, IL 60611-4267
312-644-6661
Fax: 312-527-6658
http://www.suburban-news.org

The following publication is available in print and at the SNA Web site:

• *Careers in Suburban Newspapers.* A brief description of newspaper careers.

608
TAPPI
Technology Park
PO Box 105113
Atlanta, GA 30348-5113
800-332-8686
http://www.tappi.org

• *When I Grow Up.* An online resource that helps young people learn about engineering and technical careers. Includes "Looking for a Great Career?," "What's Your Major?," and "Where to Begin."

609
TEN SPEED PRESS
PO Box 7123
Berkeley, CA 94707
800-841-BOOK or 510-559-1600
Fax: 510-559-1629
http://www.tenspeed.com

• *Job Hunting on the Internet.* ($12.95 plus shipping) 110 pages. Pocket directory of Web sites useful for those selecting a career or searching for a job.

610

TEXAS HIGHER EDUCATION COORDINATING BOARD

Division of Student Services
PO Box 12788
Capitol Station
Austin, TX 78711-2788
512-427-6340
http://www.thecb.state.tx.us

• *Financial Aid for Texas Students.* 50 pages.

611

TEXAS SEA GRANT

1716 Briarcrest, Suite 702
Bryan, TX 77802
979-845-3854
Fax: 979-845-7525
http://texas-sea-grant.tamu.edu

• *Gulf of Mexico Directory of Marine and Coastal Education Programs.* 40 pages. A listing of marine-coastal education programs in the five Gulf states (Texas, Louisiana, Mississippi, Alabama, and Florida).

• *Questions About Careers in Oceanography.* 18 pages. Brochure providing concise and informative answers to questions about oceanographic careers. Aimed at high school and college students, teachers, and guidance counselors.

• *Vocational-Technical Marine Career Opportunities in Texas.* 22 pages. Assists high school counselors, teachers, and students better understand the career opportunities available in the Texas marine industry. Provides job descriptions, training and educational requirements, and contact information of organizations and schools for reference.

The following is available in print form or online at Texas Sea Grant's Web site:

• *Marine Education: A Bibliography of Education Materials Available from National Sea Grant Programs.* 68 pages. Listing of Sea Grant Programs and institutions that publish books, reports, or videos on their sea grant programs available for free or at a nominal cost. Helpful tool for use in grades K-12 classrooms or community education classes.

612

TINSLEY COMMUNICATIONS, INC.

PO Box 651
Hampton, VA 23669
757-229-1736
info@minorityscholarships.com

• *The Minority Guide to Scholarships and Financial Aid.* ($7.98) 32 pages. Lists close to 200 undergraduate and graduate programs and, for each, a program sponsor, award amount, eligibility requirements and restrictions, and the deadline.

613

TOOLING AND MANUFACTURING ASSOCIATION

1177 South Dee Road
Park Ridge, IL 60068-9809
847-825-1120
Fax: 847-825-0041
bpahl@tmanet.com
http://www.tmanet.com

• *How Valuable Is Your Future? This Short Quiz Could Make Your Career Dreams Come True.* 10 pages. Describes the duties of precision metalworkers, as well as interning, education, salary, and advancement opportunities.

• *The Tooling & Machinery Industry.* 7 pages. Discusses the industry as well as its customers, benefits, and opportunities.

• *Why Metalworking Careers Are Very Attractive.* 2 pages. Compares the metal trades to construction using 25 different criteria.

• *Apprentice Training Courses in Related Classroom Instruction.* 23 pages. Contains registration information, entrance and testing requirements, attendance requirements, and course descriptions. See the Association's Web site for more information.

614
U.S. NEWS & WORLD REPORT
Best Colleges
Department 363
PO Box 51790
Livonia, MI 41851
800-836-6397
Fax: 602-870-4760
http://www.usnews.com/usnews.edu

• *America's Best Colleges.* ($7.95) 280 pages. Lists by state the colleges and universities offering baccalaureate degrees. Contains information on choosing a school, how to get in, application procedures, paying for college, and grants and loans.

• *America's Best Graduate Schools.* ($7.95) 164 pages. Contains exclusive ranking for schools of business, law, medical, engineering, and other disciplines.

The Web site contains helpful information about colleges and career solutions and is a comprehensive tool for anyone planning to go to college or grad school. Sections include choosing a college, finding financial aid, pursuing graduate school or a career, and learning about aspects of college life outside the classroom.

615
UNITED FARM WORKERS OF AMERICA
PO Box 62, La Paz
Keene, CA 93531
661-823-6105
Fax: 661-823-6174
http://www.ufw.org

Visit the UFWA Web site to view additional publications.

• *Jobs for Dignity: Volunteer a Little of Your Life to Help Save Lives.* 6 pages.

616
UNITED FOOD AND COMMERCIAL WORKERS INTERNATIONAL UNION
Education Office
1775 K Street, NW
Washington, DC 20006-1598
202-223-3111
Fax: 202-466-1587
http://www.ufcw.org

• *UFCW Occupational Briefs.* 6 pages. Free publications, available in English or Spanish for the following careers: barber and cosmetologist, footwear worker, insurance sales professional, nursing aide, packinghouse worker, pharmacist, registered nurse, retail clerk, retail meat cutter, and seafood worker.

617
UNITED NEGRO COLLEGE FUND, INC.
Program Services Department
8260 Willow Oaks Corporate Drive
PO Box 10444
Fairfax, VA 22031-4511
800-331-2244 or 703-205-3538
http://www.uncf.org

- *College Guide: 39 Places to Expand Your Mind.* 47 pages. Lists and describes the 39 historically black colleges and universities.

- *Student Handbook.* 16 pages. Advises on choosing a college and includes a directory of UNCF's member schools and the types of programs offered.

618
UNITED STATES COAST GUARD
14180 Dallas Parkway, Suite 326
Dallas, TX 75240-4373
800-GET-USCG
http://www.uscg/jobs/

- *Get M.O.R.E. Out of Life.* 8 pages. Describes the Minority Officer Recruiting Effort.

- *Get to the Top Faster: Become a United States Coast Guard Officer.* 10 pages.

- *Missions of the United States Coast Guard.* 8 pages.

- *Montgomery G.I. Bill: Get up to $14,998 for College, Plus a Whole Lot More.* 6 pages.

- *Officer Candidate School: How Do You Get to the Top Faster?* 10 pages.

- *Opportunities for Action: Enlisted Career Guide.* 43 pages.

- *Things to Remember When You Visit Your Coast Guard Recruiter.* 6 pages.

- *United States Coast Guard: Ready for Action?* 10 pages.

- *United States Coast Guard: Unique Education, Unique Opportunity.* 8 pages.

- *United States Coast Guard Academy: This Is More than 4 Years in the Classroom.* 10 pages.

- *United States Coast Guard Reserve: Want to See Some Action This Weekend?* 10 pages.

619
UNITED STATES COMMISSION ON CIVIL RIGHTS
Publications
624 Ninth Street, NW
Washington, DC 20425
202-376-8128
Fax: 202-376-7597
http://www.usccr.gov

- *Catalog of Publications.* 13 pages. Lists various reports and studies on national, regional, and local civil rights matters.

- *Civil Rights Journal.* A magazine published annually by the U.S. Commission on Civil Rights. Available from the Superintendent of Documents, Government Printing Office, Washington, DC 20402. Features a variety of articles on civil rights issues.

• *Civil Rights Update.* A quarterly pamphlet containing a selection of timely articles about civil rights matters.

620
UNITED STATES DEPARTMENT OF AGRICULTURE
Office of Human Resources Management
Workforce Planning, Employment and Development Division
Attn: Summer Internship Program
Jamie L. Whitten Federal Building
Room 316-W
1400 Independence Avenue, SW
Washington, DC 20250-0002
202-720-6104
Fax: 202-720-7850
http://www/usda.gov/da/employ/intern.htm

• *Summer Internship Program.* Offers paid internships that may be administrative, professional, scientific, or technical, depending on the agency.

621
UNITED STATES DEPARTMENT OF EDUCATION
Office of the Secretary
400 Maryland Avenue, SW
Washington, DC 20202-0001
202-708-5366

• *A Teacher's Guide to the United States Department of Education.* 94 pages. A resource guide for teachers about the support programs, services, and publications available from the Department of Education. Provides a general description of programs and their relative location within the department, as well as a reference to which teachers can turn for specific needs or questions.

622
UNITED STATES DEPARTMENT OF EDUCATION
Information Resource Center
400 Maryland Avenue, SW
Washington, DC 20202-0498
800-USA-LEARN
customerservice@inet.gov
http://www.ed.gov

Available at the Web site:

• *The Student Guide.* Comprehensive resource on financial aid. Includes information on grants, loans, and work-study.

• *Funding Your Education.* General information about federal student financial aid programs.

• *Looking for Student Aid.* Brochure covering sources of free information about student aid and scholarship services.

• *Getting Ready for College Early.* Suggests steps to take during middle and high school years to get ready for college.

• *Parents' Guide to the Internet.* Introduction to the Web for anyone, regardless of current technical knowledge.

623
UNITED STATES DEPARTMENT OF LABOR
Bureau of Apprenticeship and Training
200 Constitution Avenue, NW
Room S4206
Washington, DC 20210
800-733-JOBS or 202-219-6871

Fax: 202-273-4793
http://www.doleta.gov

• *50 Questions Commonly Asked About Apprenticeship.*

624
UNITED STATES DEPARTMENT OF LABOR
Employment and Training
Administration
200 Constitution Avenue, NW
Room S4206
Washington, DC 20210
800-733-JOBS or 202-219-6871
http://www.doleta.gov

• *Tips for Finding the Right Job.* 27 pages.
Offers information on resumes, cover
letters, and interviewing.

• *Train for Skills and Success: Training
Opportunities in Job Corps.* 66 pages.
Directory of vocational courses offered
at 113 Job Corps centers located in 46
states, the District of Columbia, and
Puerto Rico. Programs offer educational
and vocational skills training through
individualized instruction combining
training and support service unique to
the Job Corps.

625
UNITED STATES DEPARTMENT OF LABOR
Assistant Secretary for Policy
200 Constitution Avenue, NW
Suite S-2312
Washington, DC 20210
202-219-6197
Fax: 202-219-9216
http://www.dol.gov/dol/asp

Available at the Web site:

• *The Small Business Handbook: Laws,
Regulations and Technical Assistance
Services.* Includes such topics as minimum wage, child labor, alien workers,
occupational safety and health, employment benefit plans, whistle-blower protection, veterans, plant closings, lie
detector tests, and family and medical
leave.

626
UNITED STATES DEPARTMENT OF LABOR
877-348-0502
Fax: 877-348-0499
http://www.acinet.org

• *America's Career InfoNet.* Includes links
to information on career exploration,
general outlook on professions, wages
and trends in today's marketplace,
employer search, state profiles, and a
resource library.

627
UNITED STATES DEPARTMENT OF STATE
Office of Academic Exchange Programs
301 Fourth Street, SW, Room 234
Washington, DC 20547
202-619-4360
Fax: 202-401-5914
http://e.usia.gov/education

• *Fulbright Scholar Program.* 157 pages.
Lists and describes the specific Fulbright
senior scholar awards available for U.S.
faculty and professionals. Includes
application for grants.

• *Fulbright U.S. Student Program.* 102 pages. Lists and describes the specific Fulbright awards for graduate study and research abroad. Includes applications for grants.

• *Fulbright Teacher and Administer Exchange Program.* 21 pages. Lists and describes specific Fulbright awards for U.S. teachers and administrators. Includes application for grants.

628

UNITED STATES DEPARTMENT OF STATE

Bureau of Educational and Cultural Affairs
Office of Global Educational Programs
Teacher Exchange Branch
301 Fourth Street SW, Room 353
Washington, DC 20547
800-726-0479 or 202-619-4556
Fax: 202-401-1433
http://www.grad.usda.gov/
international/ftep.html

• *Fulbright Teacher Exchange Program.* 22 pages. Describes the exchange opportunities for U.S. university faculty, as well as secondary and elementary school teachers and administrators, to teach abroad; lists available positions by country; and includes application form.

629

UNITED STATES DEPARTMENT OF STATE

Recruitment Division SA-1
2401 E Street, NW, 5th Floor
Washington, DC 20522
http://www.state.gov

Available at the Web site:

• *Internships Index.* Listing of opportunities for students to get experience in foreign affairs environment through firsthand knowledge. Opportunities available spring through fall in Washington, DC, or at an embassy overseas. Internships are both paid and unpaid.

• *Student Programs Index.* Information on how students can get experience in foreign affairs through on-the-job experience.

630

UNITED STATES FISH AND WILDLIFE SERVICE

Office of Public Affairs
U.S. Department of the Interior
Washington, DC 20240
202-208-5611
Fax: 202-208-7409
http://www.fws.gov

The following publication is available in print and online formats:

• *Careers With the U.S. Fish and Wildlife Service.* 20 pages. More color photos than text, this book highlights the problems addressed by the service (pollution, deforestation, preservation of wildlife habitat) and describes the academic background required for its jobs.

631

UNITED STATES GEOLOGICAL SURVEY

507 National Center
Reston, VA 20192
888-ASK-USGS
Fax: 703-648-5548

ask@usgs.gov
http://www.usgs.gov

- *Selected References on Careers in Earth Science.* 4 pages. Lists pamphlets, leaflets, booklets, books, audiovisual aids, and related organizations.

632
UNITED STATES GOVERNMENT PRINTING OFFICE
Superintendent of Documents
PO Box 371954
Pittsburgh, PA 15250-7954
202-512-1800
Fax: 202-512-2250
http://www.access.gpo.gov

- *Employment Outlook: 1996-2006: Job Quality and Other Aspects of Projected Employment Growth.* ($8.50) 108 pages. Provides an overview of industry and occupational projections, focusing on fields that will generate the largest portion of the projected job growth.

- *Careers in Transportation: Moving Everyone and Everything, Everywhere.* ($9) 101 pages. Information on jobs in the transportation industry.

- *Directory of Cultural Resource Education Programs at Colleges, Universities, and Trade Schools in the United States.* ($9.50) 105 pages. Information on training or education programs related to the preservation and management of cultural resources and heritage in the U.S. Arranged by type and state.

- *High School Counselor's Handbook.* ($11) 111 pages. Designed to help counselors advise students about financial aid,

especially student aid provided by the Department of Education. Includes supplementary materials to encourage high school students on to post-secondary schools as a pathway to career success.

- *Job Outlook In Brief: 1996-2006.* ($3.25) 37 pages. Presents job title, estimated employment, percentage change in employment, and prospects for the future.

- *Learning to Work: Making the Transition from School to Work.* ($7.50) 114 pages. Assesses the potential and problems of work-based training as a component of school-to-work transition programs.

- *Nontraditional Education: Alternative Ways to Earn Your Credentials.* ($2) 14 pages. Describes nontraditional ways to earn education credit in high school and college.

- *Occupational Outlook Quarterly Subscription.* ($9.50) Year subscription to a magazine to help guidance and career counselors, employment analysts, and young people to keep up on employment developments. Each issue contains articles on new occupations, training opportunities, salary trends, career counseling, and other new studies.

- *Preparation for Work.* ($4.25) 22 pages. Illustrates how high school classes, college courses, and student work experience can help prepare a young worker for the labor force.

- *Core Subjects and Your Career: English, Math, and Science.* ($1.50) 16 pages.

- *Directory of Nontraditional Training and Employment Programs Serving Women.* ($9.50) 165 pages. Provides information on 125 programs and services to women seeking jobs in trades and technology. Includes appendices.

- *Five Articles on College Graduates: Outlook, Earnings, and More.* ($4.25) 52 pages. Examines college graduates' position in the labor market.

- *Is There Another Degree in Your Future?: Choosing Among Professional and Graduate Schools.* ($1.25) 13 pages. Provides useful information for people who want to continue their education. Addresses typical questions about choosing a school.

Other titles are available. Contact the Superintendent of Documents office for more details.

633
UNITED STATES MILITARY ENTRANCE PROCESSING COMMAND
2500 Green Bay Road
North Chicago, IL 60064-3094
847-688-3680
info@mepcom.army.mil
http://www.mepcom.army.mil/

- *Military Careers: A Guide to Military Occupations and Selected Military Career Paths.* 427 pages. A collection of military occupational, training, and career information. Used as a reference source for educators and students to aid in learning about the diverse opportunities available to young people in the military. Contains descriptions of 152 enlisted and officer occupations.

634
UNITED STATES NAVY
800-USA-NAVY
http://www.navyjobs.com

The following information is available and can be ordered through the Web site:

- *Information for Those Ages 15 and Under.* Includes information on what navy life is like, frequently asked questions, navy stories, and an interactive game called "The Mission."

- *For the High School Student or Graduate.* Explores jobs and training available, opportunities to earn money for college, information on navy life and frequently asked questions (FAQs).

- *For the College Student or Graduate.* Links to information on college money programs, benefits, career opportunities, Navy life, hot jobs, and FAQs.

- *Professional Links.* Includes information on the following job positions: chaplains, dentists, lawyers, medical services, nurses, and physicians. Each job link includes information on professional development with the Navy, career opportunities, hot jobs, benefits available, and frequently asked questions.

635
UNITED STATES OFFICE OF PERSONNEL MANAGEMENT
http://www.usajobs.opm.gov

- *USA JOBS Web Site.* Lets you tailor your job search, view daily updated listings, and receive other general information, including how to apply for a federal job, federal salaries and benefits, warnings against federal job scams, outplacement assistance, and student employment.

636
UNITED STATES PATENT AND TRADEMARK OFFICE
U.S. Department of Commerce
Box Patent Application
Assistant Commissioner for Patents
Washington, DC 20231
800-786-9199
Fax: 703-305-7786
http://www.uspto.gov/

• *Basic Facts about Patents.* 7 pages. Answers some of the most frequently asked questions about getting a patent.

• *Basic Facts about Trademarks.* 32 pages. Contains instructions and forms for registering a trademark for a product or service.

• *Internet Information.* 3 pages. Describes U.S. patent and trademark information available on the Internet.

637
UNITED STATES SECRET SERVICE
Office of Government Liason and Public Affairs
950 H Street, NW, Suite 8400
Washington, DC 20001
202-406-5708
http://www.treas.gov/usss

Available at the Web site:

• *Frequently Asked Questions.* With separate answers for kids and adults, this site covers topics such as descriptions of the job, how to become an agent, educational requirements, and more.

638
UNITED STATES SMALL BUSINESS ADMINISTRATION
Publications, Mc 7111
409 3rd Street, SW
Washington, DC 20416
http://www.sba.gov

The following publications are available at the Web site:

• *Planning and Goal Setting for Small Business.* Lists management techniques for planning.

• *Checklist for Going into Business.* Also available in Spanish, highlights the important factors in reaching a decision to start a business.

• *How to Buy or Sell a Business.* Lists several techniques for determining the best price to buy or sell a small business.

• *Handbook for Small Business.* Information for getting started in a new business. Developed by SBA's Service Corps of Retired Executives (SCORE).

• *Ideas into Dollars.* Identifies the main challenges in product development and provides a list of resources to help investors and innovators take their ideas into the marketplace.

• *Avoiding Patent, Trademark and Copyright Problems.* (#P102) Tips on how to avoid infringing upon the rights of others and how to protect your own rights.

• *Resource Directory for Small Business Management.* 6 pages. A list of SBA publications and videotapes for starting and managing a successful small business.

639
UNIVERSITY OF CALIFORNIA
Environmental Design Library
Moffitt Library, 5th Floor
Berkeley, CA 94720-6000
510-642-4818
http://www.lib.berkeley.edu/
ENVI/jobs.html

The following publication is available in print and online:

• *Job Hunting in Planning, Architecture, and Landscape Architecture.* Selectively annotated guide to help job seekers in the professions of city and regional planning, architecture, and landscape architecture. Highlights useful information on job hunting, researching prospective employers, creating resumes and portfolios, interviewing for jobs, and negotiating for salaries.

640
UNIVERSITY OF CALIFORNIA
Department of Anthropology
Berkeley, CA 94720-3710
510-642-3616
http://ls.berkeley.edu/dept/anth/
handbook.html

• *Anthropology: A Handbook for Undergraduate Majors.* Provides career information.

641
UNIVERSITY OF DELAWARE SEA GRANT COLLEGE PROGRAM
Marine Communications Office
Newark, DE 19716-3530
302-831-8083
Fax: 302-831-2005
marinecom@udel.edu
http://www.ocean.udel.edu/seagrant

• *Marine Careers.* ($15) 18 minutes. Video describing the many opportunities in marine transportation; science and technology; recreation and tourism; uniformed services; environmental management; and commercial fishing.

The following publications are available in print form or are accessible online:

• *Marine Careers: The Scientist.* (single copy is free; multiple copies are $.15 each) 4 pages. Covers educational requirements and outlook for marine science careers, including marine biologist, marine chemist, marine geologist, physical oceanographer, and ocean engineer. Also contains sources of additional marine career information.

• *Delaware Aquaculture Resource Guide.* (single photocopy is free) Lists contacts for technical information and assistance in Delaware; regional and national programs; newsletters, reference books, and manuals; aquaculture equipment and suppliers; and aquaculture associations.

• *University of Delaware Sea Grant Reporter.* (free subscription) Published twice a year, this newsletter reports on the research, education, and outreach activities of the University of Delaware Sea Grant College Program. Includes research highlights, educational features, listings of other publications, events, and seafood recipes.

642

UNIVERSITY OF ILLINOIS AT URBANA-CHAMPAIGN

Department of Agricultural Engineering
338 Agricultural Engineering Science Building
1304 West Pennsylvania Avenue
Urbana, IL 61801
217-333-3570
Fax: 217-244-0323
http://www.age.uiuc.edu

• *We've Got an Eye on Your Future and TSM Brochures.* Promotional brochures for the Department of Agricultural Engineering containing general information on the Agricultural Engineering program and the Technical Systems Management program.

• *Discover Magazine.* Distributed by the American Society of Agricultural Engineers (ASAE). Features fields of agriculture, food, and biological engineering that offer a wide variety of career opportunities.

• *Explore Magazine.* Distributed by ASAE. Describes many diverse and interesting job opportunities awaiting Agricultural Engineering graduates in the technical systems management field.

643

UNIVERSITY OF ROCHESTER

Career Center
302 Meliora Hall
Rochester, NY 14627
716-275-2366
Fax: 716-461-3093
mngr@mail.rochester.edu
http://www.rochester.edu/careercenter

• *Thinking about a Career in Law.* 1 page. SASE. Suggests the educational route for undergraduate students to follow in preparation for law school.

644

UNIVERSITY OF TORONTO PRESS

10 St. Mary Street, Suite 700
Toronto, Ontario M4Y 2W8, Canada
416-978-2239
Fax: 416-978-4738
http://utpress.utoronto.ca

• *The Education Planner.* ($2) 32 pages. Contains a 138-question survey to match interests and abilities to major areas of study; summarizes admission requirements and programs for Canadian institutions.

645

UNIVERSITY/RESIDENT THEATRE ASSOCIATION, INC.

1560 Broadway, Room 414
New York, NY 10036
212-221-1130
Fax: 212-869-2752
urta@aol.com
http://www.urta.com

• *U/RTA Theatre Directory of Member Training Programs and Associated Theatres.* ($5) 50 pages. Lists professional training programs (contact information, type of programs offered, period of engagement, stipends available, degree programs, and planned productions for the season) and provides similar details on U/RTA producing companies.

646
USA TODAY
Education
1000 Wilson Boulevard, T1-19
Arlington, VA 22229
703-276-3400
http://www.education.usatoday.com

• *Virtual Career Quest.* Using the Web site, click on the "Career Quest" icon to get real world tools and information to assist students in career planning. Leads students through self-assessment activities and introduces them to role models.

647
VINCENT/CURTIS
224 Clarendon Street
Boston, MA 02116
617-536-0100

• *Vincent/Curtis Educational Register.* 200 pages. Lists private day and boarding schools, camps, and summer study programs by region.

648
VIRGINIA EMPLOYMENT COMMISSION
CareerConnect
http://www.careerconnect.state.va.us

Available at the Web site:

• *CareerConnect.* Includes links to colleges, universities, community colleges, vocational and technical schools, financial aid opportunities, and general labor market information for the state of Virginia.

649
VIRGINIA VIEW
Virginia Polytechnic Institute and State University
205 West Roanoke Street
Blacksburg, VA 24061-0527
540-231-7571
Fax: 540-231-4979
http://vaview.vavu.vt.edu/

• *Career Hunt.* An annual newspaper providing educational and occupational information, including brief descriptions of 300 occupations. Meets the needs of adults in the planning, seeking, or transition stages of their careers.

• *CrossRoads.* An annual newspaper offering high school students and young adults career exploration and planning resources. Includes post-secondary training and educational resources and comes with a teacher's guide.

• *VIEWStarts 1, 2, and 3.* Three annual newspapers providing career-related activities for children in grades K-8. Also includes a teacher's guide.

• *Interactive VIEW.* A software program containing information on 600 occupations, a career interest inventory, financial aid, licensing, and military information. Available on disks or CD-ROM.

• *College Search.* A software program containing extensive information on national colleges, including two-year, four-year, and graduate programs. Available on disks or CD-ROM.

• *Career Information Line.* Call 800-542-5870 (toll free in Virginia). Provides access to up-to-date career information, software programs, print materials, and resources on the Internet. Discusses occupational outlook, work requirements, salaries, post-secondary education, apprenticeships, and other topics. Also provides referrals to local, state, and national agencies related to career information. Career Information Line hours are Monday through Friday, 8:00 a.m. to 5:00 p.m.

Visit Virginia VIEW's Web site for more information and links to career and educational resources, disability resources, volunteerism, and labor market information. Provides resources for educators, counselors, and job seekers.

650
VISION
Claretian Publications
205 West Monroe Street
Chicago, IL 60606
312-236-7782
editor@visionguide.org
http://www.visionguide.org

• *Vision 2000.* Published annually by the National Religious Vocation Conference through Claretian Publications, this publication is a comprehensive resource available for those seeking information on religious life.

Available at the Web site:

• *Five Reasons NOT to Enter Religious Life.*

• *How I Followed My Call to Religious Life.*

• *Mission Took Me to Federal Prison.*

• *16 Questions About Vocations.*

• *What to Expect From Generation X.*

• *Vision Directory.* Online guide of American religious communities.

651
VISTA MAGAZINE
999 Ponce de Leon Boulevard, Suite 600
Coral Gables, FL 33134
800-521-0953 or 305-442-2462
Fax: 305-443-7650
jlobaco@hisp.com

• *The Scholarship Guide for Hispanics: College Financial Assistance Opportunities.* 95 pages. *Vista Magazine,* together with Chrysler Corporation, compiled this book, which is distributed by Montemayor y Asociados, 70 Northeast Loop 410, Suite 870, San Antonio, TX 78216.

652
VOCATIONAL BIOGRAPHIES, INC.
PO Box 31
Sauk Center, MN 56378-0031
800-255-0752
Fax: 320-352-5546
VocBio@aol.com

• *Vocational Biographies.* Choose from 875 titles. Each four-page brief discusses careers ranging from the traditional to the newly emerging and talk about real-life experiences of actual people. Call or write for a complete Vocational Biographies Career Library index.

653

WATER ENVIRONMENT FEDERATION
601 Wythe Street
Alexandria, VA 22314-1994
703-684-2400
Fax: 703-684-2492
http://www.wef.org

• *Test the Waters! Careers in Water Quality.* SASE. 8 pages. Highlights career and employment opportunities, as well as the required training and skills for a number of jobs.

654

WEED SCIENCE SOCIETY OF AMERICA
PO Box 1897
Lawrence, KS 66044-8897
800-627-0629
Fax: 913-843-1274
http://www.uiuc.edu/ph/www/wssa/

• *Career Opportunities in Weed Science.* 6 pages. Describes the field, scope of the work, employment opportunities, and edcuational requirements.

655

WEST VIRGINIA BUREAU OF EMPLOYMENT PROGRAMS
Research, Information, and Analysis Division
112 California Avenue
Charleston, WV 25305-0112
304-558-2660
Fax: 304-558-1343
jarvij0@wvnvm.wvnet.edu
http://www.state.wv.us/bep/lmi

• *Employment and Earnings Trends.*

• *Employment and Wages.*

• *Licensed Occupations in West Virginia.*

• *Occupational Wage Survey.*

• *Special Report on Veterans: State of West Virginia.*

• *West Virginia County Profiles.* County-by-county description of basic economic, employment, and demographic data.

• *West Virginia Economic Summary.* Monthly data on employment, unemployment, industry, and civilian labor force.

• *West Virginia Occupational Projections.*

• *West Virginia Youth and the Labor Market.*

656

WEST VIRGINIA OCCUPATIONAL INFORMATION COORDINATING COMMITTEE
West Virginia Department of Education
Barron Drive
PO Box 487
Institute, WV 25112-0487
304-766-2687
Fax: 304-766-2689
stewart@mail.drs.state.wv.us

• *West Virginia Careers.* 60 pages. A tabloid containing valuable career information geared toward the high school and college student. Provides insights into the job market, identifies growing job fields, discusses required education, and lists additional resources for information.

657
WIDER OPPORTUNITIES FOR WOMEN
815 15th Street, NW, Suite 916
Washington, DC 20005
202-638-3143
Fax: 202-638-4885
info@wowonline.org
http://www.w-o-w.org

- *Fact Sheets.* ($3 each) Available titles include:
- *Overview: Women in the Workforce;*
- *Women and Nontraditional Work;*
- *Women, Work and Age;*
- *Women, Work and Child Care;*
- *Women, Work and Family;*
- *Women, Work and the Future; and*
- *Women, Work and Health Insurance.*

658
WILDLIFE SOCIETY
5410 Grosvenor Lane
Bethesda, MD 20814-2197
301-897-9770
Fax: 301-530-2471
tws@wildlife.org

- *A Wildlife Conservation Career for You.* ($.50) 12 pages. Describes careers in wildlife management, related opportunities, education needed, and personal requirements.

- *Universities and Colleges Offering Curricula in Wildlife Conservation.* 6 pages. Lists North American campuses that have special curricula related to the fields of wildlife conservation and management.

659
WINDS OF CHANGE: A MAGAZINE FOR AMERICAN INDIAN EDUCATION AND OPPORTUNITY
AISES Publishing Inc.
4730 Walnut, Suite 212
Boulder, CO 80301
303-444-9099
http://www.winds.uthscsa.edu

- *Annual College Guide for American Indians.* ($10) Describes the top colleges for Native Americans and lists summer college-prep programs available. Also includes information about writing college application essays, contacts for college guidance, and financial aid requirements.

660
WISCONSIN CAREER INFORMATION SYSTEM
Center on Education and Work
University of Wisconsin at Madison
Room 1074 Educational Sciences, Unit I
1025 West Johnson Street
Madison, WI 53706
800-442-4612 or 608-263-2725
Fax: 608-262-3063
wisconsincareers@education.wisc.edu
http://wiscareers.education.wisc.edu

- *Wisconsin Careers.* 8-16 pages. A tabloid newspaper published two times a year.

661
WISCONSIN DEPARTMENT OF WORKFORCE DEVELOPMENT
Workforce Development Library
PO Box 7946
Madison, WI 53707-7946
608-266-2832

Fax: 608-261-7979
pugina@dwd.stste.wi.us
http://www.dwd.state.wi.us/dwelmi

- *Civilian Labor Force Estimates.* Monthly statistics include monthly and annual averages for civilian labor force and unemployment rates.

- *Employment Review.* Monthly release of the most current information on employment and unemployment rates for each of the nine local labor market regions. Also includes articles about local labor market events and industry trends.

- *Labor Market Information: A Directory of Wisconsin Publications, 1997 Edition.* Describes all publications of labor market statistics and information produced by the Wisconsin Bureau of Workforce Information. Also includes contacts in the administrative office and a list of the regional labor market analysts throughout the state.

662
WOMEN'S BUREAU
U.S. Department of Labor
200 Constitution Avenue, NW
Room S-3311
Washington, DC 20210
800-827-5335
Fax: 202-219-5529
http://www.dol.gov/dol/wb

The following publications are available by mail or can be accessed on the Web:

- *Worth More Than We Earn: Fair Pay for Working Women.* Describes the wage gap, its causes, and what employers, unions,

and working women can do to help close the gap.

- *What Works: Fair Pay for Working Women.* Profiles employers across the country who have improved pay scales for women (and men) in traditionally female jobs.

- *Don't Work in the Dark—Know Your Rights Series.* Brochures that discuss various discrimination issues such as disability, age, pregnancy, and sexual harassment.

- *Women at the Millennium.* Addresses steps women should take to benefit from opportunities of the new century.

- *Women, Work, and Wages.* Provides women with valuable knowledge to find a job with a well-deserved salary. Includes a general overview of the existing wage gap between men and women workers and explains how to negotiate a fair salary.

- *Women of Hispanic Origin in the Labor Force.*

- *Black Women in the Labor Force.*

- *Hot Jobs for the 21st Century.*

- *Women Business Owners.*

- *Women in Management.*

- *Domestic Violence: A Workplace Issue.*

- *Nontraditional Occupations for Women in 1999.*

More titles are available from the Women's Bureau. Call or visit the Web site for more information.

663
WOMEN'S SPORTS FOUNDATION
Eisenhower Park
East Meadow, NY 11554
800-227-3988 or 516-542-4700
Fax: 516-542-4716
wosport@aol.com
http://www.womenssports
foundation.org

• *Women's Athletic Scholarship Guide.*

• *Award, Grant & Scholarship Summary.*

• *Parent's Guide to Girls' Sports.* ($3)

More materials are available. Call or write for a resource order form.

664
WOODS HOLE OCEANOGRAPHIC INSTITUTION
Woods Hole Sea Grant Program
193 Ocean Pond Road, MS #2
Woods Hole, MA 02543-1525

• *Oceanography Reading List.* (#WHOI-L-95-002) ($2.50 includes postage) 52 pages. Bibliography listing oceanography reading materials, films, videos, and research Web sites listed by category.

• *Women in Science: Good Girls Don't.* (WHOI-R-90-001) ($1.50 includes postage) 6 pages. Article describing the trials faced by women in science, as well as the changes taking place in attitudes and institutions. Includes personal stories illustrating the wide array of marine science careers that exist and the women who pursue them.

665
WORCESTER POLYTECHNIC INSTITUTE
Fire Protection Engineering and Center for Firesafety Studies
100 Institute Road
Worcester, MA 01609-2280
508-831-5000
http://www.wpi.edu

The following are available online:

• *Career Opportunities.* Describes the career paths available to engineering graduates in the field of fire protection engineering (FPE). Includes job descriptions, employers, the job market, educational requirements, and internship programs.

• *Employers.* A list of companies known to employ Fire Protection Engineers.

• *Colleges and Universities.* A list of worldwide institutions that offer programs in fire protection engineering.

• *Careers Video.* 10-minute video presentation on careers in the field of fire protection engineering. Available as a video cassette or a CD-ROM or simply download from the Web site.

666
WORKING FOR AMERICA INSTITUTE
815 16th Street, NW
Washington, DC 20006
800-842-4734 or 202-638-3912
Fax: 202-783-6536
info@workingforamerica.org
http://www.workingforamerica.org

- *It's Your Job...These Are Your Rights.* 13 pages. A guide to young workers' rights under federal laws. Includes information on wages, health and safety, and family and medical leave. Also available in Spanish.

- *Coping with Downsizing and Closings: How Unions Can Help.* Provides information for workers who have been laid off.

- *Survivng Layoff.* Provides an overview of the services available to displaced workers. Also available in Spanish.

- *Working with People Who Have Disabilities.* Highlights the Institute's services to people with disabilities, their unions, and their employers.

CAREER SITES ON THE WORLD WIDE WEB

Following is a sampling of career sites on the World Wide Web. Professional associations, Internet clearinghouses of job information, employment services, online career centers, and other sites are represented. This will give you an idea of the variety of career information available for free on the Internet.

AMERICAN ASSOCIATION OF COLLEGES OF NURSING

http://www.aac.nche.edu

The AACN, an organization founded as the voice for the nation's leading nursing educational programs, hosts a Web site providing useful information to those interested in a career in nursing or for those who want to keep abreast of the changing dynamics of the industry. The site includes online press releases, publications, conference listings, job leads, and lists 550 AACN-member schools for nursing.

AMERICA'S JOB BANK

http://www.ajb.dni.us

A national clearinghouse operated by both the public Employment Services and the U.S. Department of Labor, this database is one of the largest online job resources available on the Internet. The site is updated every night, adding approximately 5,000 new job listings daily. Job seekers can post resumes, create cover letters, and establish a personal

online career account to track their job search progress. Links to other government-run job resources are available, including "Career Infonet," which provides industry trends and employer profiles, and the "Learning Exchange," which provides online training and educational resources.

BUREAU OF LABOR STATISTICS

http://stats.bls.gov

This site offers the latest economic information including news releases, surveys, publications, research, and regional information. Economic data for states and industries nationwide are easily accessible, such as cost of living index, unemployment rates, average compensation, productivity versus cost figures, working conditions, and more.

THE CAREER KEY

http://www.ncsu.edu/careerkey

On this Web site, students can determine their personality type through an online quiz, then build a list of jobs that fit that personality type. The self-assessment also helps students choose an appropriate training program or college major.

CAREER MAGAZINE
http://www.careermag.com

This online magazine is a helpful resource for not only job seekers, but also anyone interested in reading about hot topics in today's workplace. Regularly updated articles cover issues such as discrimination on the job, work ethics, and tips to career enrichment and success. The site also provides job-searching tools such as resume boards, job match engines, employer profiles, job fair listings, and other career links for more information.

CAREER MANAGER
http://www.doi.gov/octc

Brought to you by the U.S. Department of the Interior, this site offers career advice to job seekers of all ages. Included on the site are comprehensive guides to using the Internet and developing a career strategy. Both use step-by-step instruction to get the most of your job search. Job listings for federal, state, and the private sector are updated regularly. Also included are useful links about networking, job fairs, resume and cover letter writing, and more.

CAREERMOSAIC
http://www.careermosaic.com

With an average of approximately 100,000 opportunities posted at a time,

CareerMosaic is a leading Web employment site. The site offers both general job searching tools such as resume tips and job posting boards, as well as industry-specific resources in fields such as accounting, health care, human resources, sales, marketing, and technology. For those entering the job market for the first time, a "College Connection" link covers issues such as internships, studying abroad, graduate school and testing information, and other general career building tips and techniques.

CAREER RESOURCE CENTER
http://www.careers.org

With the overwhelming amount of online career resources available, this site helps job seekers navigate the Net through a directory of online career sites. Links are organized in different ways depending on personal job searching needs, such as by state, industry, or educational and experience levels.

CAREERPATH.COM
http://www.careerpath.com

Sponsored by various national newspapers and employers, this Web site provides current job listings posted in help wanted ads around the country. No listing remains on the site for more than two weeks. All openings can be found by region, employer, job type, or keyword. Also included on the site are spotlights on different industries, salary statistics, and internship opportunities.

CAREERPLANIT
http://www.careerplanit.com

A helpful resource for graduating seniors, this site offers guidance for beginning job seekers. Their resource page offers advice on interviewing, internships, resume building, and choosing a career, and includes a list of other recommended online job search sites. CareerPlanit also provides an employer database, internship leads, and a discussion board to post questions and opinions about job searching challenges.

COLLEGENET
http://www.collegenet.com

This site offers search engines to help students locate two-year, four-year, vocational, technical, business, medical, or nursing programs nationwide. Flexible search criteria include state or region of the country, enrollment, tuition, majors and sports offered, and average GPA. Students can even apply to many of the institutions online.

COOLWORKS
http://www.coolworks.com

Job openings posted on this site are located in areas "where others only visit," such as national parks, vacation resorts, campgrounds, and ski lodges. Openings are categorized by job type or location and include full descriptions and contact information. Also included are past employee profiles and international worker requirements.

DISABILITY ONLINE
http://www.wdsc.org/disability

Brought to you by the federal Employment and Training Administration, this site is a helpful tool to any workers with disabilities. Contact information for national organizations and disability workers are provided for more assistance or information. Online reports cover facts and myths about disabled workers and profile stories of employers and successful workers with disabilities who together overcame job accommodation challenges.

DISCOVER ENGINEERING ONLINE
http://www.discoverengineering.org

Designed for young students, this site sheds light on the abstract engineering field by pointing out the important role engineers play in our society. Students can learn about specific areas of the field, such as aerospace engineering, chemical engineering, environmental engineering, and more. Also available are links to FAQ's about salaries, hours, travel opportunities, and educational requirements.

EDUGATE
http://www.acq.osd.mil/ddre/edugate

This site offers an overwhelming amount of federal opportunities available to high school, college, graduate, or post-doctorate students. Includes information on apprenticeships, mentoring and tutoring opportunities, scholarships, fellowships, tuition assistance, grants, stipends, and more.

EMORY UNIVERSITY: CAREER PARADISE

http://www.emory.edu/CAREER

This campus site is helpful to all students preparing to enter the workforce, offering resources such as pre-law and pre-med school advice, and recommended steps to take when finding a job or selecting a field. Also included on the site is a "Colossal List of Links" to additional informative career Web sites.

EMPLOYMENT LINKS

http://www.asae.org/jobs

As part of the American Society of Agricultural Engineers larger Web site, this page lists a number of employment resources available online for all career interests.

ENGINEERING NET

http://www.jets.org

Aimed at high school students curious about engineering, this site offers engineering job descriptions, suggestions for high school classes and activities, news updates, and an online directory of accredited schools, institutions, and associations of engineering.

ENGINEERING: YOUR FUTURE

http://www.asee.org/precollege

Created by the American Society for Engineering Education, this Web site answers common questions about choosing a major in the field and the resulting career options that will become available after graduation. The site includes press releases, assessment tests, homework help, and information about choosing (and paying for) a college or university.

ENVIRONMENTAL CAREERS ORGANIZATION

http://www.eco.org

This site highlights internship opportunities for people interested in environmental careers. Also included are conference listings, diversity initiative programs, helpful hints and frequently asked questions regarding opportunities available and the application process..

ENVIRONMENTAL PROFESSIONAL'S HOMEPAGE

http://www.clay.net

Priding itself on being a "quick-load, no-nonsense work platform," this Web site provides links to resources, such as federal and state government agencies, environmental associations, conferences, and training courses. Also includes job postings and announcements from employers in the industry.

GOOD WORKS

http://www.essential.org/goodworks

Providing alternatives to work available outside the corporate structure, Good Works represents over 1,000 social change organizations. Their Web site lists available publications related to social policy and working in the field, an online student guide to alternative careers, and a nationwide job search engine for those looking for a job in the public interest.

HEADHUNTER.NET
http://www.headhunter.net

This site offers job leads in fields such as informational technology, finance and accounting, sales and marketing, engineering, customer service, health care, and human resources. Job seekers can search jobs internationally by category, salary range, or keyword. The site also includes "Career BYTES," including news and humor for the college graduate or experienced professional. This page includes college tips, interesting new and hot jobs, and other expert advice.

HEALTH CAREER WEB
http://www.healthcareerweb.com

This site contains job listings, career resources, and a resume board for those looking for a career in health care. Their job database is updated regularly, with hundreds of new listings added daily. With "JobMatch," job seekers can request that relevant job leads be automatically e-mailed to their account. The site also has an online bookstore, career FAQs, and informative articles covering the medical field.

THE HELP-WANTED PAGE
http://www.helpwantedpage.com

Created by GTR Advertising, this site's job searching database contains thousands of advertised occupation openings, updated daily. Other links include searching tips, job fair schedules, industry reports, salary statistics, resume help and databases, and additional sources of information.

HOMEFAIR.COM
http://www2.homefair.com

Designed for relocating job seekers, this site offers "The Salary Calculator" which compares the cost of living among hundreds of U.S. and international cities. With a mouse click, people can see if their current salary is enough to cover expenses when relocating to a new city.

HOMEWORKERS.COM
http://www.homeworkers.com

This site is designed specifically for those that work out of the home, in various fields such as freelance writing, telecommuting, administration, computer programming, and more. Information available includes career-specific pages, job opportunities, discussion boards, and other links to additional information.

THE HUMAN RESOURCE PLANNING SOCIETY
http://www.hrps.org

HRPS offers online networking opportunities, publications to order and read on the site, and a calendar of workshops and conferences for human resource and business professionals. Also includes a link to other useful Web sites for additional information and HR career resources.

THE INTERNET JOB SOURCE
http://www.statejobs.com

A useful link to various state-run Web pages, this site offers college or employment resources to students and professionals. Jobs and colleges can be searched by keyword, state, category, or date posted.

INTERNSHIPPROGRAMS.COM
http://www.internshipprograms.com

As the largest internship source on the Internet, this site offers a giant database for students. In addition to listing internship opportunities by state and category, the site also contains online resume and college essay writing tips, career articles, and frequently asked questions.

JOB OPTIONS
http://www.joboptions.com

With over 6,000 employers in their database, Job Options offers a search engine that runs by location, job category, or chosen keyword. With "Job Alert," job seekers can post their resume and request updated E-mails regarding jobs that fit their interests. The site also offers links to other sites for help on interviewing, resume building, or additional information.

JOBTRAK.COM
http://www.jobtrak.com

A leader in the online career resource industry, Jobtrak can help students post resumes, search jobs, read about employers, research scholarship opportunities, network with career contacts, or browse online career fairs. With its huge database of employers and career resources, this site is a great starting point in the job search.

KAPLAN
http://www.kaptest.com

Kaplan may be best known for their test preparation materials, but they also offer more general career advice. Aimed at college students, this site provides suggestions for preliminary career planning, such as taking elective courses, joining campus and community organizations, and using campus career centers. Students can also explore their various career options with descriptive profiles of fields and the opportunities available.

MANUFACTURING IS COOL!
http://www.manufacturingiscool.com

Developed by the Society of Manufacturing Engineers, this site is designed for those curious about a career in manufacturing. Includes general facts about the field, contest and camp announcements, a listing of accredited colleges and universities, and industry information such as salary ranges, educational requirements, and employment trends.

MICHIGAN CONSTRUCTION CAREERS
http://www.miconstructioncareers.org

This site provides salary statistics, job offerings, and listings of apprentice schools in Michigan and the surrounding areas. Online job descriptions offer information such as the scope of work, working conditions, apprenticeship requirements, and other contacts for more information. Career descriptions include boilermakers, cement masons, electrical workers, ironworkers, laborers, sheet metal workers, and more.

MONSTER.COM
http://www.monster.com

With links to information on practically all aspects of the job search, this site is a great place to start. Monster includes a job search engine that categorizes openings by employer, state, job, and date. Job seekers can post their resume and establish a personal career account or browse through tips on interviewing, salary negotiation, and relocating. Included on the "Career Center" page are self-assessment tools to give direction to young job seekers or for those looking for a career change.

MY FUTURE
http://www.myfuture.com

Designed for the high school graduate, this site describes alternatives to the college path, such as military opportunities, volunteering, internships, apprenticeships, or vocational school. A career page provides helpful tools such as personality and self-assessment tests, advice on resumes and cover letters, interviewing tips, and lists hot job leads and workforce trends.

JOBWEB
http://www.jobweb.org

JOBWEB is a large career resource site containing information ranging from industry news and events to employer information and career services. The site was developed by more than 1,700

career centers at four-year, two-year, graduate, and vocational schools and HR departments in businesses and non-profit organizations. Included on the site is "Catapult," a link to additional career and job-related sites helpful to college students and recent graduates.

NACADA'S ACADEMIC ADVISING AND CAREER COUNSELING
http://www.psu.edu/dus/ncta/links.htm

Created by the National Academic Advising Association, this site offers links to information about academic and career search materials, such as choosing a major, college admissions sites, financial aid, studying abroad, study skills, and other innovative ways to use the Internet in your search.

NURSING CENTER
http://www.nursingcenter.com

This site offers important information for both nursing students and those in practice. Includes health care news, online journals, peer forums, career opportunities and sources for continuing education. Also available are links to job opportunities, strategies for success, information about certification, and other Web sites for additional nursing resources.

NURSING NET
http://www.nursingnet.org

Nursing Net is a comprehensive site with general nursing information, nursing school listings, research databases, and job search engines. Field descriptions include neonatal, critical care, OB-GYN, geriatric, nurse practitioners, and more. The site also includes employment Web boards and a mentoring program to connect nursing students to practicing professionals.

NURSING WORLD
http://www.nursingworld.org

Created by the American Nursing Association, this site offers a wealth of information about the field, including publications to order or read online, and news releases about professional standards and other important issues in the workplace. On the "Nursing Links" page, professionals and students can access sources of continuing education, federal and private grant opportunities, tutorials, international organizations, and answers to frequently asked questions.

OCCUPATIONAL OUTLOOK HANDBOOK
http://stats.bls.gov/ocohome.htm

This nationally recognized career guide offers detailed job descriptions in the following areas: management, professional and technical, sales, administrative support, service, mechanics, construction, production, transportation, laborers and helpers, and the armed forces.
Information includes nature of the work, working conditions, employment outlook, educational and training requirements, earnings, related professions, and sources for additional information.

PAM POHLY'S NET GUIDE TO MANAGEMENT RESOURCES FOR HEALTH CARE & MANAGED CARE EXECUTIVES
http://www.pohly.com

Designed for health care professionals seeking job enhancement, employment, or professional development, this site offers resources such as hot job profiles, listings of health care recruiters and health professional organizations, and health care employment links. Career resources include interviewing tips, salary surveys, and links to career and relocation Web sites.

PETERSON'S
http://www.petersons.com

Peterson's, an expert in career and educational resources, offers information on colleges, universities, graduate programs, distance learning courses, study abroad opportunities, and English training courses. Young job seekers can also search career education links in fields such as business, information technology, culinary, paralegal, and visual communications.

THE PRINCETON REVIEW
http://www.review.com

More than just a test preparation resource, the Princeton Review offers information on choosing a college, postgraduate education, internships, and deciding on a career. Career resources include self-assessment tests, job search engines, and expert career advice covering salary negotiation, building a strong resume, and using the Internet in your job search.

PRINCETON UNIVERSITY'S OUTDOOR ACTION WEB SITE

http://www.princeton.edu/~oa

This site contains resources for students interested in an outdoor or environmental career. An career guide provides job descriptions, tips on choosing a career, job leads, print resources, and information on graduate programs in environmental education. The site also contains a guide to additional outdoor and environmental Web sites available on the Internet.

QUINTESSENTIAL CAREER AND JOB HUNTING RESOURCES GUIDE

http://www.stetson.edu/~rhansen/careers

Sponsored by Dynamic Cover Letters, this site provides information and resources to young job seekers. Career resources include tips on networking and researching companies, cover letter and resume help, interview conversation skills, and more. The site also has a job search engine organized by location, type of position, or experience required.

RENSSELAER'S CAREER DEVELOPMENT CENTER

http://www.cdc.rpi.edu

Through their "Career Links" site on the student homepage, college students and recent graduates can research career options, costs of living and compensation nationwide, employers, graduate school options, salary statistics, and much more. Links to career resources are also grouped by college major or field for easy access.

THE RILEY GUIDE: EMPLOYMENT OPPORTUNITIES AND JOB RESOURCES ON THE INTERNET

http://www.rileyguide.com

This site is a useful resource for job seekers, with an extensive employer database containing leads for internships, seasonal or temporary work, and full-time positions. Jobs can be searched by location, employer, or industry. Also included on the site are salary surveys, networking tools, and tips for searching on the Internet, including suggestions for formatting resumes for online use.

UBIQUITY ENVIRONMENTAL CAREERS PAGE

http://www.geocities.com/rainforest/8974

Created for people who are dedicated to preserving the environment, this site offers general and specific career advice for students, such as tips on choosing college courses, interviewing, and creating resumes and cover letters. Job descriptions help students to define their career plans. Other career resources include job links, internship openings, and tips on how to use the Web efficiently to job search.

USA JOBS

http://www.usajobs.opm.gov

Provided by the United States Office of Personnel Management, this is the official guide to jobs and employment information for the federal government. Includes a variety of job openings for both full- and part-time work, and covers how to apply for openings, federal salary and benefits information, and warns against federal job scams.

USDA FOREST SERVICE
http://www.fs.fed.us

This site offers general employment information about deciding on and obtaining a federal Forest Service job. Topics covered include salary and benefits, grant availability, locating paid and volunteer positions, and training required. The site also contains a link to a governmental job search engine, USA Jobs.

U.S. NEWS
http://www.usnews.com/usnews/edu

Students can access national rankings for colleges and graduate schools, research financial aid opportunities, and job search all at this one site. Ranks are grouped by location, type of institution, majors offered, and tuition costs. The career section of this site is impressively packed with resources such as job search engines, internship opportunities in the U.S. and abroad, and career outlooks for major industries. Also includes tips on assessing your skills, interviewing, writing resumes and cover letters, and how best to use the Web in the job search.

WORK4WOMEN
http://www.work4women.org

This useful site highlights non-traditional occupations (NTOs) available to women of all ages. A separate page is dedicated to girls exploring career options early and dispels myths about working in high-wage NTOs. Women can research job and training opportunities, talk to women in NTOs, and browse an online clearinghouse of books, videos, and other Web sites about career choices.

WORKING WOMAN
http://www.workingwoman.com

This new site offers businesswomen the tools, knowledge, and industry connections to succeed in today's working world. Includes an online business exchange to buy and sell products and services, networking connections to communicate with working women around the world, salary surveys, and other articles of interest to women.

YAHOO! CAREERS
http://careers.yahoo.com

This popular search engine also has impressive career resources, such as a job search engine with more that 1,000,000 positions in their database, and a resume posting and editing board. Job seekers can research employers, salaries, and industry outlooks, and gain advice on resume and cover letters. A special section is dedicated to college students and contains tips for searching and securing that first job, as well as internship opportunities to gain valuable experience.

SECTION VI

RELATED REFERENCE BOOKS

(Dates of publication are not cited because most of these books are revised annually or periodically.)

Career Guide to Industries. U.S. Department of Labor, U.S. Government Printing Office, Superintendent of Documents, Mail Stop: SSOP, Washington, DC 20402-9328.

Catalog of Federal Domestic Assistance. U.S. Government Printing Office, Superintendent of Documents, PO Box 371954, Pittsburgh, PA 15250-7954.

Create Your Own School Career Information Centre. North York Career Centre, 44 Appian Drive, North York, Ontario, M2J 2P9 Canada.

Developing a Career Information Centre. Canadian Career Information Association, 720 Spadina Avenue, Suite 300, Toronto, Ontario M5S 2T9, Canada.

Encyclopedia of Careers and Vocational Guidance. Ferguson Publishing Company, 200 West Jackson Boulevard, Chicago, Illinois 60606.

Ferguson's Guide to Apprenticeship Programs. Ferguson Publishing Company, 200 West Jackson Boulevard, Chicago, Illinois 60606.

Free Stuff from Uncle Sam. Profit Source Publishing, PO Box 1366, Windermere, FL 34786.

Government Job Finder. Planning Communications, 7215 Oak Avenue, River Forest, Illinois 60305.

How to Plan and Develop a Career Center. Ferguson Publishing Company, 200 West Jackson Boulevard, Chicago, Illinois 60606.

Internships. Peterson's Guides, Inc., Box 2123, Princeton, New Jersey 08543-2123.

The Internship Bible. Random House, Incorporated, 201 East 50th Street, New York, New York 10022.

Internships: A Directory for Career-Finders & Career-Changers. Macmillan Publishing Company, Incorporated, 345 Park Avenue South, New York, NY 10010-1707.

Job Hunter's Sourcebook. Gale, 275 Drake Road, Farmington Hills, Michigan 48331-3535.

National Trade and Professional Associations of the United States. Columbia Books, 1212 New York Avenue, Suite 330, Washington, DC 20005.

Free and Inexpensive Career Materials

Non-Profits Job Finder. Planning Communications, 7215 Oak Avenue, River Forest, Illinois 60305.

Occupational Outlook Handbook. U.S. Department of Labor, U.S. Government Printing Office, Superintendent of Documents, Mail Stop: SSOP, Washington, DC 20402-9328.